MIDDLE ENGLISH LITERATURE

BRITISH ACADEMY GOLLANCZ LECTURES

MIDDLE ENGLISH LITERATURE

British Academy Gollancz Lectures

SELECTED AND INTRODUCED BY
J. A. BURROW

Published for THE BRITISH ACADEMY
by THE OXFORD UNIVERSITY PRESS

Oxford University Press, Walton Street, Oxford OX2 6DP
Oxford New York Toronto
Delhi Bombay Calcutta Madras Karachi
Petaling Jaya Singapore Hong Kong Tokyo
Nairobi Dar es Salaam Cape Town
Melbourne Auckland
and associated companies in
Berlin Ibadan

Oxford is a trade mark of Oxford University Press

Published in the United States
by Oxford University Press, New York

British Library Cataloguing in Publication Data
Middle English literature : British Academy
Gollancz lectures.
1. English literature, 1066–1400 –
Critical studies
I. Burrow, J. A. (John Anthony)   II.
British Academy
820.9′001

ISBN 0-19-726085-3

Printed in Great Britain by
Billing & Sons Ltd, Worcester

CONTENTS

NOTE ON CONTRIBUTORS

Professor Derek Brewer, *Master of Emmanuel College, Cambridge; Professor of English, University of Cambridge*

Professor John A. Burrow, *Winterstoke Professor of English, University of Bristol; Fellow of the British Academy*

Sir William A. Craigie (1867–1947), *Fellow of the British Academy*

Professor Norman Davis, *formerly Merton Professor of English Language and Literature, University of Oxford; Fellow of the British Academy*

Professor E. J. Dobson (1913–1984), *Fellow of the British Academy*

Dorothy Everett (1894–1953), *Lady Margaret Hall, Oxford*

Dr Pamela Gradon, *St Hugh's College, Oxford*

Professor Phyllis Hodgson, *formerly Professor of English Language and Medieval Literature, Bedford College, University of London*

Professor Elizabeth Salter (1925–1980), *University of York*

Professor Geoffrey Shepherd (1918–1982), *University of Birmingham*

INTRODUCTION

By J. A. BURROW

In 1924 Mrs. Frida Mond endowed a new series of British Academy lectures. The prescribed subjects were: 'Old English or Early English Language and Literature, or a philological subject connected with the history of English, more particularly during the early periods of the language, or cognate subjects, or some textual study and interpretation'. R. W. Chambers delivered the first lecture in 1926 on 'The Saga and Myth of Sir Thomas More', and the series has continued every other year since then. It commemorates the work of Sir Israel Gollancz (d. 1930), the first Secretary of the Academy; and, as he would no doubt have wished, most of the lectures have concerned either Old English or Middle English literature.

The present volume includes all the Sir Israel Gollancz Memorial Lectures on Middle English subjects that have been delivered since the Second World War, together with one wartime piece on Scots (Craigie, 1942). All but one of the lectures are reprinted photographically here, with little more than occasional correction of printing errors. However, Professor Norman Davis has revised his 1954 lecture on 'The Language of the Pastons' to bring its quotations and references, and also some other details, into line with his own edition of the Paston Letters, which has superseded the older edition by James Gairdner to which he then referred. The present editor is grateful to Professor Davis for agreeing to produce this revision of his lecture, which itself now supersedes the 1954 version.

The ten lectures are presented in the order in which they were delivered, over a period of forty years from 1942 to 1982. Three of them (Salter, Shepherd, and Gradon) are mainly or exclusively concerned with William Langland, and two (Everett and Brewer) with Geoffrey Chaucer. The rest are devoted to a variety of texts: some neglected Scottish poems (Craigie), the Paston Letters (Davis), *The Orchard of Syon* (Hodgson), *Ancrene Wisse* (Dobson), and Thomas Hoccleve (Burrow). A few of these lectures have already been reprinted elsewhere; but gathered together, as they are here, they serve to represent certain advances in the scholarly and critical study of Middle English

literature since the Second World War. On the one hand, there is
that kind of scholarly work, represented by the lectures of Davis,
Dobson, and Gradon, which depends upon exact chronology to
display medieval writers in their most immediate contexts. Here,
a few years either way can be shown to make a difference: to
what the authors of *Ancrene Wisse* or *Piers Plowman* read and
thought, or again to the forms of English used by different
members of the Paston family—tiny linguistic variations such as
together go to make up that large abstraction, the Development
of the English Language. Studies of this meticulously detailed
kind serve as a corrective to drastically foreshortened views of the
medieval period, and as a reminder that even in the Middle Ages
a year (as one monk calculated) contained no less than 365 days,
8760 hours, 525,600 minutes, or more than 31 million seconds,
just like a modern year. Yet there is a place also for those
discussions of author, genre, or period in which their general
characteristics are painted with a much broader brush, as in the
lectures by Salter, Shepherd, and Brewer; for it is here that new
ideas—about rhetoric, or 'figural' writing, or traditional tales, or
autobiography—find their way into these pages.

THE SCOTTISH ALLITERATIVE POEMS

By SIR WILLIAM CRAIGIE

Fellow of the Academy

Read 21 October 1942

THE Scottish alliterative poems form a sequel and epilogue to that section of English literature to the study of which so many contributions of great value were made by the distinguished scholar whose name is commemorated in the title of this lecture. All students of Middle English literature owe a great debt to Sir Israel Gollancz for his editions of a number of the most important alliterative poems, which illustrate the beginnings and development of a type of poetry now best known by the work which, in its subject and plan, stands apart from all the others—the Vision of Piers the Plowman. It is with the later stages and final fortunes of this poetry that the present lecture is concerned.

About or shortly after the year 1500 the Scottish poet William Dunbar, who is rightly reckoned among the Scottish Chaucerians, so far departed from the Chaucer tradition as to compose his longest poem, not in any of the Chaucerian metres, but in the unrhymed alliterative verse which forms so strong a contrast to these. Thus, while the Golden Targe opens with the regular lines

> Ryght as the stern of day begouth to schyne,
> Quhen gone to bed war Vesper and Lucyne,
> I raise, and by a rosere did me rest,

the other 'tretis' begins with

> Apon the Midsumer ewin, mirriest of nichtis,
> I muvit furth [in] ane meid, as midnicht wes past,
> Besyd ane gudlie grein garth full of gay flouris,
> Hegeit of ane huge hicht with hawthorne treis,
> Quhairon ane bird on ane bransche so birst out hir notis,
> That neuer ane blythfullar bird was on the beuche hard.[1]

Some fifty years earlier an older Scottish poet, Richard

---

[1] In quoting this and other passages in the course of this lecture, I realize that some of the lines may sound so unfamiliar as to be unintelligible, but I feel it necessary to read them in order to bring out clearly the special character of the metre. It may also be of interest to hear how Scots of the sixteenth century must have read these poems, for Scottish pronunciation has not materially altered since that time.

Holland, who fortunately took care to record his own name, also chose to express himself in alliterative verse, but of the type which combined this feature with end-rhymes and stanzaic form. His poem consists of seventy-seven stanzas of thirteen lines each, of which the first runs as follows;

> In the myddis of May, at morne, as I ment,
>> Throw myrth markit on mold, till a grene meid,
> The bemes blythest of ble fro the son blent,
>> That all brichtnyt about the bordouris on breid;
> With alkyn herbes of air that war in erd lent
>> The feldis flurist, and fret full of fairhed;
> So soft was the sessoun our Souerane dovne sent,
>> Throw the greable gift of his Godhed,
> That all was amyable owr the air and the erd.
>> Thus throw thir cliftis so cleir,
>> Withoutin fallow or feir,
>> I raikit till ane reveir,
>> That ryally apperd.

In neither of these two instances was the poet using a form of verse characteristic of the earlier poetry of Scotland. The model in each case, as much as in the adoption of the Chaucerian types, came from the south, and apparently both of these southern models, the alliterative and the Chaucerian, became effective about the same time, the middle of the fifteenth century. By that time, to all appearance, the alliterative school had ceased to be productive in England, but what had already been produced was extensively copied in the first half of that century and must still have had a large number of readers.

Although the origin and earlier history of this remarkable body of poetry does not really call for investigation here, something may usefully be said regarding this, since it was the vogue which it attained during its most flourishing period which enabled it to survive long enough to be imitated in Scotland at a later date.

In Anglo-Saxon poetry the alliteration which was an essential feature of the verse was combined with other principles which limited the number of admissible variations of the line, although these were never so severely restricted as they were in Old Norse and Icelandic. Apart from other changes in the language, observance of correct Anglo-Saxon metre was certain to break down sooner or later when the sense of quantity was lost. In speech this had evidently taken place by the time of Ælfric, since he was of opinion that quantity in Latin applied only to verse and not to prose, and was unable to understand why the Welsh should pronounce *pater* with a short *a* instead of reverently giving it the long vowel, 'since God is not to be subjected to the art of grammar'. Deprived of quantity, the alliterative line of real verse naturally fell together in many instances with the looser alliterative line which Ælfric himself extensively employed, and may have been the first to use. This line, though with less regularity, continued to be used in lives of saints and other religious works, and the reading aloud of these must have kept the use of alliteration familiar to the ear throughout part at least, if not the whole, of the thirteenth century. That the tradition was also carried on in secular poetry of a similar form is not improbable; that there is little evidence for the existence of this is not surprising. Such a tradition may account for Laȝamon's use of alliterative lines as well as rhyming couplets, but Laȝamon as a priest would also naturally be familiar with the alliterative type of homily and religious discourse.

The important point to be noticed is that all indications point to a definite locality in which the alliterative tradition was preserved, namely, the more southern part of the West Midlands. It is therefore natural that when alliterative poetry again becomes an important feature in English literature about the middle of the fourteenth century, it should, to all appearance, have its beginnings in precisely this area, that is, in the counties of Gloucester, Worcester, and Hereford. Few of the poems give any precise indication of their place of origin, but three are respectively associated with Gloucester, the Malvern Hills, and Bristol.

It is not necessary to accept the view that this use of alliterative verse was a deliberate revival of something that had been quite discontinued, or that it was a conscious adoption of a national form in opposition to that which had been introduced under French influence, and which had been in constant use for at least a century and a half. The possibility is not excluded that a fresh literary impulse simply made use of a form of verse already familiar, and in some respects better adapted for long narratives or sustained discourse than any form based on the use of rhyme. The time was undoubtedly favourable for the rise of a new literature. The successful wars of Edward III, with the victories of Cressy and Neville's Cross, and the growing prominence of social, economic, political, and religious questions, were all fitted to stimulate a lively national feeling which, as at other times and in other countries under similar conditions, found expression in the creation of a vigorous national literatuie. In the west this took the form of the alliterative poems; in the London area, somewhat later, it produced the poetry of Chaucer and Gower, which was destined to become the more lasting of the two. Having the advantage of an earlier start, however, the alliterative movement was able to extend northwards for a time without a rival, and to produce within some fifty years a voluminous literature, especially of romances, of which it is certain that only a portion has been preserved.

The typical alliterative poem, of which the bulk of this literature consists, is composed of unrhymed lines sometimes grouped in stanzas of four lines, but more commonly running on in sections of indeterminate length. The only limit to the length of the poem itself is the subject with which it deals; that on the Destruction of Troy extends to over 14,000 lines, nearly twice as many as in the final text of Piers Plowman. There was indeed nothing to stop the alliterative poet, even if he took some care to observe the elementary rules of the metre, and still less if he was prepared to be lax in adhering to them. There was, however, another and more difficult type of alliterative verse, which was less suitable for long compositions and of which fewer specimens have been preserved. This apparently originated in a combination of two pre-existing types of verse. One of these was a stanza of eight alliterative lines with alternate rhymes, of which specimens occur about 1300, also in the western area. The other was a tag of four or five short lines attached to a stanza of four long lines, current about the same date. By a combination of these a stanza of thirteen lines was produced, of which the first eight had four stresses, the ninth only one, and the remainder two; the ninth line rhymed with the thirteenth, the other three of the tag rhymed with each other. This is the metre of the Pistill of Susan (i.e. the story of Susanna and the elders) and the Quatrefoil of Love. It must have been obvious, however, that the very short ninth line awkwardly broke the flow of the stanza, and that a much better effect was produced by giving it the same length as the previous eight; this improvement is found in the Aunters of Arthur, and was adopted by the Scottish poets with only one or two unimportant exceptions.

The northward extension of the alliterative movement must have begun early and made rapid progress, as some of the best specimens are clearly of north midland origin. That it had come to be associated with the north before the close of the

fourteenth century is evident from the prologue to the Parson's
Tale:

> I am a Southren man,
> I can nat geste *rum, ram, ruf* by lettre.

The northward limit, however, cannot be fixed with any
certainty, and there is no direct evidence how early, and to
what extent, copies of any of the alliterative poems were carried
farther north into Scotland. Relations between Scotland and
England, and especially between the parts on each side of the
Border during the fourteenth and fifteenth centuries, were not
favourable for literary intercourse, though no doubt some Scots
would be sufficiently interested in poetry to annex any manuscript which they might come across in the course of a 'reiving'
expedition. We cannot judge by the surviving specimens how
numerous such manuscripts were in the northern English shires.
The fact that Robert Thornton, apparently in an out-of-the-way
part of Yorkshire, was able to collect so much material, including the important alliterative Morte Arthure, indicates that
literary interests must have been fairly widespread, at least in
that county; and there is similar evidence for Lancashire.
Peaceful intercourse between the two countries was of course
not entirely wanting, as at the meetings of the wardens on both
sides of the Border, and an occasional English minstrel may well
have ventured north of the Solway to entertain a Scottish
audience.

For early Scottish acquaintance with alliterative poetry,
however, we have only one slender piece of evidence, the
mention by Andrew of Wyntoun, writing his chronicle about
1420, of three pieces attributed by him to the otherwise unknown Huchown of the Awle Ryale. From the titles of these,
the Gret Gest of Arthure, the Awntyre of Gawane, and Pystyll
of Swete Swsane, there is every reason to suppose that certain
alliterative pieces are implied, of which the first and third, and
possibly the second, can be reasonably identified with texts still
extant. In that case, however, a common authorship is most
improbable, and the attribution of all three to the unidenti-
fiable Huchown becomes suspect; Wyntoun may merely have
made a wrong inference from finding the three pieces in the
same manuscript. He was not, however, the only person
acquainted with the Gest Hystorialle, since he defends Huchown
against some who had unjustifiably criticized him.

The assumption that Wyntoun's mention and defence of
Huchown implies that he was a Scottish poet has led to a whole

series of speculations into which it is unnecessary to enter, since they run counter to all probability. They involve the view that the Pistill of Susan, for example, was a Scottish composition, although the language bears no trace of such an origin, and that it had been composed and carried south early enough for an anglicized copy of it to occur in a southern manuscript written before 1400. (All the extant copies, in fact, are English.) This would be a complete reversal of all that is otherwise known of the literary relations between Scotland and England at that period, and of the history of the alliterative movement. So far as the Scottish alliterative poems are concerned, Huchown, whatever foundation Wyntoun's account of him may have had, may safely be left out of account.

The course of early Scottish literature from the composition of Barbour's 'Brus' in 1375–6 is sufficiently clear. This, and other compositions of the late fourteenth and early fifteenth centuries, including Wyntoun's chronicle and the Buke of Alexander, are in the usual octosyllabic rhyming couplet common in English works from about 1250. No change in technique appears until about the middle of the fifteenth century, when southern influence asserts itself in the two forms which had become dominant during the previous hundred years, viz. the south-eastern school of Chaucer, Gower, Hoccleve, and Lydgate, on the one hand, and on the other the alliterative poetry of the west and north. These two new models no doubt reached Scotland by different channels, but to all appearance became effective about the same time. The earliest specimen of the Chaucerian type which can be dated is a translation, in the Liber Pluscardensis, of part of a French elegy on the Dauphiness Margaret, who died in 1445; the translation, in ten-line stanzas, is obviously not much later than this. The same chronicle closes with a poem of good advice to a king, which can hardly be later than 1460. The earliest of the Scottish alliterative poems are practically of the same date.

While in England the continuous unrhymed type of alliterative verse is represented by numerous compositions which individually and collectively far exceed in quantity those in rhyming stanzas, there is no evidence that these were either generally known or imitated in Scotland during the fifteenth century. Possibly their obvious lack of regular form did not appeal to the Scottish poets, who by this time showed a much finer sense of rhythm and regularity in verse than their English contemporaries or their immediate predecessors. This makes it difficult to account for Dunbar's choice of this type of verse for his account of the talk between the two married women and the widow, for which, so far as we know, he had no model to follow. It is clear that the suggestion for the theme came from the Wife of Bath's prologue, and he may have wished to avoid the obvious comparison with this if he used the same metre, but it is quite as likely that he saw in alliterative verse greater opportunity for easy composition, racy discourse, and a free use of the abusive epithets which the three women agree in applying to their husbands. In this respect his choice was justified; there is far more vigour in these rapid unfettered lines than either he or Kennedy displayed in the equally outspoken, but regular, verses of the Flyting. It may be assumed that Dunbar in composing the piece, and Chepman and Myllar in printing it, knew that the metre, although already antiquated, would not be unfamiliar to Scottish readers. This implies that copies of at least some of the English poems had found their way over the Border, although no trace of these has been preserved. We cannot be certain, either, that no Scottish poet before Dunbar had made use of the metre, since there are so many examples of Scottish compositions of the fifteenth century existing only in single copies, and many indications of others that have completely disappeared. Even in the unique copy of Chepman and Myllar's print the first hundred lines (about one-fifth of the whole) are missing, and the beginning of the poem would thus have been lost but for the copy in the Maitland Folio, written about 1575. The title here given is no doubt the original: 'Heir beginis the tretis of the tua mariit wemen and the wedo, compylit be maister William Dunbar.' The authorship is corroborated at the end of the print by the words 'Quod Dunbar'.

After the opening lines which I have already quoted, the poet describes how his attention was attracted by loud voices in a garden, and how, on pressing into a hawthorn hedge, he saw sitting there, talking and drinking, 'three gay ladies', two of whom 'wedded were with lords', while the third was a widow of wanton manners. In describing in detail the persons and their setting as being clearly seen by him between midnight and daybreak the poet is not imagining the impossible; in the latitude of Edinburgh there is no real darkness on midsummer night. Having introduced the speakers, Dunbar immediately allows them to begin to talk, which they proceed to do with the utmost freedom, quite unaware of the listener behind the hedge.

While Chaucer found it quite sufficient to have one Wife of Bath, Dunbar presents three of similar character, each even more shameless and outspoken than their prototype. The nature of their discourse may be inferred from the fact that for their husbands, past and present, they have more than forty contemptuous or abusive names. The widow, who is the third speaker, and talks at greater length than the other two combined, couples her own frank admissions with much good advice on the importance of keeping up the appearance of virtue, a lesson which the others declare they will take to heart, 'and wirk eftir hir wordis, that woman wes so prudent'. After a few lines describing the dawn, which brought the party to a close, Dunbar ends by putting to his 'honorable auditoris' the difficult question

> Of thir thre wantoun wyffis, that I haue written heir,
> Quhilk wald ʒe waill to ʒour wyf, gif ʒe suld wed ane?

Of this incursion by Dunbar into the field of alliterative verse it can at least be said that he appears to have been original in his choice of a subject for this form of verse. The choice in itself may well be an indication that the metre was no longer taken seriously, and was regarded as more suitable for matter of this kind than for a tale of chivalry or the discussion of social problems. However this may be, the Tua Mariit Wemen and the Wedow, and the slightly later English poem of Scottish Field, form not only a belated, but a lame, conclusion to a literature which included such masterpieces as the Vision of Piers the Plowman, the Wars of Alexander, the Morte Arthure, and Sir Gawain and the Green Knight.

If Scotland contributed so little to the usual type of alliterative verse it made up for this in the more elaborate rhyming stanza, in which it certainly surpassed its models, if these are fairly represented by the extant specimens. There is no direct evidence how many such pieces of English origin found their way north, but they must have included either the Pistill of Susan and the Aunters of Arthur, or two others similar to these, the one with the short, and the other with the long, form of the ninth line. The Scottish poets preferred the latter, the only exception being two or three short pieces, in which the ninth line, however, has two stresses instead of only one. It is most probable that the immediate model followed by the Scots was a tale of romance like the Aunters of Arthur, since two of the Scottish poems are of this class. These, however, are not so early as the third piece, the Buke of the Howlat, by Holland, which must have been composed about 1450. The other two, the Tale of Rauf Coilȝear and the Knightly Tale of Golagros and Gawane, are obviously later, but are earlier than 1500, and may be conjecturally dated as 1470 or 1475. It is only by the merest chance that all three have been preserved. Of Golagros and Gawane there is a single printed copy of 1508, of Rauf Coilȝear one of 1572; copies of both, which were among the later contents of the Asloan MS., are now lost. Of the Howlat there are two manuscript copies which may have been made from a print known only from a fragment containing two stanzas. The existence of these prints is good evidence that this form of alliterative poetry still appealed to Scottish readers in the sixteenth century to an extent which encouraged the printer to produce them.

The three poems are very different in character. The Howlat is the most original, Rauf Coilȝear the best story, and Golagros and Gawane a good specimen of the ordinary romance of chivalry. Its main defect is lack of variety, the matter being mainly limited to descriptions of castles and of single combats between armed knights. Basing the story on two episodes in the Old French romance of Percival le Gallois, the poet displays great facility in metre, and employs a rich vocabulary, not overcharged with archaisms or rare words. The result is a vigorous and well sustained poem of 1,360 lines, the seriousness of which is relieved only by the incident in which Sir Kay snatches a roasted bird from the spit in the kitchen of a castle which he has entered, is knocked down by an indignant knight, and retires in undignified haste. Within its limits, Golagros and Gawane is an excellent example of the use of this form of verse for both rapid and detailed description, the metre giving the necessary swing to the narrative and the alliteration demanding the use of many words that might not naturally have occurred to the poet. Thus when King Arthur pitches his camp for the night:

Thai plantit doun ane pailyeoun vpone ane plane lee,
    Of pall and of peloure that proudly wes picht,
With rapis of rede golde, riale to see,
    With grete ensenyes of the samyne, semly by sicht;
Bordouris about, that bricht war of ble,
    Betin with brint gold, burely and bricht;
Frenyeis of fyne silk, fretit ful fre.
    With deir dyamonthis bedene, that dayntely wes dicht.

Or in the combat between Golagros and Gawane:

> With ane bitand brand, burly and braid,
>> Quhilk oft in battale had bene his bute and his belde,
> He leit gird to the grome, with greif that he haid,
>> And claif throw the cantell of the clene schelde.
> Throw birny and breist-plait and bordour it baid,
>> The fulye of the fyne gold fell in the feild.

That similar descriptions of hard fighting are repeated several times in the poem would not strike the readers or hearers as superfluous, especially as the wording is varied; such encounters are part of the stock material of the romances of chivalry, as they have continued to be of Icelandic *rímur* down to the present day. Though it is inferior in interest to the Aunters of Arthur, and especially has no counterpart to the impressive scene in which the ghost of her mother appears to, and addresses, Queen Gaynour (i.e. Guinevere), it is no unworthy addition to Arthurian literature by a Scottish contemporary of Sir Thomas Malory, whose name has not been preserved either in the poem itself or by the printer. According to Dunbar, a certain Clerk of Tranent wrote 'the anteris of Gawane', but this title does not quite fit a tale which recounts only one adventure of that knight. The apparent date of Clerk, however, would agree quite well with that of the poem.

'Rauf Coilȝear', a tale of the days of Charlemagne, is throughout in a lighter strain. It is a variant of the adventure of the king who by accident is parted from his followers, and has to be indebted to a man of low degree for food and shelter overnight. The poem opens with the storm by which the king and his men are dispersed, and his falling in with the charcoal-burner. There is great vigour in the description of the storm, and much humour in the account of Rauf's entertainment of the king, even to the extent of knocking him down to teach him politeness—humour which is also maintained in the arrival of Rauf at the court in Paris, in spite of the efforts of Sir Rolland to stop him by the way and of the porter at the gate to bar his entrance. There is, however, a distinct falling off of interest after the king has related his adventure to the assembled nobles and has conferred the honour of knighthood on Rauf to show his gratitude 'To him that succourit my life in sa euill nicht', and the piece ends rather lamely with an incident in which Sir Rauf and Sir Rolland encounter a Saracen, the latter giving up the combat and accepting Christianity in the same easy manner as Otuel and Ferumbras. Unless the poet had some

French original to follow which has not been discovered, it may be suspected that he had some difficulty in finding a good ending to his tale, and had recourse to one of the conventional situations for want of anything better.

The ease and liveliness with which the story is told is partly helped by the poet not troubling too much about the alliteration, which is less fully and less strictly observed than in the Golagros and Gawane. This is not so noticeable at the outset, the opening stanza being quite regular in this respect.

> In the cheiftyme of Charlis, that chosin chiftane,
>   Thair fell ane ferlyfull flan within thay fellis wide,
> Quhair Empreouris, and Erlis, and vther mony ane,
>   Turnit fra Sanct Thomas befoir the ȝule tyde;
> Thay past vnto Paris, thay proudest in pane,
>   With mony Prelatis and Princis, that was of mekle pryde,
> All thay went with the King to his worthy wane;
>   Our the feildis sa fair thay fure be his syde;
> All the worthiest went in the morning,
>   Baith Dukis and Duchepeiris,
>   Barrounis and Bacheleiris,
>   Mony stout man steiris
>   Of town with the King.

Even in the third stanza, however, the regular line

> His steid aganis the storme staluartlie straid

is immediately preceded by one in which alliteration is altogether wanting,

> He saw thair was na better bot God at the last,

and similar lines occur here and there throughout the poem, though the poet never forgets that alliteration is a cardinal principle of the metre, and at times shows his mastery of it by extending it to the couplet instead of limiting it to a single line:

> Thow fand me fechand nathing that followit to feid,
>   I war ane fule gif I fled, and fand nane affray;
> Bot as a lauchfull man my laidis to leid,
>   That leifis with mekle lawtie and labour in fay;
> Be the Mother and the Maydin that maid vs remeid,
>   And thow mat me ony mair, cum efter quhat sa may,
> Thow and I sall dyntis deill quhill ane of vs be deid,
>   For the deidis thow hes me done vpon this deir day.

When David Laing brought out the first modern edition of Rauf Coilȝear in 1822 he made the following just remarks with regard to its style. 'Although, like most poems of the same age and character, many words are introduced merely for the sake of alliteration, the language is by no means obscure. The narrative is simple and circumstantial; the characters are well described; and a vein of comic humour runs through the whole.' To this it may be added that both the language and the humour are so thoroughly Scottish that it is doubtful whether any but Scots to whom their native dialect is perfectly familiar can fully understand the one and appreciate the other. It is to be regretted that the name of a poet of so much merit should not have been handed down along with the poem. There is no clue to justify even a guess at his identity. Possibly he was one of those mentioned by Dunbar, of whom nothing is known beyond the name.

More original in design and execution than either Rauf Coilȝear or Golagros is the earlier poem of the Howlat by Holland, the framework of which is the fable of the owl who by his complaints to Nature was granted a feather from each of the other birds, and on that account became so vain and arrogant that he had to be reduced to his original ugliness. There is no evidence that there was any personal allusion in this, as in Stewart's alleged application of it to Wallace before the battle of Falkirk, which may imply a knowledge of the poem on the part of Blind Harry, but Holland may have had this reason for his choice of a theme without making the application plain to all. Into the framework of the tale he has cleverly fitted an enumeration of the birds summoned by the Pope, who is the peacock, to each of which an appropriate ecclesiastical character is assigned, and of those attending the Emperor, the eagle. The latter's pursuivant, the woodpecker, gives occasion for a description of several coats of arms, viz. those of the Pope, of the Emperor of Almaine, of France, of Scotland, and of the Douglasses. The latter are clearly introduced merely because the poet wishes to celebrate that family, since the account of them occupies no less than twenty stanzas out of the seventy-seven.

> That word is so wonder warme and euer ȝit was,
> It synkis sone in all part
> Of a trewe Scottis hart,
> Reiosand ws inwart
> To heire of Dowglas.

After this digression the poet returns to the birds; there is a feast given by the Pope, at which minstrels sing a hymn to the virgin and play on a variety of instruments, a juggler performs remarkable feats of conjuring, and the rook as 'a bard out of Ireland' addresses the company in Irish and imperfect Scots, demanding meat and drink under the threat of 'ryming' (i.e. satirizing) them. After some rough play with the bard and two other birds the poem proceeds in a more sedate strain to the end, the last stanza giving the author's name and the place of composition, Darnaway in Morayshire.

While each part of the poem has its merits, the poet reaches his highest level in the stanzas which relate how James of Douglas took the heart of Bruce to the Holy Sepulchre, hallowed it there, and carried it hung to his neck when he went to fight the Saracens.

> He gart hallowe the hart, & syne couth it hyng
> About his hals full hende & on his awne hart,
> > Oft wald he kiss it and cry,
> > 'O flour of all chewalry,
> > Quhy leif I, allace, quhy,
> > > And thow deid art?'
>
> Thus in defence of the faith he fure to the ficht,
> > With knychtis of cristindome to kepe his command,
> And quhen the battallis sa brym, brathly and bricht,
> > War joyned thraly in thrang, many thousand,
> Amang the hethin men the hert hardely he slang,
> > Said, 'Wend on as thou was wont,
> > Throw the batell in bront,
> > Ay formast in the front,
> > > Thy fays amang.'

There is nothing in Scottish poetry of the fifteenth century, except some of the best passages in the 'Wallace', that can be compared with ten or twelve of the stanzas in this part of the poem. Whatever the merits of the Chaucerian verse which was coming into favour at the same period, it may be doubted whether any passage of similar force and beauty could have been composed in it. These stanzas alone justify the poet in his choice of the alliterative metre for his tale.

The author of the Howlat was an ecclesiastic and a public notary, of whose career some particulars are known. While the two romances are anonymous, it is evident that they also were composed by men of some learning, who were acquainted not only with the technique of alliterative verse but with the proper setting of a tale of chivalry, and were familiar with the external and internal aspects of castles and halls, with the armour of knights and all the details of jousting and single

combat, and with the names of the douzepers and the knights
of the Round Table. In neither of them is there anything to
suggest the work of a mere minstrel addressing himself to
unlettered hearers. In this respect they agree with the majority
of the longer English alliterative poems, which have clearly a
background of literary culture.

So far the Scottish poets had maintained alliterative poetry
at as high a level as it had attained in its native England. But
even while they were doing so, signs of a lowering of the status
of the form begin to appear, and it may be significant that the
poet who exemplifies this is Henryson, who as a pronounced
Chaucerian may have had no respect for the rival type of verse-
making. There were English anticipations of a burlesque use
of alliterative verse, but these are so rare that it cannot be
assumed that Henryson knew and imitated them. It is, however,
noteworthy that he chose this metre for the only scurrilous and
indecent piece attributed to him, one of seven stanzas entitled
'Sum practysis of medicine', in which the alliteration is well
maintained. This is apparently a piece of bitter sarcasm
addressed to some pretender to medical knowledge, with mock
recipes for various ailments, and in its own way has some merit,
though the best lines are those which least bear quotation.

This burlesque use of the metre is continued in a short poem
(possibly by Dunbar) of three stanzas on the theme of Kynd
Kittok, her adventures on the way to heaven, and her fortunes
there. There is considerable humour in the absurdities of these,
but in form the piece is defective, alliteration being altogether
lacking in many of the lines. This is better observed in another
piece of the same length, of uncertain date, relating to a 'gyre
carling' (i.e. a female ogre), a certain Blasour who was in love
with her, and the king of Faerie. This is a deliberate piece of
nonsense with no particular point in it, and the use of the metre
for such a theme is in all probability indicative of the low
estimation in which it had come to be held.

A few years later than Dunbar, Gavin Douglas made use of
the alliterative stanza in the prologue to the eighth book of his
translation of the Aeneid. Part of this is a vigorous denunciation
of the corruptions of the times, but there is no sequence in the
practices or persons denounced, and the tone is far from serious.
The setting also is an indication that the metre has been chosen
to give the prologue a different character from any of the others.
The later stanzas are introduced by an altercation between the
poet and the stranger whom he meets in his dream, and include

an account of the medley of subjects dealt with in a roll which the latter hands to him. Douglas could hardly write anything without merit, and the prologue is distinctly above the level of the piece by Henryson and the two others already mentioned, but does not indicate any higher appreciation of the value of alliterative verse as a poetic form.

For some seventy years after this there is but scanty evidence of further attempts in this field. Sir David Lyndsay's Satire of the Three Estates opens with a single stanza; this may have been suggested by a knowledge of one of the York Mystery Plays. As this is the latest specimen that has any serious purpose, and as the rules are fairly well observed, it may be worth while to quote it.

> The fader, foundar of faith and felicitie,
>> That ȝour fassone formit to his similitude,
> And his sone, our saluiour, scheild in necessitie,
>> That bocht ȝow frome bailis, ransonit on the rude,
> Replegeing his prissonaris with his pretious blude,
>> The haly gaist, gouernour and grundar of grace,
> Of wisdome and weilfair bath fontane and flude,
>> Save ȝow all that I se seisit in this place,
>>> And scheild ȝow fra syn,
>>> And with his spreit ȝow inspyre;
>>> Till I haif schawin my desire,
>>> Scilence, soveranis, I requyre,
>>>> For now I begin.

A modified form of the nine-line stanza is also used by Rolland in one of the 'moralities' inserted at intervals in his version of the Seven Sages. This is noticeable only because it agrees with Douglas's prologue in being used for denunciation.

The last expiring flash of alliterative verse breaks out about 1580 in the 'Flyting' of Montgomerie and Polwart, and indicates clearly the level to which it had fallen by that time. Montgomerie first uses it in twenty-two stanzas, giving an imaginary account of Polwart's birth and baptism, and the curses showered on him by the weird sisters. The verses are mainly made up of a long list of diseases and other evils laid upon the infant, and an account of the witches calling upon the fiends to carry out their imprecations. In Polwart's reply there are six stanzas in the same metre, much less vigorous and having little point.

Most of the Flyting would be unintelligible, even to a Scot, if read aloud, and few of the verses are worth quoting as anything but specimens of violent and vulgar invective. A single stanza, not so obscure as most of the others, may, however, be cited to show that alliterative poetry, even in this final stage, still gave the poet an opportunity for producing some vigorous lines.

> Be the hicht of the hevins & the howness of hell,
>> Be the windis, and the weirdes, & the Charlewaine,
> Be the hornes, the handstaffe, and the kinges Ell,
>> Be thunder, be fyreflauchtes, be drouthe, & be raine.
> Be the poles, and the planetts, & the signes all twell,
>> Be the mirknes of the moone—lett mirknes remaine—
> Be the elementes all, that our craftes can compell,
>> Be the feindis infernall, and the fureis in pane.
> Be all the gaistis of the dead, that dwels thair doune
>> In Lethe and Styxe the stinkand strands,
>> And Pluto, that 30ur courts commands,
>> Receive this howlet aff our hands,
>>> In name of Mahoune.

The conclusion which would naturally be drawn from the Flyting as to the light in which alliterative verse had now come to be regarded is confirmed by the place given to it in the 'short treatise' by King James on the rules to be observed in 'Scottis poesie', which was printed in 1584. James approved entirely of alliteration. 'Lat all your verse be literall, sa far as may be, quhatsumeuer kynde they be of, but speciallie Tumbling verse for flyting.' He then cites as a good specimen a sadly overloaded line from one of Montgomerie's verses:

> Fetching fude for to feid it fast furth of the Farie.

Later on in the treatise he writes: 'For Flyting or Inuectives, vse this kynde of verse following, callit Rouncefallis or Tumbling verse', and illustrates it by the second stanza of the same piece, beginning with the lines

> In the hinder end of haruest, vpon Alhallow ene,
>> Quhen our gude nichtbors rydis (nou gif I reid richt).

Thus, both in respect of the matter which it was made to present, and the intention with which it was written, the career of alliterative verse came to an inglorious end, a full century after it had last been used for poetry worthy of the name. It was a fate to which one might fittingly apply the words with which Burns pointed his epigram on the Earl of Galloway

> So ran the far-famed Roman way,
>> And ended in a mire.

Although they came so late into the field, and produced so

little in comparison with their English predecessors, the Scottish alliterative poets had one advantage over these. They wrote in the common language of the country, with only a limited number of archaic or rare words, and could thus command a large body of readers. In consequence of this, almost everything that they are known to have written found its way into print in the sixteenth century and the early part of the seventeenth. In England, on the contrary, the dialectal features of so many of the poems must have prevented a wide circulation outside of the area in which they originated. On this account, and because a general interest in them had clearly declined in the latter part of the fifteenth century, the early printers had no inducement to employ their presses in printing them. With the exception of the Vision of Piers the Plowman, which Crowley printed in 1550, not a single piece has survived except in manuscript, and of many only a unique copy is extant.

This difference in respect of language was not entirely due to dialectal variations in the English poems or to the later date of the Scottish. The principles of alliterative verse partly compelled, but also encouraged, the poet to make full use of the vocabulary which he had at his command, in order to provide every line with at least two or three, and sometimes four or five, words beginning with the same letter. Those who had a copious fund of language took full advantage of the opportunity, bringing into the verse a large number of rare words, and sometimes increasing the demand for these by running on the alliteration for two or three, or even more, lines. This richness of language is especially noticeable in the more northerly poems, such as the Wars of Alexander, the Morte Arthure, and Sir Gawayne and the Green Knight, in which a Scandinavian element is added to the English and French vocabulary of the more southern texts. The preservation of many of those Scandinavian words is entirely due to their usefulness for alliteration. The result is that the alliterative poems are a real storehouse of Middle English, and from that source alone a very full dictionary could be compiled. If this had been done some fifty or sixty years ago, when the serious study of the poems began, it would have prevented many hasty conclusions as to common authorship or mutual relationship, based on comparison of only two or three texts.

Most of this special vocabulary is limited to the period when alliterative poetry was at its highest point, and only certain elements of it were retained by the Scottish poets. One of these was the convenient variety of synonyms for 'man' or 'men', which run through most of the alphabet, and from which the poet could select whichever suited the other words in the line. They included for example: bern, carl, freke, gome, grome, hathill, lede, renk, sege or segg, swain, and wy. In addition to these the Scots took over various rhyme-tags, and some English forms which were convenient for rhyme, as 'bold' or 'more' in place of the native 'bald' and 'mare'. They also followed their English models in using a large stock of adjectives, usually of commendation, which similarly covered most of the alphabet, as: bald, blithe, clere, courtes, cruel, cumly, digne, doughty, fre, fresche, gay, grim, gude, hende, kene, prise, proud, pure, stalwart, stout, strang, sture, traist, vailyeand, wicht, yape. A liberal use of these was of great service to the poet, especially if their appropriateness to the person or occasion was not too closely considered. Some of them, however, now seem unsuitable merely because the modern application is different, as when Douglas is made to call Bruce 'my singular sovereign', or 'a prise knight' is mentioned in alliteration with 'pity'. Most of the adjectives employed for this purpose were words in common use, and on the whole the Scottish poets are not given to go outside of the traditional vocabulary of poetry, or even of ordinary speech. When a violent storm is called 'a ferlyfull flan', neither of the words would have sounded strange to a Scot of that time or of a much later generation. In three verses of the Howlat there are respectively eleven, six, and seven words which would be unfamiliar to a modern English reader, but only five or six of these do not belong to the ordinary Scottish tongue of the period, and even those would be perfectly understood by any one acquainted with the language of poetry.

In several of the English poems there is clear evidence that they were intended to be read aloud or recited as a means of entertainment, and the textual variations in some of the shorter pieces can best be accounted for by oral transmission; they had been learned by heart, and written down from memory or dictation. In the Scottish poems the only suggestion of hearers, rather than readers, is Dunbar's question addressed to his 'auditoris most honorable, that eris has gevin onto this uncouth aventure', but it is not certain that this is to be taken literally, although the poet may quite well have read his tale to an audience not so refined as to be scandalized by its coarseness. In this or any of the Scottish pieces there is no sign of oral transmission; the texts clearly rest upon manuscript and printed copies.

In respect both of extent and variety of subject the Scottish alliterative poems as a whole fall far short of the English, though in one of the types they hold the higher place. Dunbar's 'Tretis' of 530 lines of the ordinary unrhymed type exceeds in length only two or three of the shortest English pieces, and is a mere trifle in comparison with the many which run into thousands of lines. His subject, it is true, is original, but does not bear comparison with poems of real genius which recount tales of ancient history or medieval chivalry, or discuss in fluent verse the political, social, and religious questions of the day. So far as works of outstanding literary value are concerned, the continuous alliterative line had reached its culminating point by the end of the fourteenth century, and neither England nor Scotland made any worthy addition to it after that date.

In the stanzaic rhyming type, on the other hand, the Scottish poets apparently surpassed their models both in quantity and quality. Their joint production extends to over 4,000 lines, rather more than double of what has been preserved on the English side. Among the older pieces, while the Aunters of Arthur may justly be placed over against Golagros and Gawane, the Pistill of Susan and the Quatrefoil of Love are uninspired and trivial in comparison with the Howlat and Rauf Coilȝear. Here, however, the record of real achievement ends; all that was produced after 1500 barely exceeds 600 lines, and enough has already been said as to its poetic value.

The English alliterative poems as a whole are anonymous. Only two Williams are known, as the authors of William of Palerne and the Vision of Piers Plowman; the surname of the former is not recorded and that of the latter is doubtful. Among the Scottish pieces, so much fewer in number, the proportion of known authorship is much higher, the only exceptions of importance being Rauf Coilȝear and Golagros and Gawane, which thus share in the general anonymity of the great body of medieval romances.

The reasons for the failure of alliterative verse to maintain itself as one of the normal forms of English poetry are not far to seek. With the loss of quantity, and lack of definite rules as to the number and placing of the alliterative words, the Middle English line became too formless and gave too much scope for careless composition, while the poet was apt to give way to the weakness of using words merely because they began with the required letter, whether they were the most appropriate or not. In the face of these defects, lines which were so irregular in their

beat compared unfavourably with those in which stressed and
unstressed syllables came alternately. Even the classical hexa-
meter, with all the authority of the Greek and Latin poets to
recommend it, has not been adopted as one of the ordinary
forms of English verse, evidently for the same reason. After
rhyme had become so thoroughly established in all other verse-
forms, its absence was no doubt felt by ears accustomed to it as
a real want in the ordinary alliterative poem, while in the
alliterative stanza the addition of elaborate rhyming did not
reconcile the ear to the stumbling (King James's 'tumbling')
effect of the line. The tradition of correct alliterative verse,
subject to strict rules, did not last long enough in England to
have the same effect as it had in Iceland. There also, about the
middle of the fourteenth century, and so contemporaneously
with the rise of the Middle English alliterative poetry, a new
type of versification was introduced, that of the *rímur*, in which
end-rhymes, previously rarely used, became regular. Here,
however, the proper number and placing of the alliterative
letters was carefully observed, and the movement of the line
was regularly trochaic, whereas in the older poetry there had
been some freedom in the placing of the heavier and lighter
syllables. As the result of these changes the many varieties of
metre employed in the *rímur*, instead of becoming antiquated
and discarded, were steadily added to, and have remained in
use right down to the present day. Unless some such change
had taken place in English practice, the alliterative metre could
not have successfully competed with other types of verse; in the
forms which it actually assumed and retained its decline and
disappearance sooner or later were inevitable.

SOME REFLECTIONS ON CHAUCER'S 'ART POETICAL'

By DOROTHY EVERETT

Read 15 November 1950

WHEN the British Academy did me the honour of inviting me to give the Gollancz Memorial Lecture, I recalled a day long ago on which I had the privilege of visiting Sir Israel Gollancz at King's College, and of consulting him about a piece of work I was hoping to undertake. This seems the fitting occasion to record my gratitude for the kindly help and encouragement he then gave to a mere beginner, who had no claim upon him other than an interest in the Middle English writings to which he devoted so much of his life.

The third book of Chaucer's *House of Fame* opens with the poet's plea to Apollo to guide him in what he is about to write, a plea that echoes Dante's at the beginning of the *Paradiso*; but, instead of continuing as Dante does, Chaucer adds,

> Nat that I wilne, for maistrye,
> Here art poetical be shewed.[1]

I am not going to consider in detail what precisely Chaucer meant by 'art poetical'; I shall assume that, in this context, the expression, like the word 'craft', which seems to be used as a synonym a few lines later, implies knowledge of how to write poetry (or skill in writing it) according to established rules. This is, I think, in line with what many medieval writers understood by 'art'.[2]

Chaucer's statement in the *House of Fame* that he does not wish to manifest such knowledge or skill reminds one of other passages in which he, or sometimes one of his characters, disclaims any power as a writer or speaker but that of plain speech. More than once what is specifically disclaimed is a knowledge of the 'colours' of rhetoric.[3] 'Thyng that I speke, it moot be bare and pleyn' says the Franklin, and adds, 'Colours ne knowe I none'. It can therefore, I think, be assumed that, to Chaucer, 'art poetical' could mean, more particularly, knowledge of poetic art (or, as we might call it, technique) as set out in such medieval treatises as Geoffroi de Vinsauf's *Nova Poetria* (which Chaucer certainly knew) and the *Ars versificatoria* of Matthieu de Vendôme—treatises in which certain parts of the old doctrine of *rhetorica* are applied to poetry. Whatever be the reason for Chaucer's disclaimers—and it should be remarked that they usually occur in works which are by no means devoid of poetic art in the sense in which I am thinking of it—they suggest a consciousness on his part, perhaps even an acute consciousness, of the kind of thing they disclaim.

The effect which the teaching of the so-called rhetoricians (Geoffroi de Vinsauf, Matthieu de Vendôme and the rest) had on Chaucer's writing has been discussed by a number of scholars, notably by the late Professor Manly.[4] Attention has been drawn to Chaucer's artificial beginnings, his use of some of the means of amplification described in the treatises, and his frequent introduction of certain rhetorical tropes and figures. The tendency in several of these discussions has been to consider such features in Chaucer's poetry more or less in isolation, and to look upon them as mere ornaments, appendages to something which could have existed without them,[5] and which, it is sometimes implied, would have been the better for their absence. This attitude is natural enough, for as one reads the late twelfth and early thirteenth century Arts of Poetry which have been mainly considered in relation to Chaucer, they do suggest a purely mechanical conception of poetry. But, to understand fully the influence which these treatises had on medieval poets, I think it is necessary to keep in mind the purpose for which they were written. Several of them were school-books, written either by school-masters, or for them.[6] They were intended for use in teaching boys who had already received instruction in *grammatica*, that is (to paraphrase one of the well-known definitions) who had been taught how to interpret authors (including poets) and how to write and speak correctly.[7] The treatises of the so-called rhetoricians seem to have been designed to carry this elementary study farther by directing attention to certain aspects of poetical composition not already considered, including the use of rhetorical tropes and 'colours'. It is likely that, as in the earlier study of *grammatica*, a boy was expected to learn both by analysis and by composition (of course in Latin).[8] Inevitably, those so trained (which means, I suppose, the majority of educated men) would come to think of poetry largely in terms of the statements and descriptions they had been taught, and, if a man were himself a poet, he would, both consciously and unconsciously, apply what he had learnt to his own writing.[9] That this resulted in some excessively ornate verse, we know; but it has of late years been recognized that there were also other, quite different, results, of more fundamental importance for literature. Professor Vinaver has claimed that it was from the study of *rhetorica* (at least partly as presented in treatises of the kind I have mentioned) that medieval French writers of romance learnt how to organize their stories so as to express a particular point of view; and he has shown that the form of, for instance, the *Suite du Merlin* is the result of using the device of *digressio* to explain the story. Writing of the general significance of the study of rhetoric in the earlier Middle Ages, Professor Vinaver says, 'The discipline which in the later Middle Ages was to be largely reduced to mere stylistic ornamentation had not at that time lost its original composing function. In a number of important works embodying the doctrine of the rhetoricians from Quintilian onwards the term *colores rhetoricae* refers, as in Cicero, not so much to formal elaboration as to the 'treatment of the matter' from the speaker's or writer's point of view'.[10] Professor Vinaver then goes on to show that there is 'a significant agreement in this respect' between Quintilian and certain medieval writers, even as late as John of Salisbury.

There is one point in this passage to which I would object—the assumption that it was no longer possible to regard rhetoric in this way in the later Middle Ages. I believe that, for a number of English poets of the late fourteenth century, *rhetorica* still had some of its old 'composing function'. In particular, I think that it can be shown that Chaucer dealt with certain problems of presentation and organization in ways which are traceable, though certainly not always directly, to rhetorical teaching.[11]

I shall begin with a simple example, the opening stanza of the *Parlement of Foules*. The first line, 'The lyf so short, the craft so long to lerne', has often been remarked on as an instance of one of the artificial ways of beginning a poem—the beginning with a *sententia*—and there are several other rhetorical devices in the stanza. But what is interesting is the way the devices are used. Chaucer's subject in the *Parlement* was to be love, a subject familiar enough in the courtly poetry of his day. His problem was to introduce it so as immediately to arrest the attention of his hearers or readers.[12] What he does is to take the well-known *sententia* 'Ars longa, vita brevis' and use it as a circumlocutory description of his subject. Its form, that of a *contentio* (two contrasted phrases, here applied to the same thing) is arresting, and

Chaucer emphasizes it by adding a second circumlocution in the same form,

> Th'assay so hard, so sharp the conquerynge.

The third line repeats the pattern with a difference, the phrase 'the dredful joye' itself containing a contrast, and being amplified by a descriptive phrase, 'alwey that slit so yerne'. Then comes the point to which Chaucer has been leading—'Al this mene I by love'. Having thus given great stress to the idea of love, and at the same time provided some indication of the kind of love he is going to write of, Chaucer amplifies the idea by another descriptive phrase suggesting love's mysterious power and something of his own attitude towards it—

> Al this mene I by love, that my felynge
> Astonyeth with his wonderful werkynge
> So sore iwis, that whan I on hym thynke,
> Nat wot I wel wher that I flete or synke.

This analysis, I hope, makes it clear that the rhetorical devices used here are not, as it were, appended to the fabric of the stanza; they are themselves the fabric. The problem of how to present the subject effectively has been solved entirely by rhetorical methods.

It may be objected that the *Parlement* is a comparatively early work, written when Chaucer was most under the influence of the rhetoricians. In answer to this, I would suggest that the opening of the *Prologue* to the *Canterbury Tales*, though more complex, is organized on lines which are not dissimilar. To present the idea of spring which, as it revivifies all things, fires men with the desire to go on pilgrimage, Chaucer once again begins with several circumlocutory descriptive phrases (each, it may incidentally be noted, displaying some 'colour' of rhetoric),

> Whan that Aprille with his shoures soote
> The droghte of March hath perced to the roote . . .
> Whan Zephirus eek with his sweete breeth
> Inspired hath in every holt and heeth
> The tendre croppes, and the yonge sonne
> Hath in the Ram his halve cours yronne . . .

Finally he comes to his point,

> Thanne longen folk to goon on pilgrimages.

From *Troilus and Criseyde* one other example may be quoted which is not, like these two, from the beginning of a work.

Chaucer has told how Troilus was struck 'atte fulle' by the god
of love, and he wishes us to see his case in wider perspective.
We are to understand that, for all his pride, Troilus could not
hope to escape love. It was his destiny, as it is every man's.
Chaucer begins with the apostrophe,

> O blynde world, O blynde entencioun!
> How often falleth al the effect contraire
> Of surquidrie and foul presumpcioun;
> For kaught is proud, and kaught is debonaire.
> This Troilus is clomben on the staire,
> And litel weneth that he moot descenden;
> But alday faileth thing that fooles wenden.[13]

The *sententia* which forms the last line of this stanza is followed
by the comparison of Troilus to 'proude Bayard', kept in check
by the whip, and this in turn by an apostrophe to 'worthi folkes
alle' to take example from Troilus not to scorn love, 'For may
no man fordon the lawe of kynde'.

I have chosen to illustrate the rhetorical presentation of an
idea, but Chaucer uses similar methods for other purposes, for
the presentation of an argument, for instance, as when the old
hag in the *Wife of Bath's Tale* discourses to her husband on the
true nature of 'gentillesse' and the virtues of poverty, or when
Pluto and Proserpyne, in the *Merchant's Tale*, dispute about
January's predicament.[14] Most of all he uses these methods in
description; but instances of descriptions rhetorically presented
are so common in his work at all periods that there is no need
for me to 'sermoun of it more'.

To catch the hearer's or the reader's attention and fix it on
an idea is one thing; it is a different matter to ensure that his
mind will retain that idea for just as long as the poet wishes.
In the early *Book of the Duchess*, Chaucer employs, for this end, a
means which, in our day, Mr. T. S. Eliot has found effective—
that of verbal repetition.[15] The opening lines of the poem, in
which the poet complains that he cannot sleep, contain a succession of phrases expressing the main idea, 'withoute slep', 'I
may nat slepe', 'defaute of slep', the last two of which occur
more than once. This might be thought accidental, but further
examination of the poem shows that it is not. There is an echo
of these phrases a little later when Chaucer is about to relate
how he took a book to 'drive the night away'; and, when he has
finished reading about Ceys and Alcyone, and is telling how
this story gave him the idea of praying to the god of sleep for
help,[16] his lines echo and re-echo with phrases containing the

words 'sleep' or 'sleeping', in the following order, 'defaute of
slep', 'For I ne myghte, for bote ne bale, Slepe', 'goddes
of slepyng', 'goddes that koude make Men to slepe', 'defaute of
slepynge', 'make me slepe', 'make me slepe a lyte', 'to slepe softe',
'make me slepe sone'. These all occur in about forty lines; they
culminate, some ten lines farther on, in the statement,

> Such a lust anoon me took
> To slepe, that ryght upon my book
> Y fil aslepe.

Other parts of the *Book of the Duchess* show a similar, though
usually less frequent and less effective, repetition of what one
may call a key-word or key-phrase. In the passage describing
the hunt, the words 'hunt', 'hunting', 'huntes' ('hunters'),
'hunten' recur, and a little later the changes are rung on the
words 'floury', 'floures'. It would, I think, be possible to show
that in the first part of the description of the poet's dream, almost
every paragraph has its own key-word or phrase, and though
the practice is less marked later, there are still signs of it, for
example in ll. 617–54, where the word 'fals', first introduced in
the phrase 'fals Fortune', appears again and again.

This kind of verbal repetition is not confined to Chaucer's
early work. There is a more restrained and more subtle use of
it in the *Prioress's Tale*. The word 'litel', several times repeated
in the opening stanzas ('A litel scole', 'A litel clergeon', 'This
litel child, his litel book lernynge'), is caught up from time to
time, later in the tale, in the phrases 'this litel child', 'hir litel
child', 'My litel child'. The reiteration of this word is doubly
effective, as recalling the boy martyr who 'so yong and tendre
was of age', and as a reminder of the teller of the tale, with whose
nature it is so perfectly in keeping. With the line, 'He Alma
redemptoris herde synge', a second *motif* is introduced, which
is reflected by the repetition, at intervals throughout the rest
of the tale, both of word 'synge' (or 'song') and of some part of
the phrase 'O Alma redemptoris mater'. The two combine in
a triumphant line when the martyred child is lying on his bier
before the high altar—

> Yet spak this child, whan spreynd was hooly water,
> And song O Alma redemptoris mater.[17]

The opening sections of the *Book of the Duchess* also provide
the first hints for another use of repetition. The repeated word
'slepe', besides sounding the key-note of a passage, serves as a
link between one paragraph and another some distance from it.

This use of repetition, as a device to link different parts of a work, is also to be found in Chaucer's later poems. An instance of it in the *Canterbury Tales*, the echo in the Merchant's Prologue of the last line of the Clerk's Envoy, is well known; but it is, I think, worth while to look at it again. The Clerk has followed up his tale of Griselda with the warning that 'Grisilde is deed and eek hire pacience', and then, addressing wives, he ironically bids them, 'sharply taak on yow the governaille'. He concludes,

Be ay of chiere as light as leef on lynde,
And lat hym [the husband] care, and wepe, and wrynge and waille.

This is too much for the Merchant, who bursts out,

Wepyng and waylyng, care and oother sorwe
I knowe ynogh . . .,

and he explains that he has a wife, 'the worste that may be', to whom he has been wedded just two months. Here the Merchant's repetition of the Clerk's words acts as a mechanical link between two tales; but it does much more than this. It reveals at once the overcharged heart of the Merchant and so prepares us for the bitter tone of the tale that follows.

A rather different effect is produced by the same device in the *Parlement of Foules*. In Chaucer's account of the *Somnium Scipionis*, Africanus tells Scipio that

what man, lered other lewed,
That lovede commune profyt, wel ithewed,
He shulde into a blysful place wende,
There as joye is that last withouten ende.

The words 'blysful place' are again used by Africanus at the end of the dream, and are kept in mind during the course of it by the phrases 'hevene blisse' and 'that ful of blysse is'. When Chaucer has ceased his reading, which has given him a hint of celestial bliss, he falls asleep and is himself led by Africanus to a gate which we shall presently know to be the entrance to the garden of love. The first inscription he reads over the gate runs,

Thorgh me men gon into that blysful place
Of hertes hele and dedly woundes cure.

So, at the moment of entering the garden of love, we are made to recall that other 'blysful place'.[18]

One more instance, from the *Merchant's Tale*. Chaucer tells us that the young wife May is so moved by pity for the squire

Damyan that she decides to grant him her grace. 'Whom that this thyng displese, I rekke noght', she says to herself. This is the prelude to her deception of her old husband and, at this point, Chaucer slips in the words which he twice uses elsewhere in the *Canterbury Tales*,

> Lo, pitee renneth soone in gentil herte!

The repetition reveals, as nothing else could, the gulf between May's pity for Damyan, and the pity of Duke Theseus for the rival lovers or of the innocent Canacee for the deserted falcon.[19]

It would be well to consider at this point how Chaucer's practice in this matter of verbal repetition is related to the teaching of the rhetoricians. They recognize, among the 'colours' of rhetoric, seven or eight varieties of verbal repetition, minutely distinguished by such characteristics as the position of the repeated words in the sentence (*repetitio, conversio, complexio*), whether the repetition is of identical or similar sounds, either in related forms or otherwise (*annominatio*), or of words with the same sound but different meanings (a species of *traductio*). Some of these rigidly defined varieties of repetition are to be found in Chaucer's writings, but most of the instances I have just been considering could not, I believe, be classified under any of the types mentioned in the treatises. Moreover, the rhetoricians do not as a rule make any suggestion as to how or why repetition should be used. It is not possible, therefore, to claim that Chaucer learnt the kind of practice which I have illustrated directly from the precepts of the rhetoricians.[20] This, however, is not what I am trying to show; but rather—to repeat what I said earlier—that in certain problems of presentation or organization he used methods adapted from the teaching of the rhetoricians or in some way traceable to its influence. Sometimes he combined a number of devices actually described in the treatises known to us, as he does at the beginning of the *Parlement of Foules* or of the *General Prologue*. Sometimes he adapted devices (that is, either devices actually mentioned by the rhetoricians or others like them) to special purposes which the rhetoricians themselves need not have considered. Here his use of verbal repetition as a linking device may possibly be included, though I think that even this is likely to be an over-simplification of the facts. This particular use of repetition is not confined to Chaucer; it appears elsewhere in medieval poetry, particularly perhaps in Middle English alliterative poetry. There are traces of it in Laȝamon's *Brut* and the alliterative *Morte Arthure*; and in *Purity* (*Cleanness*) the repetition of part, or the whole, of the text of the homily helps to link the several Biblical stories which illustrate it.[21] Chaucer may have known in earlier or contemporary poetry something which gave him a hint of the possibilities of repetition as a linking device, and he may have been consciously influenced by that. In that case his use of the device is traceable to the teaching of the rhetoricians only in the widest possible sense—that a poet trained in that teaching could hardly have failed to observe it and to consider its value for purposes of presentation.

It was necessary to make a distinction between a slavish imitation of the devices which the rhetoricians describe, and the adaptation of these devices, or others like them, to individual ends, because most of the examples of Chaucer's methods which I am going to consider next may not seem to have any connexion with the Arts of Poetry. All these examples have to do with a major problem of organization, the layout (or *dispositio*) of a poem as a whole, or of a large part of it; and more than one critic has pointed out that the rhetoricians have little to say about this.

For my first example I turn once again to the *Book of the Duchess*. We have here the unusual advantage of knowing the occasion for which it was written. We can say with certainty that, in the poet's dream of the Black Knight who is grieving for the loss of his dead lady, Chaucer figures the loss which John of Gaunt suffered in the death of his wife Blanche. Before this dream begins, however, there is a long introductory passage which includes the story of Ceys and Alcyone. Chaucer gives a reason for the inclusion of this story when he tells us that the reading of it gave him the idea of praying to Morpheus for sleep. But there is another, unstated reason, of much more significance for the poem as a whole. The real point of the story for Chaucer was that it told of a wife's grief for the loss of her husband, and thus provided a parallel, with a difference, to the main theme of the poem. (That Chaucer meant it to be so understood is clear from his omission of the beautiful end of Ovid's story; for the transformation of Ceys and Alcyone into birds, and their happy reunion, have no part in the parallel.)[22] To the medieval mind, accustomed to look behind appearances to the inner meaning, this story, and the dream of the Black Knight, could be two examples of the same theme—the loss of a loved one and the grief of the one who is left. Looked at in this way, Chaucer's organization of this poem could, I think, be regarded as a special application of Geoffroi de Vinsauf's first means of amplification, *interpretatio*, of which he writes, 'let the same thing

be covered in many forms; be various and yet the same' ('multiplice forma dissimuletur idem; varius sis et tamen idem'.)[23]

There is an obvious similarity between the layout of the
Book of the Duchess and that of the earlier part of the *Parlement
of Foules*. In the *Parlement* the poet places side by side two visions,
the one read in a book and concerned with the blissful place
that awaits the righteous who work for common profit, the
other concerned with that blissful place, which, to some, is the
'wey to al good aventure', but brings others to the 'mortal
strokes of the spere'—that is, the garden of love. The two visions
are linked, not merely verbally, but by the fact that Africanus
is the guide in both.[24] But the similarity of this arrangement to
that of the *Book of the Duchess* is only partial, for the two stories
in the earlier poem are parallels, but the two visions in the
Parlement are parallel only in form; in significance they present
a contrast. This is never stated, for the contrast between heavenly
and earthly bliss, which Chaucer makes explicitly at the end of
Troilus and Criseyde, would be too weighty a matter for this
much lighter poem. Yet I think it is just hinted at in the lines
at the end of the first vision where the poet tells us that, on
finishing his book, he went to bed,

> Fulfyld of thought and busy hevynesse;
> For bothe I hadde thyng which that I nolde,
> And ek I nadde that thyng that I wolde.[25]

Later in this poem another contrast is suggested by the descriptions of the two goddesses, Venus and Nature. Chaucer
first describes Venus lying in a dark corner of the temple which,
he has told us, is filled with the sound of 'sykes (sighs) hoote
as fyr .... Whiche sikes were engendered with desyr'. Then
he presents Nature, the deputy of that almighty Lord who knits
the discordant elements into a harmony. Nature sits, surrounded
by the birds, on a hill of flowers, and Chaucer remarks that her
halls and bowers were made of branches. Again no explicit
contrast is made; the two juxtaposed descriptions merely hint
at the difference between courtly love and the natural love of
creature for creature which will culminate in the unions of the
lesser birds.

This method of presenting, in more or less parallel forms, two
things which are essentially to be contrasted cannot be directly
related to anything recommended by the rhetoricians, though
Matthieu de Vendôme's portraits of Helen and Beroe, which
present the antithesis of beauty and ugliness, could possibly

have provided some suggestion for it.[26] But it may well have been developed by Chaucer himself from his use of parallels in the *Book of the Duchess*. The more complex scheme was perhaps more after Chaucer's mind. Certainly he makes a masterly use of it in the *Canterbury Tales*, when the Miller 'quits' the Knight's noble tale of the rivalry of Palamon and Arcite for Emelye with the low comedy of the rivalry of the two Oxford clerks for the carpenter's wife. Here, too, there is a verbal link, when the line spoken by the dying Arcite is applied to Nicholas in his neat chamber—'Allone, withouten any compaignye'.

I turn next to some of Chaucer's tales, and I shall begin with the *Knight's Tale*, the presentation of which has, perhaps, something in common with what I have been describing, though it is, of course, far more complex. But, before I can go 'streght to my matere', I must digress a little to consider, though very sketchily, some of the ways in which parallels are used by other medieval story-tellers. Parallelism, of one kind or another, is, of course, a marked feature of medieval story-telling. In its simplest form, it consists in a repetition of the same incident with some variation in detail. This is what we often find in folk-tales, and in many medieval romances which are derived from them. There is an instance of it in Chaucer's *Man of Law's Tale* where, as in other versions of the Constance story known to us, the heroine is twice set adrift in an open boat. In this form the parallelism can have nothing to do with rhetorical teaching, though it witnesses, I suppose, to some primitive feeling for an ordered narrative. But this simple device was developed in various ways by story-tellers who had something of their own to express. One development has been explained by Professor Vinaver in his introduction to the French romance of *Balain*. In this romance, Balain has many and various adventures which appear to be quite unconnected with one another, but, as Professor Vinaver has shown, they are actually 'parallels' in the sense that they all illustrate the same thing, the *mescheance* ('ill-fortune') which finally overwhelms Balain.[27] (It may be remarked, incidentally, that this seems to have something in common with Chaucer's method in the *Book of the Duchess*. To it, too, one could apply Geoffroi de Vinsauf's words, 'multiplice forma dissimuletur idem'). This way of presenting a story does, as Professor Vinaver claims, render it coherent and emotionally satisfying; but it has the obvious disadvantage of leaving it shapeless. Yet, in parallelism itself there are the beginnings of design, as we can see from folk-tales; and this

potentiality was also developed in medieval poetry. The Middle
English romance of *Sir Gawain and the Green Knight* is an outstanding example of how, by means of parallel incidents and
descriptions, a narrative can be fashioned into a comprehensive
pattern. The poet of *Gawain* was not, however, content merely
to produce a formal order. His interest was in knightly virtue,
and particularly the virtue of 'courtesy', as illustrated in the
character of Gawain; and the incidents of the story have meaning
and coherence because they throw light upon the various
aspects of Gawain's 'courtesy', just as Balain's many adventures
are given meaning by the underlying theme of *mescheance*. The
Gawain poet has, in fact, seen how to use his parallels in two ways
at once, so as to produce both an internal and an external order.

Chaucer never wrote anything quite like this, but his *Knight's
Tale*, though less completely patterned, is nevertheless an example of a narrative comprehensively organized for a particular
end; and again the organization largely depends on a skilful use
of parallelism. In a recent article, to which I am very much indebted in what I shall say about this tale, Mr. William Frost
remarks that:

> Much of the beauty of the Knight's Tale . . . resides in a certain
> formal regularity of design. Thus the May-songs of Emelye and Arcite
> . . . come at two crucial points in the plot; while early May is also the
> time of the final contest that will make one hero happy and the other
> glorious. Thus the Tale begins with a wedding, a conquest and a
> funeral; and ends with a tournament, a funeral and a wedding.[28]

These are, of course, relatively unimportant parts of the design,
but they are interesting because they indicate how comprehensive the design is. At the centre of it, so to speak, there are the
two knights, Arcite and Palemon, and, in order that our attention may not be distracted from them, Emelye's part in the
action is diminished (as compared with that of Boccaccio's
Emilia),[29] so that she is little more than the beautiful object of
their desire.

Mr. Frost has remarked on the 'systematic and delicately
balanced parallelism' of Chaucer's presentation of Arcite and
Palemon, and on the fact that this parallelism intensifies the
problem of who shall win Emily. It should also be noticed that
it throws into relief the one point in which the heroes differ.
Though Chaucer makes them similar in age, rank, and fortune,
and in general individualizes them little, he does differentiate
them in the one point that matters for the story—their behaviour
as lovers. Moreover, he remodels Boccaccio's account of their

first sight of Emelye so that the impact of love immediately reveals this difference. In Chaucer's story it is Palemon who first sees Emelye, and it is only he who takes her to be the goddess Venus.[30] Arcite knows at once that she is a woman, and is quick to recognize that henceforth he and Palemon are rivals. It is he who casts aside the ties of friendship, declaring,

> Ech man for hymself: ther is noon oother.

The significance of this scene is well brought out by Mr. Frost. It marks the beginning of the conflict and at the same time prepares the way for the resolving of it. For Arcite, who has shown himself to be what is now called a 'realist' in love and in friendship, will pray to Mars for victory in the tournament, believing that thereby he will win Emelye; but Palemon will care nothing for victory and will simply beg Venus, 'Yif me my love, thow blisful lady deere'. So, when Mars and Venus are allowed to grant the two suppliants what they asked for, it follows that Arcite will be victorious, but must die before he can possess Emelye, and that Palemon will be defeated, but will win Emelye in the end. Chaucer leaves no loose end; even the broken friendship is repaired in the dying Arcite's generous words about Palemon. The conclusion is a neat and, one might almost say, logical result of the one difference in the two men who were in so many ways alike.

If this were all there is to the tale, I think one would object that it is too neat and logical to be just. Certainly one might feel this strongly in the case of Arcite, who cannot be thought to have fully deserved his cruel fate. But there is, of course, another aspect of Chaucer's tale. He inherited from Boccaccio's *Teseida* the conflict between Mars and Venus, of which the conflict between the two knights is a reflection on the earthly plane; he also inherited the parallelism between Saturn's function, as arbiter between Mars and Venus, and Theseus's function, as arbiter between the knights. The parallelism between Saturn and Theseus Chaucer developed farther. The story of Palemon and Arcite becomes in his hands an illustration of the power which destiny wields over man. This theme is emphasized at the beginning by the victims themselves. 'Fortune hath yeven us this adversitee', says Arcite, of their imprisonment, 'We moste endure it; this is the short and playn'; and a little later Palemon is railing at the 'crueel goddes that governe This world with byndyng of youre word eterne'. As they complain, they are the prisoners of Theseus, who at all times in the story has power of life and death over them. So, the control which the gods have over man is made manifest in the material world by the power of Theseus; he is (to quote Mr. Frost again) the 'executant of destiny' on earth, and in this respect, too, he parallels the functions of the planetary powers and, more particularly, of Saturn. But, according to the Boethian philosophy, which Chaucer is reflecting in this poem, the planetary powers are not the final arbiters. It is fittingly left to Theseus, who stands outside the conflict and can see a little more than the other human actors, to recall the 'Firste Moevere', 'the prince and cause of alle thyng', who, when he first made the fair chain of love, 'Wel wiste he why, and what thereof he mente'. With this concluding speech Theseus removes the human conflict, and its apparently unjust resolving, to a yet more distant plane where earthly affairs, however they may seem to men, are part of an established order, a plan in which, though man cannot hope to understand it, he should acquiesce.

I have tried to show only the main features of the organization of the *Knight's Tale*, but there is much on a lesser scale which reveals similar methods. I will mention one instance only. It is well known that, in place of Boccaccio's diffuse account of the many champions who come to fight for Palemon and Arcite, Chaucer describes two champions only, Lygurge and Emetreus. Thereby his story obviously gains in brevity, neatness, and vividness. What is more important, it also gains in significance. The two champions stand as representatives of the two opposing forces in the coming tournament, and so, ultimately, as representatives of the two rival knights. The two descriptions, though entirely different in detail, are alike in manner, suggesting the same kind of parallelism as between Palemon and Arcite, between things similar yet dissimilar. In several ways this comparatively minor piece of reorganization could be said to epitomize what Chaucer does in his tale as a whole.

It is a far cry from this finely ordered tale to the treatises of the rhetoricians, and I can produce no logical proof of a connexion between them. I can only hope that the various links which I have tried to establish between the Arts of Poetry and Chaucer's practice are sufficiently strong to support my feeling that this kind of order is the product of a genius which has known the discipline of a training in medieval rhetoric, or, more properly speaking, in the 'art' of poetry.

As my last examples I shall take three tales—the tales of the Pardoner, the Manciple, and the Nun's Priest—in which the

methods of presentation are much more directly related to
rhetorical teaching. Indeed, it can be said of all three, diverse
as they are in subject and mood, that in them Chaucer used
rhetorical methods more or less as the rhetoricians themselves
intended. Manly remarked of the *Pardoner's Tale* that the story
of the three rioters displays Chaucer's 'advanced method' (by
which he meant that the rhetorical influence in it is slight) and
that 'the long passages of rhetoric, placed between the opening
twenty lines, . . . and the narrative itself, are thoroughly explained and justified by their function as part of the Pardoner's
sermon'.[31] This, I think, gives a false impression. The *Pardoner's
Tale* does not consist of a more or less unadorned story plus
some passages of rhetoric. On the contrary, the whole discourse
which is known as the tale of the Pardoner is a closely integrated
unity. In the opening twenty lines to which Manly refers, the
Pardoner provides the setting for a story by describing a company
of 'yonge folk that haunteden folye'. As he explains, these
young folk spent their time whoring, playing at dice, eating
and drinking excessively, and swearing oaths,

> so greet and so dampnable
> That it is grisly for to heere hem swere.

The Pardoner then pauses to dilate upon some of these sins,
in particular upon lechery, gluttony, gambling, and swearing.
He uses for this purpose various means of amplification, apostrophe and *exemplum* being his favourites. When he has finished
inveighing against the sins, he tells the terrible tale of the three
rioters.[32] This is an impressive illustration, not only of his
favourite theme, 'Radix malorum est cupiditas,' but also of what
may befall those who commit the sins he has preached against,
and he rounds it off with a final apostrophe against homicide,
gluttony, hasardry, and swearing. The story and the tirade
against the sins are so closely connected with one another that
one can either regard the story as an *exemplum* illustrating the
tirade, or one can consider the story as the central point and
the dilations upon the sins as amplifications of it. Either way,
the whole tale is organized according to rhetorical methods.

But this organization is for a special purpose. By his words
at the end of his Prologue,

> A moral tale yet I yow telle kan
> Which I am wont to preche . . .

the Pardoner has led the reader to expect something related to
a sermon. What Chaucer gives him is not a sermon constructed

according to the elaborate rules of the *Artes praedicandi* (which would, in any case, have been unsuited to the Pardoner's usual audience, and his present one); but a tale so presented that it will create the illusion of a sermon. It has some of the regular features of a sermon. The theme is known, for the Pardoner has said that he has only one. His final apostrophe against the sins acts as a peroration, and is followed by a benediction.[33] In his dilations upon the sins of hasardry and swearing there is a slight suggestion of the 'division' of the theme, so essential a part of the medieval sermon; for these are branches of avarice, as appears from a passage in the treatise on the seven deadly sins which forms part of the *Parson's Tale*—a passage which is actually echoed by the Pardoner.[34] But, for the most part, the illusion depends upon the Pardoner's examples, especially the Scriptural ones at the beginning, and on his direct attacks upon the sins, or the sinner—

> O glotonye, ful of cursednesse!
> O cause first of oure confusioun!

and,

> O dronke man, disfigured is thy face . . .

It depends, that is, on a few common rhetorical devices—devices fitting for a preacher and appropriate in the mouth of the Pardoner, who has told us that, as he preaches,

> Myne handes and my tonge goon so yerne,
> That it is joye to se my bisynesse.

So the tale is shaped for its ultimate purpose, the completing of the portrait of the Pardoner; but that purpose is only fully achieved by the complex pattern of irony which Chaucer has woven into it. The Pardoner, who feels himself to be so much cleverer than his victims, delights in and confidently exploits the cheap irony of his preaching against his own vice,

> I preche of no thyng but for coveityse.
> Therfore my theme is yet, and evere was,
> Radix malorum est cupiditas.

He is not, however, as clever as he believes himself to be, for the Host is not gulled by him. But this is a small part of his self-deception; its full extent is revealed by his own sermon. In his tale of the three rioters, who went out to seek for death and —after they had given up the search—found it at one another's hands, there is an irony which cuts so much deeper than any the Pardoner shows himself to be conscious of, that we feel him, equally with them, to be the victim of it. He understands no more than they that the wages of sin is death.[35]

It is a descent from this tale to the Manciple's. Yet, in its method, the *Manciple's Tale* resembles the Pardoner's, and even more closely the Nun's Priest's, and I doubt whether it is any more dependent for its form on rhetorical devices than they are. When, therefore, it is condemned as being over-rhetorical, it would seem to be condemned for the wrong reason. The real difference between it and the other two tales is that, in it, Chaucer appears to have been interested in rhetorical devices only for their own sake; there is no motive for the amplification of the story of Phoebus and the crow.

In the *Nun's Priest's Tale* Chaucer uses almost every means of amplification known to the rhetoricians, *interpretatio*, *comparatio*, *prosopopeia*, apostrophe, digression, description; and he uses them precisely as the rhetoricians intended, to amplify, or extend, the little tale of the cock and the fox. It may be objected that this is a different case altogether, that here Chaucer is ridiculing the rhetoricians and he used their own methods to show them up. He is, of course, amusing himself at their expense; this would be clear if there were no echoes of Geoffroi's *Nova Poetria*[36] and no allusion to his famous apostrophe on the death of Richard I,

> O Gaufred, deere maister soverayn . . .
> Why ne hadde I now thy sentence and thy loore
> The Friday for to chide, as diden ye?

But, when this mockery is quoted (as it sometimes is) to prove that Chaucer saw the folly of applying rhetorical methods to poetry, it should be remembered that, if he is here attacking rhetorical methods, he is at the same time attacking much of his own most serious poetry. The apostrophe, 'O destinee, that mayst nat been eschewed!' is not in itself more ridiculous than some of Troilus's bitter outcries against Fortune. The joke lies in the incongruity between the high-sounding line and the farmyard birds to whose fate it refers—

> O destinee, that mayst nat been eschewed!
> Allas, that Chauntecleer fleigh fro the bemes!
> Alas, his wyf ne roghte nat of dremes!

The joke is a better one if it is recognized that fine apostrophes and tragic *exempla* have their proper functions. It is the best joke of all for those who, like Chaucer and presumably his readers, had been taught the rhetorical doctrine of the three styles, and knew that the only fitting style for the farmyard was the *stylus humilis*.[37]

I would ask you to consider for a moment what would happen to the *Nun's Priest's Tale* if all traces of rhetorical amplification were to be removed from it. (This means the delightful descriptions of the cock and the hens as well as Chauntecleer's examples of prophetic dreams, the apostrophes, asides, and so on.) There would be nothing left but the bare bones of the story, something utterly different in kind from the subtly humorous poem which Chaucer created for a quick-witted and sophisticated audience. It is inconceivable that Chaucer should not have been aware of the extent to which the structure of his story, and all that gave it its special quality, depended on rhetorical methods. Chaucer often makes fun of things for which he had a serious regard, and particularly in the *Nun's Priest's Tale* he mockingly alludes to many things in which he elsewhere shows deep interest—the significance of dreams, for example, and the question of predestination and free will. So it seems to me likely that if, as we read the *Nun's Priest's Tale*, we laugh too heartily and unthinkingly at the rhetoricians, there is a danger that Chaucer may be laughing at us.

NOTES

1. *House of Fame*, 1094–5. Quotations are from *The Complete Works of Geoffrey Chaucer*, ed. F. N. Robinson.
2. Several medieval definitions of art are given by E. de Bruyne, *Études d'esthétique médiévale*, ii (1946), 371 ff. He sums up as follows: '... le Moyen-Âge ... distingue nettement le théoricien (artifex theorice) de celui que nous appelons le créateur (artifex practice). Le premier parle de l'art, le second agit par art. Mais chez l'un comme chez l'autre, la dignité de l'art vient de sa participation à un savoir organisé. Le Moyen-Âge ne s'imagine pas un artiste qui "ignore" les règles de son métier' (p. 374).
3. See *Canterbury Tales, Franklin's Prologue*, F 716–27, *Squire's Tale*, F 34–41, 102–8. The eagle in the *House of Fame* (853 ff.) is proud of his power to explain things simply. Pandarus deliberately eschews 'subtyl art' (*Troilus and Criseyde*, ii. 255 ff.)
4. See J. M. Manly, *Chaucer and the Rhetoricians* (Warton Lecture on English Poetry, xvii, 1926); T. Naunin, *Der Einfluss der mittelalterlichen Rhetorik auf Chaucers Dichtung* (Bonn, 1929); F. E. Teager, 'Chaucer's Eagle and the Rhetorical Colors', *PMLA* xlvii (1932); M. P. Hamilton, 'Notes on Chaucer and the Rhetoricians', *PMLA* xlvii (1932). The following also deal, in various ways, with the relations between Chaucer's writings and rhetorical teaching: R. C. Goffin, 'Chaucer and "Reason",' *M.L.R.* xxi (1926) and 'Chaucer and Elocution', *Med. Aev.* iv (1935); C. S. Baldwin, 'Cicero on Parnassus', *PMLA* xlii (1927) and *Medieval Rhetoric and Poetic* (1928); B. S. Harrison, 'Medieval Rhetoric in the

"Book of the Duchess",' *PMLA* xlix (1934) and 'The Rhetorical In-consistency of Chaucer's Franklin', *S in Ph.* xxxii (1935); J. W. H. Atkins, *English Literary Criticism: The Medieval Phase* (1943).

5. An exception is G. Plessow's discussion of the *Manciple's Tale* (*Des Haushälters Erzählung*, Berlin and Leipzig, 1929), in which he shows that the tale is largely built up by means of rhetorical devices (see especially pp. 17 ff., pp. 126 ff.).

It is not, of course, to be denied that some of Chaucer's rhetorical devices are mere 'appendages'. Many of those in the *Man of Law's Tale*, for instance, are obviously so. This tale, indeed, appears to be an experiment in the application of rhetorical ornament to a simple story. If the experi-ment is not, on the whole, to the taste of the modern reader, yet it has to be granted that the best thing in the tale, the simile beginning 'Have ye nat seyn somtyme a pale face . . .' (ll. 645–51), is, equally with the apostro-phes and *exempla*, a rhetorical ornament.

6. Matthieu de Vendôme taught grammar at Orléans. Évrard the German, whose *Laborintus* was written as a guide to the teacher of Grammar and Poetry, mentions Geoffroi de Vinsauf's *Nova Poetria* and Matthieu de Vendôme's *Ars versificatoria* in his list of authors suitable for boys to study (see *Laborintus*, ll. 665 ff., in *Les Arts poétiques du XIIe et du XIIIe siècle*, by E. Faral). Évrard himself probably taught at Bremen (see Faral, pp. 38–39).

7. 'Grammatica est scientia interpretandi poetas atque historicos et recte scribendi loquendique' (Rabanus Maurus, *De institutione clericorum*, iii. 18).

8. The practice in England at the time when Chaucer was educated can only be conjectured. John of Salisbury's famous description of the teaching of Bernard shows how authors were studied at Chartres in the twelfth century. He refers to composition in prose and verse (*Metalogicon*, ed. Webb, i. xxiv). Gervais of Melkley, who must have written his *Ars versificaria* in the early years of the thirteenth century, also speaks of composition (see résumé by Faral, op. cit., pp. 328 ff.; on Gervais of Melkley, see Faral, pp. 34 ff.) For an early fourteenth-century reference to the practice of composition in England, see A. F. Leach, *The Schools of Medieval England*, pp. 180–1. The Oxford statute to which Leach refers suggests that composi-tion must have been practised by intending schoolmasters as well as by boys learning Grammar, and the statutes made for St. Alban's Grammar School (1309) also indicate that it was practised by older pupils (see Leach, p. 186).

9. The unconscious application of rhetorical rules is recognized by Gervais of Melkley, who (according to Faral, p. 328), speaks of 'un sens naturel, d'où vient que, même sans penser à la théorie, le génie des écrivains ap-plique les règles d'instinct et fait spontanément des trouvailles heureuses'.

10. See *The Works of Sir Thomas Malory*, ed. E. Vinaver, i, pp. xlviii–lxvii. For Professor Vinaver's discussion of the *Suite du Merlin*, see his introduction to *Le Roman de Balain*, ed. M. D. Legge, especially pp. xii ff. Reference is made here to Professor Vinaver, because his statements appear most relevant to the present discussion; but it is not possible to write on the influence of rhetoric on medieval literature without being indebted to the work of H. Brinkmann (in *Zu Wesen und Form mittelalterlicher Dichtung*, 1928) and of E. R. Curtius (in *Europäische Literatur und lateinisches Mittelalter*, 1948, and in many articles.)

11. I am assuming that Chaucer was trained in *grammatica* and *rhetorica* (or perhaps 'poetria') in his youth. In fact, of course, we know nothing about his education except what can be deduced from his works. His service in the household of the Countess of Ulster need not, I take it, preclude his having been so trained, either previous to it or during it (possibly by a *grammaticus* especially hired for him and other youths in her service). His earliest extant works (or what are generally taken to be such), the *A B C* and the *Book of the Duchess*, reveal the influence of rhetorical teaching; and his knowledge of the standard medieval school-reader, the *Liber Catonianus*, is some slight indication that he had received instruction in Grammar. For information about this book and Chaucer's knowledge of it, see R. A. Pratt, 'Chaucer's Claudian', *Speculum*, xxii (1947), *A Memoir of Karl Young*, pp. 45 ff. (privately printed, New Haven, 1946), and 'The Importance of Manuscripts for the study of Medieval Education as Revealed by the Learning of Chaucer', *Progress of Medieval and Renaissance Studies*, Bulletin No. 20 (1949). It may be worth recalling that a copy of the *Liber Catonianus* was left in 1358 by William Ravenstone, a former master, to the Almonry School of St. Paul's Cathedral, the school which, it is held, Chaucer is most likely to have attended (see E. Rickert, *Chaucer's World*, p. 123, and n. 51).

12. The importance of engaging the hearer's attention and goodwill at the beginning of a speech is stressed by Quintilian and the writer of *Ad Herennium*. See Quintilian on the *exordium* (principium), 'Causa principii nulla alia est, quam ut auditorem, quo sit nobis in ceteris partibus accommodatior, praeparemus' (*Institutio Oratoria*, IV. i); see also *Ad Herennium* (ed. F. Marx, p. 4): 'Exordiorum duo sunt genera: principium, quod Graece prohemium appellatur, et insinuatio.... Principium est, cum statim auditoris animum nobis idoneum reddimus ad audiendum. Id ita sumitur, ut attentos, ut dociles, ut benivolos auditores habere possimus.' While most of the twelfth- and thirteenth-century rhetoricians are interested in ways of beginning, they do not consider why an author should take special pains with this part of his work.

13. *Troilus and Criseyde*, i. 211 ff. The apostrophe and the reference to Troilus's ignorance of his fate are in Boccaccio's *Il Filostrato* (Part I, st. 25), but not the metaphor of Troilus climbing the stair, nor the *sententia* with which Chaucer's stanza ends. The following three stanzas (ll. 218–38) have no parallel in *Il Filostrato*.

14. See *Wife of Bath's Tale*, D 1109–1206 (ll. 1177–1206 provide a particularly good example of rhetorical presentation) and *Merchant's Tale*, E 2237 ff., especially Proserpyne's reply (ll. 2264–2304). The argument by which Pandarus persuades Troilus to tell him who it is he loves (*Troilus*, i. 624–714) is another example. Comparison of this passage with *Il Filostrato*, ii, sts. 10–13 shows that, while most of the main points of the argument were taken by Chaucer from the earlier poem, he added almost all the rhetorical amplification. The odd thing is that Pandarus's argument, for all its rhetorical devices, does not sound less 'natural' than Pandaro's, but rather more so. Boccaccio's passage is perhaps too straightforward to be quite convincing as the speech of one friend to another at a time when both are under the stress of emotion.

15. See Helen Gardner, *The Art of T. S. Eliot* (1949), pp. 51 ff. As Miss Gardner points out, however, the meaning of Mr. Eliot's repeated words

does not remain constant, as with Chaucer; 'it is deepened or expanded by each fresh use'. In aim and effect Mr. Eliot's use is rather nearer to the *Pearl* poet's practice of ringing the changes on the various meanings of some of his refrain words (*cortaysye, ry3t*, for instance), though close analysis would reveal some interesting differences between them.

16. *Book of the Duchess*, 221 ff.

17. There are also in the *Prioress's Tale* some slight traces of stanza linking by repetition, notably in ll. 1838–9, but see also ll. 1691–2, 1726–7, 1866–7.

A study of the various kinds of verbal repetition in Chaucer's works (both those which are recognized by the rhetoricians and those which are not), and of their effects, might give interesting results. Even when the practice is technically the same, the results are often different. For instance, the repetition noted in the *Book of the Duchess* and the *Prioress's Tale* makes its appeal to the emotions, but the repetition in the *Wife of Bath's Tale* of the words *gentillesse, gentil, gent(e)rye* (D 1109–76) and of the word *poverte* (1177–1206) helps to drive home the arguments, that is, its appeal is to the intellect. In the latter part of this argument Chaucer is using the rhetorical device of *repetitio* (the repetition of the first word of a clause), which he also frequently employs elsewhere, again with varying effects. Compare, for instance, the repetition in *Manciple's Tale* H 318 ff. with that in *Knight's Tale* A 2918 ff. or that of the words 'Thou seist' ('seistow') in the *Wife of Bath's Prologue*. (It may incidentally be remarked that *Manciple's Tale*, 318 ff. exemplifies the difficulty of making clear-cut distinctions between some of the rhetoricians' terms. Naunin, op. cit., p. 45 calls the figure here used *repetitio*, while Plessow labels it *conduplicatio*. In fact, Geoffroi's definition of either term could cover it.)

18. Another slight verbal link between these two passages (compare l. 62 'welle of musik and melodye' and l. 129 'welle of grace') may or may not be intentional.

19. See *Merchant's Tale*, E 1986, *Knight's Tale*, A 1761, *Squire's Tale*, F 479. The line, as used of Canacee, comes after the *Merchant's Tale* in our modern editions; but uncertainty about the chronology of the tales and about their order (particularly the order of those in Groups E and F), combined with what can now be called the certainty that Chaucer never finally arranged them, leaves it an open question whether Chaucer wrote the *Merchant's Tale* before or after the *Squire's*, and how he would ultimately have placed them in relation to one another.

20. Some of Geoffroi de Vinsauf's own verses in *Nova Poetria*, especially those composed to illustrate *gradatio* (ll. 1145 ff.) and *conduplicatio* (ll. 1169–72), might have provided some suggestion for the kind of repetition found in the *Book of the Duchess*, however.

An exception to the statement that the rhetoricians do not indicate why repetition should be used is to be found in Geoffroi's definition of *conduplicatio*—'Conduplicatio est quando motu irae vel indignationis idem conduplicamus verbum' (*Summa de Coloribus Rhetoricis*, ed. Faral, p. 324). See also Geoffroi's remarks under *interpretatio* (Faral, p. 325).

21. In the story of Lear as told by La3amon the phrases 'hauekes & hundes' and 'feowerti hired cnihtes' (or slight variations of them) provide a link between some important stages of the story (see *The Brut*, ed. F. Madden, ll. 3256–8, 3274–5, 3295–9, 3560–3).

Verbal repetition, though very common in the alliterative *Morte*

Arthure, is not generally used there as a linking device, at least not in the way Chaucer uses it. In ll. 3523–78, however, it does act as a link between Sir Cradok's news of Modred's treachery and Arthur's recital of the news to his council and it is effective as suggesting Arthur's state of mind, his stunned horror at what he has been told.

In *Purity*, the text which forms the theme of the whole poem, 'Beati mundo corde, quoniam ipsi Deum videbunt', is paraphrased in ll. 27–28, and immediately after (ll. 29–30) the converse is stated,

'As so saytz, to þat syȝt seche schal he never
Þat any unclannesse hatz on, auwhere abowte.'

The second part of the text (Vulgate 'Deum videbunt') is echoed in varying forms throughout the poem, often in the transitional passages from one part of the matter to another, but also elsewhere. At the end of the parable of the man without a wedding garment, comes the phrase 'Þenne may þou se þy Savior' (l. 176); the words 'Ne never see hym with syȝt' (l. 192) come at the end of section II, and 'þe syȝte of þe Soverayn' just after the story of the Flood (l. 552), and so on (see ll. 576, 595, 1055, 1112). The words 'clannesse', 'clene', and their opposites 'unclannesse', 'fylþe,' representing the first part of the text, also echo through the poem, and the two parts are once more combined at the end,

'Ande clannes is his comfort, and coyntyse he lovyes,
And þose þat seme arn and swete schyn se his face' (1809–10).

22. It is for the same reason that the death of Alcyone is dismissed so abruptly (see *Book of the Duchess*, 212–17).

23. I am not suggesting that Geoffroi de Vinsauf himself had anything like the organization of the *Book of the Duchess* in mind when he used these words. In part of what he says about *interpretatio* in the *Nova Poetria* (ed. Faral, 220–5) he is almost certainly thinking only of verbal variation (cf. 'Sub verbis aliis praesumpta resume; repone Pluribus in clausis unum'); and this seems to be all that is in his mind in the *Documentum de arte versificandi* (Faral, p. 277). Even so, a creative mind, occupied with problems of organization, might have found in his words a hint for variation on a larger scale.

The parallelism between the story of Ceys and Alcyone and the theme of the poet's dream is pointed out by W. Clemen in *Der Junge Chaucer* (1938), pp. 39 ff., but his interpretation of it differs from mine.

24. Chaucer twice draws attention to this connecting link, see ll. 96 ff., 106–8.

25. The significance of these lines is made clearer by reference to their source in Boethius's *Consolation*. They echo a speech made by Philosophy in the course of her discussion of true and false 'blisfulnesse' (see *Boece*, iii, pr. 3).

On the similarity between *Parlement* 50–70 and *Troilus* v. 1807–20, and the implied contrast in the *Parlement* between heavenly and earthly bliss, see B. H. Bronson, *In Appreciation of Chaucer's Parlement of Foules* (University of California Publications in English, iii, 1935).

26. See *Ars versificatoria*, ed. Faral, pp. 129–32. Faral (p. 77) remarks that Matthieu treats these two portraits 'en manière de pendants antithétiques' and he notes other medieval examples of 'opposed' descriptions. Nearly related to these is the passage in *Sir Gawain and the Green Knight*, ll. 943 ff., which describes Morgan le Fay and the lady of the castle antithetically.

What Chaucer does in the *Parlement* is obviously much further removed from Matthieu.

It is perhaps worth noting that Chaucer's presentation of the two visions has a good deal in common with the presentation of ideas in the rhetorical figure of thought known as *contentio*, of which Geoffroi de Vinsauf writes 'quando res comparo, secum Contendunt positae rationes' (*Nova Poetria*, 1253–4). Chaucer uses *contentio* (both the figure of thought and the figure of words) rather frequently in the *Parlement*, and it seems possible that these figures, and the layout of the poem, reflect his state of mind at the time the poem was written.

27. See the introduction to *Le Roman de Balain*, especially pp. xxv ff.

28. See W. Frost, 'An Interpretation of Chaucer's Knight's Tale', *R.E.S.* xxv (1949). That I am indebted to this article for some fundamental ideas about the *Knight's Tale* is easily apparent; but I cannot accept Mr. Frost's views completely. He appears to me to lay more stress on the *motif* of friendship than Chaucer does, and I do not agree that the 'conflict between love and comradeship in the hearts of the two knights is the emotional focus of the story'. As I understand the story, the 'emotional focus' is their rivalry in love. The fact that they are kinsmen and sworn brothers adds poignancy to the situation, and their final reconciliation helps one to acquiesce in the solution; but these things appear to me to be subordinate in interest to the theme of rivalry in love.

Some of the expressions which Mr. Frost uses of the tale seem unfortunate, as when he writes of its 'theological' interest ('the theological interest attaching to the method by which a just providence fully stabilizes a disintegrating human situation', p. 292) and of its teaching 'a deep acceptance of Christian faith' (p. 302). Chaucer develops the wider issues of the story in the light of Boethian thought, as expounded in the *Consolation of Philosophy*, and its solution is in line with that thought. The general terms used by Mr. Frost, while not actually misleading, do not adequately convey the conceptions that lie behind the tale. As for the term 'tragic' (see pp. 299–301), I doubt whether the word, in any sense in which it is used in serious criticism today, or was understood in the Middle Ages, is properly applicable to this tale.

While it is not to be denied that the tale is sufficiently well suited to the Knight to arouse no questions in the reader's mind, it cannot safely be maintained that it is 'an important function' of the tale 'to present the mind and heart' of the Knight; for what little evidence we have suggests that it was written, substantially as it is, before Chaucer began the *Canterbury Tales*.

It may be noted that the 'symmetry' of the *Knight's Tale* is again emphasized in C. Muscatine's article, 'Form, Texture, and Meaning in Chaucer's "Knight's Tale"', *PMLA* lxv (1950), which I did not see until after the delivery of this lecture.

29. See *Teseida*, iii, sts. 18–19, 28–31, iv, sts. 56–58, 61, v, sts. 77 ff. There is nothing in the *Knight's Tale* to correspond to any of these passages.

30. Contrast *Teseida*, iii, st. 13.

31. See *Chaucer and the Rhetoricians*, p. 20.

32. Actually, although Chaucer writes, 'Thise riotoures thre of which I telle' (C 661), he has not previously mentioned them. This has led some critics to suspect that the tale of the three rioters was not originally connected

with the preceding 'homily on the sins of the tavern' (see Carleton Brown *The Pardoner's Tale*, 1935, for an exposition of this view). If Carleton Brown is right, and it is not a mere oversight that the three rioters are not mentioned in the opening lines of the *Tale*, one can only marvel at the skill with which two originally distinct elements have been amalgamated and inter-related.

33. See C 895–903, and 916–18.

34. See *Parson's Tale, De Avaricia* (Robinson's ed., p. 301) 'Now comth hasardrie with his apurtenaunces, as tables and rafles, of which comth deceite, false othes, chidynges and alle ravynes, blasphemynge and reneiynge of God, and hate of his neighebores, wast of goodes, mys-spendynge of tyme, and somtyme manslaughtre.' Compare with this passage, *Pardoner's Tale*, C 591–4. The tale of the three rioters gathers up most of the sins mentioned in the passage in the *Parson's Tale*.

35. I am indebted to Miss M. M. Lascelles for some suggestions about Chaucer's handling of the *Pardoner's Tale*, and the *Nun's Priest's Tale*, but she is not responsible for any statement made here or any opinion expressed.

36. On these echoes, see Marie P. Hamilton, 'Notes on Chaucer and the Rhetoricians', *PMLA* xlvii (1932), K. Young, 'Chaucer and Geoffrey de Vinsauf', *Modern Philology*, xli (1944) and a brief note by R. A. Pratt, 'The Classical Lamentations in the "Nun's Priest's Tale"', *M.L.N.* lxiv (1949).

37. On the doctrine of the three styles see Faral, pp. 86 ff., and, for a more recent discussion, De Bruyne, *Études d'esthétique médiévale*, ii. 41 ff.

THE LANGUAGE OF THE PASTONS

By NORMAN DAVIS

Read 19 May 1954*

In the prologue to his translation of the *Eneydos*, printed in 1490, William Caxton wrote these familiar words: 'And certaynly our langage now vsed varyeth ferre from that whiche was vsed and spoken whan I was borne.' It was the shifting currency of words that impressed him most: 'And thus bytwene playn, rude, and curyous, I stande abasshed; but in my iudgemente the comyn termes that be dayli vsed ben lyghter to be vnderstonde than the olde and auncyent Englysshe.' But he must have noticed also movements in pronunciation, in the spellings that represented it—for his treatment of which he has sometimes been unjustly censured—and in some of the few remaining inflexions. We know, in a general way, the directions in which these features of English were changing during the fifteenth century; but there is a great deal still to be learnt, by close study of dated and localized texts, about the speed and the distribution of the changes. How might the usage of each new generation differ from that of the earlier? How far could the language of a single individual develop during his adult life? How much might members of the same community differ from one another in the details of language? What was the 'social status' of particular forms of speech at different periods within the century?

It is with Caxton's words in mind—and so from a point of view a little different from that of earlier studies—that I wish to begin by examining briefly some features of the language of the Paston family as we find it in their surviving letters. The great collection of 'Paston Letters' includes over 400 letters and memoranda written by or for members of the family, of which the earliest

* When this paper was written the only relatively complete modern editions of the Paston Letters were those of James Gairdner described in note 1 below, and all references were necessarily given to them. Since then the documents have been re-edited in *Paston Letters and Papers of the Fifteenth Century*, ed. N. Davis, Part I (comprising letters written by members of the family) (Oxford, 1971); Part II (with select index) (Oxford, 1976). References in the present reprint have been brought into conformity with the new edition (*PLP*); and a few other small changes have been made where later work has shown some details to require correction.

autograph document is credibly dated 1425, and the latest 1503.[1]
The collection thus covers a span a little longer than Caxton's life
(*c.*1422–91), and almost identical with it. The letters are good
evidence, for we know something of most of the writers, and the
dates can usually be fixed within at any rate a year or two. Many
of them are informal, written to other members of the family on
current business, so that they seldom pretend to grace of style or
originality of thought. Apart from the conventional opening and
closing phrases,[2] and many obvious echoes of legal phraseology,

[1] Almost all the family letters are now in the British Library, most of them in
Additional MSS. 27443–6, 34888–9, 43488–91, and a few in 33597, 35251,
39848. One is in the library of Pembroke College, Cambridge, Case II,6. The
first modern edition, a selection only, was by John Fenn, *Original Letters,
Written during the Reigns of Henry VI, Edward IV, and Richard III* ... (London,
vols. i and ii 1787, iii and iv 1789, v 1823). The most quoted edition, much
augmented but still not complete, is by James Gairdner, *The Paston Letters,
1422–1509*, 6 vols. (London and Exeter, 1904), which is a rearranged and
slightly corrected reprint of his four-volume edition (Westminster, 1901).
    The manuscript of the letters in Fenn's vols. i and ii were for many years in
private hands. They were bought for the British Museum in 1933, and were
eventually bound, after the Second World War, in Add. MSS. 43488–91, with
a valuable index of writers, hands, and dates. Some account of the history of
the manuscripts is given in *PLP* vol. i, pp. xxiv–xxxiii; more particulars of
certain episodes may be found in Gairdner's Preface to the introductory
volume of his 1901 edition. An indispensable key to the numbering of the
manuscripts and their transcripts in Gairdner's editions appears in H. S.
Bennett, *The Pastons and their England* (Cambridge, 1922, 1932, and reprints). I
am indebted to the authorities of the British Library and the librarian of
Pembroke College, Cambridge.
    In references below individual words are not referred to the letters in which
they occur when *O.E.D.* quotes the relevant passage.
[2] These epistolary conventions are already so firmly standardized that the
tradition of letter-writing in English must have been of long standing. The
usual form of address to a friend or acquaintance was *Right worshipful sir, I
recommend me to you*; and this, with slight variations, was common between
brothers: *Ryght worschypful and verrely welbelouyd brothere, I hertely comande me to yow*
(John II to John III, *PLP* no. 236); and, with more elaborate expressions of
respect, from son to father or mother: *Ryth reuerent and worchepfull fadyr, I
recomand me on to you, besechyng yow lowly of yowr blyssyng* (John III, no. 319);
Ryght wyrshypfull and my moste kynde and tendre moodre, I recomaund me to yow (John
II, no. 285). Margaret always addressed her husband in similar terms: *Ryth
wyrchypful hwsbond* (e.g. no. 128); and Margery also: *Ryght reuerent and wortschep-
full syre, jn my most vmbill weysse I recomaunde me to you* (no. 419), though she once
allowed herself *Myne owyn swete hert, jn my most humylwyse I recomaund me on to you*
(no. 418). Only Agnes wrote *Dere housbond, I recomaunde me to yow* (no. 13).
Husbands to their wives were generally more reserved. John I, if he troubled
to use any opening phrase at all, nearly always said only *I recomaund me to yow*
(e.g. no. 76), but once went so far as *Myn owne dere souereyn lady* (no. 77). John

they must often present an only slightly formalized version of the speech of the writers. They are therefore a much better guide to the real state of the spoken language than any literary work, conscious of tradition and seeking special effects, can ever be.

Only about half of the letters are in the handwriting of the authors. The earliest group of autograph letters, a small one, was written by William Paston of Paston in Norfolk, who lived from 1378 to 1444, and was a justice of the Common Pleas from 1429.[3] He was survived by four sons, John, Edmond, William, and Clement, born in 1421, 1425, 1436, and 1442,[4] letters from each of whom are extant. The judge's earliest letter is of 1425, his latest of 1442; the earliest of the new generation, a single letter written by Edmond, probably of 1447, so that the gap is only of some five years. Over thirty years pass before the last letter of the second generation, by William, in 1480. John, the judge's eldest son and heir, lived until 1466[5] and had five sons from whom letters survive: two named John, born in 1442 and apparently 1444,[6] Edmond, Walter, and William, born in 1459.[7] This is by

III said simply *Mastress Margery, I recomand me to yow* (no. 389). Different addresses were used by parents to children. Both Agnes and Margaret began their letters to their sons with some such form as *Sone, I grete yow well and send you Godys blyssyng and myn* (no. 26), *Ryght welbelouyd son, I grete you well and send you Cristes blissyng and myne* (no. 224). This last form may be traced back in English to the early twelfth century: see F. E. Harmer, 'The English Contribution to the Epistolary Usages of Early Scandinavian Kings', *Saga-Book of the Viking Society*, xiii (1949–50), 115–55, esp. 150. See also N. Davis, 'A Note on *Pearl*', *R.E.S.*, N.S. xvii (1966), 403–5, and N.S. xviii (1967), 294.

The earliest known English letter, written by Sir John Hawkwood in 1392–3, begins *Dere S. I grete you well* (C. L. Kingsford, *Prejudice and Promise in XVth Century England* (Oxford, 1925), p. 23. *O.E.D.* records this use of *Dear* only from 1503–4). The Zouche letters of 1402 have *Ryȝth wel by loued frend, I grete yow well* (Edith Rickert, 'Some English Personal Letters of 1402', *R.E.S.*, viii (1932), 257–63).

[3] See *D.N.B.*

[4] The judge's will, dated 31 January 1444 (extracts in *PLP* no. 12), gives the ages of Edmond and William as 18 and 7. It also gave Clement's age, but the passage is illegible. John's is given only as *xx annorum et amplius*. According to Blomefield, *History of Norfolk* (London, edn. of 1807), vi. 479, the inquisition post mortem (misdated 1443) found John to be 23, Edmond 18, and Clement 1 year old.

[5] Inq. p.m. 6 Edward IV, no. 44. See also *PLP* no. 900.

[6] The inquisition gives the eldest son's age as over 24. The inquisition on Sir John is lost, and we depend for the age of the second son on Sandford's genealogy of 1674, now Cambridge University Library Additional MS. 6968. See F. Worship, 'Account of a MS. Genealogy of the Paston Family', *Norfolk Archaeology*, iv (1855), 1–55.

[7] The date of Edmond's birth is not known. That of William's appears from

far the best represented of all the generations that appear in the collection. There is no gap between it and the earlier generation: indeed, the two younger Johns' letters, beginning in 1461, overlap their father's by several years and their uncle William's by many years. The latest letter, written by the youngest John, is apparently of 1503. This John, who fell heir to his brother in 1479, had a son William, the fourth of that name, who is represented by only one short letter, of about 1495. Thus four generations of Pastons—though only three at adequate length— exhibit, in their own handwriting, the current usages of epistolary English.

And these are only the men. Three generations of women also appear: Agnes, wife of the judge; Margaret, wife of the first John, and Elizabeth, his sister; and Margery, wife of the third John.[8] Some of the women's letters are among the most interesting and important of all, but they do not give as precise linguistic evidence as the men's; for it does not appear that any of them are autograph. Agnes must have employed several clerks: six of her seventeen letters are in one hand, two in another, and the rest in eight or nine more. Margaret's 104 letters are in an extraordinary variety of hands, some found in as many as twenty letters, many in only one.[9] Margery's six are in four different hands; and Elizabeth's two are in different hands. It does not seem possible to prove that no single one of the hands that appear in the letters of Agnes or of Margaret is that of the author of the letter, though many of them can be identified; but neither is it possible to prove that any one of them *is* that of the author. Certainly no considerable group can be shown to be autograph. The fact that both women employed so many clerks suggests that they could not write themselves, or at any rate did not find writing easy and did not like it. Margaret could perhaps read; but *schewe* in her son Sir John's injunction to his brother, 'I praye yow schewe ore rede to my moodre suche thynge3 as ye thynke is fore here to know'

Sir John's statement in a letter dated 1473 (no. 282): *my brother William whyche shall nott be off age thys vij yeere.* Walter was not twenty-four in 1479, for he could not be given a benefice (no. 733).

[8] The letters and papers of Agnes run from about 1440 to probably 1466; those of Margaret, much the most voluminous correspondent of all, from about 1441 to 1478; Elizabeth wrote only two, in 1459 and perhaps 1467; Margery's run from 1477 to 1489.

[9] See further on this and related points N. Davis, 'The Text of Margaret Paston's Letters', *Medium Ævum*, xviii (1949), 12–28, esp. 15; 'A Scribal Problem in the Paston Letters', *English and Germanic Studies*, iv (1951–2), 31–64; 'A Paston Hand', *R.E.S.*, N.S. iii (1952), 209–21.

$(1470)^{10}$ may mean only 'make known' (*O.E.D. show* v.23). It does not follow that she could write; and another indication that she did not may be seen in a suggestion made by the youngest John in 1477. He has prepared a draft of a letter to be sent in her name, and he introduces it thus: 'Wherfor, modyr, if it please yow, myn advyse is to send hyr answer a yen in thys forme folowing, *of some other manys hand.*'[11] Both of Elizabeth's letters are certainly in secretaries' hands. Margery could write, but only just: three of her letters bear conventional subscriptions in the same tremulous, totally unformed hand, quite distinct from that of the body of each letter, and this must be her own.[12] The letters of the women, then, cannot be taken as preserving the language of their authors undisturbed. They can probably be trusted, since they were presumably dictated, to preserve the words and even the syntax of the authors, but they cannot be trusted for the details of form, or for such limited information about sounds as spellings may reveal.

The Pastons at this date were a rising provincial family, all the men born and largely brought up in Norfolk, but with strong and continuing interests in London. Some of them had legal training; several were at Oxford or Cambridge; some served noble families.[13] John the eldest, after a time at Trinity Hall and then at Peterhouse, was at the Inner Temple, and used to lodge there during his many long visits to London in the course of interminable litigation over his inheritance of Sir John Fastolf's lands. The elder Edmond was at Clifford's Inn, the younger Edmond for a time at Staple Inn. The second William was at Cambridge, and later had the large house in London which had belonged to the Earl of Warwick; he married Anne Beaufort, daughter of the Duke of Somerset. The second John, knighted on coming of age in 1463—his father had paid a fine a few years earlier in consideration of not being knighted—was often at court or in the king's forces, especially at Calais at intervals from 1473 to 1477. The third John as a young man was attached to the household of the Duke of Norfolk; he became sheriff of Norfolk and Suffolk in 1485, was knighted at the battle of Stoke in 1487, and later appears as a 'right trusty and right welbelouyd Councellor' of the Earl of Oxford. The third William was educated at Eton. He, too, entered the service of the Earl of Oxford, but, having

[10] no. 248.
[11] no. 378.
[12] nos. 417, 418, 420.
[13] For a brief account of the family, with references, see *PLP* i.xl–lii.

become 'troubelid with sekenes and crasid in his mynde', had to
be dismissed. Walter took his degree at Oxford, but died soon
afterwards. And the fourth William's one letter was evidently
written while he was a Cambridge undergraduate. From such
associations, we may expect to find usages characteristic of local
dialect mingled with metropolitan forms.

This is not the place to discuss in detail minute differences of
spelling, sounds, inflexions, and syntax. But I must offer some
examples of the kind of variation that exists, and for this purpose
I shall use only the writings of the men, and for the most part
only a few critical features which provide a fairly clear series of
comparisons: in spelling, the treatment of the final group of
sounds in syllables that ended in -*ht* in Old English, as in 'right',
'thought', 'daughter'; in sounds, the lowering of *i* as shown by the
writing of *e*, as *heder* 'hither', *wretyn* 'written', which, even if its
interpretation is sometimes open to doubt, cannot be without
phonetic significance;[14] in forms, two points: first, in the pronoun
of the third person plural, the alternation of the English *her* and
hem in possessive and objective cases with the originally Scandinavian *ther* and *them*; and second, in the verb, the incidence of
final -*n* in infinitive, present and past plural, and strong past
participle.

The first William, the judge, as the sole representative of the
first generation, must be the starting-point. His spelling was
generally close to the practice of good manuscripts of his time,
such as the Ellesmere Chaucer, and he always used -*ght* in words
like 'right' and 'thought'. In words like 'written' he used *i*, not *e*.
In the pronoun, he used only *here* and *hem* for 'their' and 'them'.
In the verb, in infinitive and present plural he occasionally used
-*n*, but markedly preferred endingless forms. A typical example
of the mixture is the following, from a set of instructions for the

[14] Forms in which *e* appears in an originally open syllable may contain a long
vowel, developed as in *week*, *evil* (see e.g. Asta Kihlbom, *A Contribution to the
Study of Fifteenth Century English* (Uppsala, 1926), p. 20). Some must have done
so, notably the verb *wete*, *weet(e)*, which is commonly so spelt. But later
developments, known both from grammarians (as cited by Luick, *Historische
Grammatik*, § 543 Anm. 1) and from spellings (as in Wyld, *History of Modern
Colloquial English*, pp. 228–9), prove that many must have kept the vowel short.
This is true especially of words in -*er*, as *hither*, *thither*, and is probably true of
participles like *wretyn*; perhaps because the -*er* and -*yn* could be reduced to a
syllabic consonant. John Paston I's frequent form *wret* confirms the shortness
of the vowel here. The verb *wete* itself could evidently have its vowel short as
well as long: *wete*, *weet(e)* are the commonest spellings, but *wet*, *wett(e)* also
occur.

building of a wall: 'and thenne þo brode sawed stones shulde euere *stonde* in þe werk betwen þe seid weel bedde[d] stonys, þat shuld *rise* but a fote in þe walle and *ben* ankered iche of hem with other; and þis werk shal *be* strong j nowe, as werkmen *seyn*, and *drawe* but litill cariage.' In the past participle, on the other hand, forms with -*n* strongly predominate—there are 11 with it against 2 without.[15]

The judge's four sons all differ from their father in all these matters, but they differ among themselves as well.

Edmond's one short letter shows important changes from his father's usage, in spelling 'right' *ryth*, 'nought' *nowth*, and 'thought' *thowte*; in using *e* for *i* in *wrete, preuye, trenyte*, and with similar effect *wheche, meche*; and in using -*n* in verbs only in one plural *ben* and one past participle *seen*: 'for sche [his mother] woll tell persones many of her counsell this day, and to morwe sche woll sey be Goddis faste þat the same men *ben* false. I haue *seen* parte of þe euydence, and þe maner hathe be purchasid ....' The ratio in the past participle, one -*n* form to 4 without, contrasts sharply with the judge's 11 to 2.

John—among whose forty-four documents, from about 1445 to 1465, only two complete letters and some brief additions and interlineations are autograph—has more variety than Edmond in the 'right' group, which mostly has -*gth*, but sometimes -*gt, ght*, as well as -*th*; but he treats the 'thought' group in the same way, with -*owth* and -*owt* about equal. His language is coloured by a preference for *e* instead of *i* in several classes of words: *wret(e)*, the past participle, occurs nine times and is his only form, and *heder, theder, leuyng, well* 'will', and probably *ded* 'did' are of the same type. The *e* in *deke* 'dike' and *lekith* 'likes' must be of similar origin. That in *besines* and *ken* (beside *kyn*) may well, but of course need not, be the same again. The prominence of *e* is further increased by *whech, sech, mech*, the usual though not exclusive forms of these words. In the pronoun, *her* and *hem* are much the commoner forms; þer and þem appear from about 1460, for the first time in the family letters, but only 6 times against 24 of the others. There is only one certain -*n* form in the verb,[16] the past

---

[15] For a fuller account of the judge's usage see N. Davis, 'The Letters of William Paston', *Neophilologus*, xxxvii (1953), 36–41. The data there are not quite complete, for they omit the forms in the 'Instruccion' (*PLP* no. 1), here quoted; but these do not appreciably alter the proportions. In all, there are 3 -*n* forms of the infin. to 57 endingless, 9 in the pres. pl. to 16 endingless; and there are only 3 cases of the past pl., all endingless.

[16] There is one infin. (no. 73) and one pres. pl. (no. 75) in which *han* would

participle *don* found 3 times, compared with 28 participles without ending—a proportion of endingless forms much higher even than Edmond's, and indeed than that of any other of the correspondents. John's language seems to show no important or consistent development throughout his writings.

The second William's letters and papers run for nearly thirty years, from 1452 when he wrote from Cambridge, and they, too, are remarkably consistent for so long a period. William usually writes both 'right' and 'thought' groups with -*th*(*e*), occasionally with -*t* only, but never with -*ght*. He uses *e* for *i* in many words, such as *heder*, *pekyd*, *leke* (some half-dozen times), *tedyng*; *abedyn*, *redyn*, *wretyn*; *contenu*, *indeferent*, *parteculer*, *pete*, *qwett*, *sperituall*; *beryed*, *besy*, *ded*. On the other hand he favours *y* instead of *e* in some words: *frynd* (3 times), *pryste* (also *prist*), and *wyll*, *will* 'well' (9 times). He uses *e*-forms also in *qweche* and *meche*, but *much*(*e*), *moche*, and *myche* as well, and only *suche*, *soche*. In the pronoun, *hem* is the usual form, though *them* does occur; but the possessive *ther*(*e*) is commoner than *here*. In the verb, -*n* is not used in normal infinitives, but it appears in perhaps 4 present plurals and one past plural,[17] and in 19 past participles (10 of them *wretyn*) against 18 without it. Some progression may be seen in this particular: though *wretyn* is regular from the first, it is only from 1459 onwards that other -*n* forms of the participle are frequent. It may not be irrelevant that in 1459 and 1460 William writes from London.

The youngest of the judge's sons, Clement, has left six letters from 1461 to 1466. He agrees with Edmond and William in spelling both 'right' and 'thought' groups mainly with -*th*(*e*) and -*t*(*e*). But he differs from all his brothers in his very limited use of *e* for *i*: he has only *dede* 'did' and *wretyn* once, elsewhere writing *y*, however he pronounced it.[18] His pronominal forms are too few to be significant. In the verb, he has no -*n* forms in infinitive or past

be a possible reading; but the writing is extremely careless, and it is more probably *hau* with -*e* left off. In these parts there are over 180 forms without -*n*. Four cases of *born*(*e*) (no. 74) are not real participles.

[17] Four of the five cases are in the same letter (no. 92), of 1467: 'Do Pampyng comyn wyth owr sperituall concell suche mater as *nedyn* there, and haue newe wretyn ye attestacion yat *lakkyn* ... Ser Jamys and Call meche *spokyn* to ye tenantys in myn lordys name', and the doubtful 'all oder materys yat *hangyng* there'. There are about 55 cases of these forms without -*n*. The weakened form of *have* appears as *an* in 'j scholere of Cambryg ... schuld *an* vtteryd ferthere to ȝowre grete schalndyr' (no. 81).

[18] A remarkable form is *styll* 'steal' (no. 114).

plural, but 4 in the present plural (3 of them *ben*), and in the participle 21 forms with -*n* to 10 without.

In the participle the difference of practice among the brothers is striking: John and Edmond are very sparing of -*n*; Clement has it twice as often as not; William takes a middle position with numbers roughly equal.

In general, the two eldest brothers, John and Edmond, tend to agree, and to differ from William and Clement—William was eleven years, Clement seventeen years, younger than Edmond. The younger brothers share an important peculiarity of spelling: the use of *qw*- and *w*- instead of *wh*- in words like 'which', 'where'. There are some differences of treatment in particular words. In William, 'which' is only *qweche*, 'whether' only *weder*; 'where', 'what', 'when', and 'while' appear both with *qw*- and with simple *w*-; and 'squire' is *swyre*. In Clement, 'which' is *qwyche* but also *wych*. The alternation with *w*- is enough to show that the *qw*- form is purely conventional, and that the pronunciation was [w]; and this is confirmed by William's spelling of 'was' as *qwas*.

Clement alone spells 'shall' and 'should' *xall* and *xwld(e)*. Both the *qw*-/*w*- and the *x*- spellings are highly characteristic of Norfolk writers, and it is remarkable that they should appear only in the hands of the two younger brothers. We hear something of Clement's education, some three years before the first of his surviving letters, in a memorandum of his mother's 'errands to London' in 1458: 'To prey Grenefeld to send me feythfully word by wrytyn who Clement Paston hath do his devere in lernyng. And if he hathe nought do well, nor wyll nought amend, prey hym that he wyll trewly belassh hym tyl he wyll amend; and so ded the last mayster, and ye best that euer he had, att Caumbrege.'[19] Perhaps Norfolk spellings were accepted at Cambridge—William had also been there; but it is surprising that they should survive so stern a schooling in London as well.

In a few things, such as the appearance of *them* and *ther*, this generation shows some trends towards more modern usage than that of the judge; but in other ways—the common lowering of *i*, the confusion of spelling in the -*ght* words, and the instability of -*n* in the past participle—none of the sons is as near to the later literary language as their father had been. It is the younger brothers who favour the less orthodox spellings, and nobody changes his habits much in the course of time.

In the generation that follows—grandsons of the judge—the

---

[19] no. 28.

evidence for the usage of two of the brothers is extremely full.[20]
Sir John the elder has left 69 autograph documents, the younger
John 74 written on his own account as well as 11 written for his
mother Margaret and parts of three more for his father and
others. Both series continue over many years, and change somewhat in language as time goes on. I must go into some detail here
to show how the changes appear.

The eldest brother's first surviving letter is, I think, one which
can be dated 1461.[21] Some features of it do not occur again.
Words like 'right', for example, are variously spelt: *rygth, mythg*;
and 'writing' is *wrythgtyng*. Words like 'thought' are similarly
unsettled: *nowgth, nogth, nowthg*, and also *thowt*. 'Much' is *myche*.
There are eight reduced forms of *have* in compound tenses: *ye
schuld a ben hurt, I schuld an had it*. The other autograph letters date
from probably 1464 onwards, and in the interval John had been
at court, had been knighted, and had evidently entered the king's
service. In the latest letters the spelling *-ght* becomes virtually
regular in the 'right' group, though in the 'thought' group there
is no set form even in the latest: *thowt, thowght, thogt* (both with
and without *-e*) all occur, but *-wt(e)* about twice as often as either
of the other two. As soon as the *-ght* type establishes itself in
words in which the spirant is historical, it appears also in words
that never had the sound: the verb 'write' is nearly always *wryght*,
and there are a few forms like *dowght*. 'Much' is nearly always
moche, with *meche* perhaps twice; and compound tenses with *have*
are fully written out. There is no change in the use of *e* for *i*,
which is common—though not regular—throughout: *thedyr, whe-
dyr* (but usually *hyddre*), *leuyd, wedowe; dreuyn, redyn, strekyn, wretyn;
contenew, peler, preuy; besy, ded*. In the pronoun, *them* and *ther(e)*

---

[20] See now N. Davis, 'The Language of Two Brothers in the Fifteenth
Century' in *Five Hundred Years of Words and Sounds. A Festschrift for Eric Dobson*,
ed. E. G. Stanley and Douglas Gray (Cambridge, 1983), pp. 23–9.

[21] no. 231. Gairdner put first no. 234, dating it 1459 on the ground that it is a
plea by John II to his father for forgiveness, and we know from a letter of
Margaret's that John I was displeased with his eldest son in that year. But
father and son were on bad terms at other times also; cf. especially no. 175 of
1463 and no. 73 of 1465. The handwriting of no. 234 is undoubtedly much
more practised and developed than that of no. 231, though not so fluent as
that of demonstrably later letters such as no. 235, which is certainly of 1465.
Gairdner's argument that after 1463 John II would have signed his letters
John Paston, K (i.e. *Knight*) is shown to be invalid by the fact that no. 235 is
subscribed *By yowre oldere son, John Paston*—precisely the same words, and even
spelling, as the subscription of no. 234. The likeliest date for the latter, as for
Margaret's letter no. 176, is 1464.

overwhelmingly predominate, with perhaps only three cases of *hem*. In the verb, no *-n* forms appear in infinitive or past plural, and only a few in the present plural (*be(e)n* six times, *seyn* once). In the past participle, on the other hand, they are well established from the first, and more or less consistent at different periods. There are about 330 with *-n* against 32 without—roughly 10 to 1. Those which are always without *-n* have stems ending in a nasal or *-nd*: *bonde, bownde, fonde, founde; bygonne, wonne*. (Yet *comen* is normal, occurring 27 times against only 2 of *com(e)*).

Sir John makes two new departures, though both remain very much in the minority. He uses *-ys* in the third person singular present indicative of verbs, only five times beside the immeasurably commoner *-yth*;[22] and he once has *yow* instead of *ye* as a nominative. These exceptional forms are all in letters to his younger brother John, the *-s* forms in 1472–4, *yow* in 1477 (no. 306).

The youngest John's hand, the most fully represented of the whole family, first appears in a group of letters written on behalf of his mother, most of them between 1460 and 1462. In this group the spelling of words like 'right' is *-yth* six times as often as *-yt(e)*, and *-ght* is not used at all; in words like 'thought' *-wt(e)* is regular. Lowering of *i* is common: *hedyr, thedyr, levith, seth(yn); wretyn; dechys, lek; indeferent; ded*; but 'which', 'much', and 'such' all usually have *y*: *whyche (wyche, qwyche), myche, swyche (syche, siche, suche* twice). The plural pronoun is *hem* twice as often as *them*, but (though numbers are small) *ther* is commoner than *her*. In the verb, *-n* appears once in the present plural *ben* and once in the past plural *redyn*; in the past participle less than one-third of the total of nearly 70 have *-n*.

John's own letters begin probably in 1461.[23] At first his forms are in all important respects the same as in the letters he had written for his mother. (There are small differences of detail; e.g. *syche*, earlier rare, now becomes normal.) As the years pass, however, new spellings and forms appear, sometimes as alternatives but sometimes altogether displacing the earlier types.

This is especially well seen in the 'right' group. The usual spelling is *-yth*, with *-yt* rarely, up to 1466. *Myght* appears first in a letter apparently written early in 1467,[24] and though there is a temporary reversion in 1468,[25] *-ght* thereafter is unchallenged.

[22] The forms are *delys, greuys, helpys, semys, shewys*.

[23] no. 319.

[24] no. 325.

[25] no. 330. This letter has *ryth, knyt* 3 times, *myght* corrected from *mygth*.

The 'thought' group is less clear-cut, but the same in tendency: -*owght* begins to appear in 1467, the same date as -*yght*; but remnants of -*owt* survive sparsely until 1470,[26] and from that date also -*ought* begins and gradually becomes commoner. Soon after the adoption of the new spellings they spread to words historically without the spirant, and *wryght* and *abowght* are John's usual forms after about 1469. In this matter the brothers agree fairly closely. Both begin by using -*yth* and -*owt*, and adopt -*ght* later, the younger man going further in finally making -*ght* his regular form after a back vowel as well as a front. The early spellings show that the spirant was no longer pronounced; and the extension of the new spellings to words with no etymological right to them proves that the change of spelling does not imply a change of pronunciation.

No such movement affects the use of *e* for *i*. The youngest John has most of the usual examples,[27] though there are a few differences of detail: from 1467, for example, 'like' is nearly always *lyek*, not *lek*. *Whyche*, *syche*, *myche* unexpectedly regularly have *y*.[28]

But the plural pronoun is complicated. Unlike his elder brother, the third John often uses *hem*, and occasionally *her*. Beside these stand *them* and *ther*, but the by-form—it may be only a spelling variant—*theym*, which appears first in 1467, is prominent enough to call for special notice. In all, *hem* occurs 58 times, *them* 36, *theym* 38; *her* only 3 times, *ther* and *thers* jointly 69. Thus the currency of the possessive *her*, compared with *ther*, is enormously less than that of the accusative-dative *hem* compared with *them* and *theym*. But the proportions change greatly within the series. Taking the ten autograph letters written up to 1467, *hem* is three and a half times as frequent as *them* and *theym* together; but in the 25 letters up to the middle of 1471, *hem* occurs 45 times out of its total of 58, *them* 29 out of its 36, but *theym* only 5 times out of its 38. There is, then, a strong increase in *th*-forms after 1467, and another strong increase of *theym*, largely at the expense of *them*, from 1471 onwards. *Her* is from the first so unimportant that its disappearance after 1472 is not surprising.

The history of -*n* forms in the verb is almost equally complicated. They occur, in normal use, only in the past participle. Over the whole series there are some 236 forms with -*n* to 70 without it—about 3·3 to 1, in contrast with the elder John's 10 to 1.

---

[26] The latest example seems to be in no. 341.

[27] e.g. *hedyr*, *thedyr*, *leue*, *wedow*; *dreuyn*, *redyn*, *wretyn*; *lek*; *aqwetans*, *consederyng*, *dener*, *pete*, *preson*, *preuy*, *vetayll*; *beryed*, *besy*, *kechyn*, *shet*; *ded*.

[28] There seem to be only one *wheche* and one *moche*.

But there are far fewer endingless forms in later than in earlier letters, and in particular there is a discernible decline from a letter dated 1475,[29] and another apparent break from 1473.[30] In the letters from 1473 to the end, the proportion of -n forms to endingless is 8·7 to 1; from 1475 to the end it is 11 to 1. After 1475 the only forms without -n in ordinary use are *be* (3 times beside *been* 18) and verbs ending in a nasal or -nd, which never have -n: *bond, bownde, com, fond*. Two minor observations may be made. The youngest John uses only *com* in the past participle, whereas his elder brother uses *comen* almost always. Two abnormal forms, the infinitive *doone*, the only -n form outside the past participle, and the past participle *shake*, without -n, have a special explanation: they are used in a poem, and in rhyme, *doone* rhyming with *soone*, *shake* with the infinitive *take*.[31] This is a trifling but neat example of the way in which the demands of rhyme may force a versifier quite away from his usual linguistic forms.

Finally, the youngest John extends the -s ending in the present indicative somewhat beyond his brother's use. There are 15 examples, 8 of them *thynkys*,[32] against Sir John's 5—a difference too great to be explained simply by the larger bulk of the younger man's writings. These forms do not begin until 1467.

It is noticeable that this is also the year that marks the first appearance of -*ght* spellings. The increase of *th*- forms of the pronoun begins in 1468, and 1473 and 1475 mark stages in the adoption of -n in the participle. Why 1467 should have seen such changes is not clear. The following year brought new experiences which may well have left their mark—John and his brother went to Bruges in the retinue of Princess Margaret, sister of Edward IV, for her marriage to the Duke of Burgundy.[33] The later dates may also have some connection with events in his life. In 1473 he made plans to go on pilgrimage to Compostela, but there is no firm evidence that he went. In 1475 he records his return from a visit to Calais: 'I haue be seek euer sythe I cam on thys syd the see, but I trust hastyly to amend; for all my seknesse that I had at

---

[29] no. 365.

[30] In and after no. 360.

[31] no. 351. Fenn, followed by Gairdner, headed this text *Verses written by a Lady in the reign of Henry VI or Edward IV. To an absent Lord with whom she was in Love.* Gairdner suggested that 'they may have been the production of Lydgate writing in the name of a lady . . .'. But the manuscript is in the hand of John Paston III, and the many corrections show that it was an original composition, not a copy.

[32] The others are *clemys, delys, preyes, sendys* (twice), *waytys, wotys*.

[33] no. 330.

Caleys, and sythe I cam ouer also, cam but of cold. But I was never so well armyd for the werre as I haue now armyd me for cold.'[34]

The next brother, Edmond, writes seven letters, or parts of letters, for his mother as well as six on his own behalf.[35] He is in some ways more individual in his usage than either of his elders, especially in spelling 'shall' and 'should', in early letters for Margaret, with x-, as his uncle Clement had done. In other things he is like his brothers. He uses e for i in many words, and them as well as hem in the pronoun—them rather more commonly, especially later. In the 'right' and 'thought' groups he uses -th(e), occasionally -te, until 1472, but, after a long interval, he adopts -ght in all but a few cases. In the verb, he has rare -n forms in the infinitive and the present and past plural, and in the past participle 24 -n forms against 2 (com, woond) endingless. He has 14 -s forms in the present indicative, in his own letters only, beginning in 1471—perhaps significantly, after living for a time in London.

The third William, eight of whose letters we have, has again characteristics of his own. He is like his elder brothers in using -ght in the 'right' group (including 'to write'), but both -wt and -wght after back vowels; and e in thedyr, mende, ded. But in the plural pronoun he is the first of the family to use exclusively th-forms—a total of 27. In the verb, he has -n forms only in the past participle, but his preference for them there is striking: of 31 examples 28 have -n, and the odd three are all come. But he does not use -s in the present. His greatest singularity is the representation of a diphthong in cawlyd, gowld, in two letters written from Eton, probably in 1478 and 1479.[36] He once uses yow apparently

---

[34] nos. 278, 284, 365.

[35] For a detailed account of Edmond's usage see 'A Paston Hand' (note 9 above).

[36] nos. 406, 407. Fenn dated the latter of these (on which the date of the former depends) 1467-8. Gairdner dated it 1479, on the ground that it was written on 23 February, and that the following Monday was the first Monday of Lent. This was true also of 1474, but 1479 seems on the whole more likely, because William was then nineteen, which would be more appropriate to the interest he expresses in a young woman of 'xviij or xix yere', and he owed money for board to Thomas Stevenson, who became fellow of Eton on 12 July 1479 (H. C. Maxwell Lyte, A History of Eton College (London, 1875), p. 80). Sir Wasey Sterry, The Eton College Register 1441-1698 (Eton, 1943), p. 258, confuses this William with his uncle, following The Visitations of Norfolk, 1563, 1589, and 1613 (Harleian Society, xxxii (1891), 216).

as a nominative: 'as for hyr bewte, juge yow that when 3e see hyr.'

Walter is of special interest in that his three surviving letters were written at Oxford, where he took his degree in 1479. In the first of them, evidently comparatively early in his undergraduate career, he spells 'shall' and 'should' with *x-*, but in the others changes to *sch-*. The 'right' and 'thought' groups are poorly represented, but offer *nyth, mythy, rytgh, rygth,* and *thowth.* In the verb, *-n* appears only in the past participle *wretyn* three times, and endingless forms in *do, forgete, wryt*—a departure from the practice of the elder brothers by this date. Walter's greatest distinction is his frequent use of *yow* in the nominative—8 times in all, 6 of them in his last letter, against a total of 5 cases of *ye*.

The third generation carries further some of the tendencies which had begun in the second. *Them* and *ther* gain ground strongly. In the verb, *-n* endings decrease still more in parts other than the past participle, in which, on the other hand, they become almost general except in words with stems ending in a nasal or *-nd*.[37] The spelling *-ght*, regular in the judge's writings but very infrequent in his sons', becomes common again; and in particular, it is preferred in the later letters of those writers who change their habits in the course of time. Some features are new. The *-s* ending in the present and the use of *yow* as nominative arise first in this generation, but remain only occasional. There is a good deal of variation among the different writers, but in some things, notably the widespread use of *e* for *i*, the judge's grandsons are farther from the central stream of development of English than he had been.

There remains the fourth William, the only representative of

---

[37] The regularity of the treatment of *-n* in these letters does not support the view that the writing of *-n* in the fifteenth century was largely a matter of spelling only. See e.g. David W. Reed, *The History of Inflexional* N *in English Verbs before 1500* (Berkeley and Los Angeles, 1950), p. 247.

It deserves notice that not all writers who changed their habits increased their use of *-n* in the past participle. The scribe of the early group of Margaret's letters discussed in 'A Scribal Problem . . .' (note 9 above) reduced it in the past participle as well as other parts, but not so drastically. In five sub-groups, written between 1448 and 1454, the percentage of *-n* endings (considering only verbs which have endings in some forms) in parts other than the past participle varies as follows: 57·1: 63·1: 58·7: 23·9: 2. The respective percentages for the past participle are 87·5: 88·5: 91·7: 50: 40.6. Thus there is a sharp break in both series after the third sub-group (1450), but the past participle, beginning with a much higher proportion of *-n* forms than the other parts, retains a much higher proportion even after heavy loss.

the fourth generation. Unfortunately his single letter is so brief
that it offers too little evidence to be worth setting against the far
fuller record of his ancestors.

From the great variety of usage revealed by this very limited
study of a few points, it is obvious that no simple statement can
answer the sort of question that I suggested at the beginning.
Each new generation does, in broad terms, show some differences
from its predecessor; but individuals go their own ways, and some
change considerably in the course of years while others retain the
habits of their youth. Perhaps the clearest result of the inquiry is
the demonstration that in roughly the third quarter of the
fifteenth century men of some education, of similar background
and interests, could choose among so many 'permitted variations'
that no two of them wrote exactly alike.

But there is, I think, more than this to be said. When all
allowance for idiosyncrasy has been made, certain trends can be
discerned. Some members of the third generation even thought it
worthwhile to alter some of their linguistic habits; those who did
so all changed in the same direction, and it was the direction of
the future literary language. It is especially interesting that the
writers who—partly as a result of these changes—seem nearest to
the general development of the language are not, as we might
have expected, those educated at Eton or Oxford, still less the
Cambridge men; but rather the courtier and soldier Sir John,
and his younger brother who also became Sir John and the
trusted servant of noble families. That such men thought it
desirable to modify their English implies that they were conscious
of a model worthy of imitation. Sir John the elder did not think
highly of ordinary Londoners. He writes of his aunt: 'She is in
many thyngys full lyke a wyffe of London and of Londone
kyndenesse, and she woll needys take advise off Londonerys,
wheche I telle here can nott advyse her howghe she scholde deele
weell wyth any body off worshyp.'[38] But it must have been from
London—no doubt from Londoners 'off worshyp'—that he and
some of his brothers learnt to adopt new forms and spellings; so
that even at this date one type at least of London speech must
have acquired something of the prestige of an incipient 'standard' language.

The linguistic behaviour of these brothers may also contribute
something to the understanding of variations of scribal practice,
or even of the spelling habits of early compositors. Clearly one

[38] no. 313.

man might in his time use many forms, sometimes changing them quite suddenly; and each so regularly that his writings could be placed in roughly chronological order on their evidence alone. If the youngest John's letters, say, had been copied by clerks or printed, we might be disposed to account for the different linguistic strata by assigning them to different writers; but his handwriting is happily unmistakable.[39]

II

I turn now from the details of grammar to more general features of vocabulary and style. They cannot well be used for precise comparison within the collection, but they help to relate it to other documents of the time.

A point of social as well as linguistic interest, well illustrated by the letters of the entire family, is the use of the pronouns and verbs of the second person. The singular 'thou' and its oblique cases are never used in normal correspondence, however intimate the writers: husband to wife, mother to son, one brother to another, even master to servant, all use 'ye' and 'you' invariably. In this they differ from the practice of some of the Celys about the same time. Richard Cely the elder uses 'thee' and 'thy' (beside 'ye', 'you', 'your') in several letters of 1477 and 1478 to his son George,[40] and Richard the younger uses *I pray thee* to his servant in 1481.[41] Where the singular occurs in the Paston letters it always implies anger, contempt, or hostility. The following extract, from an account by Margaret in 1448 of an attack by a certain Wymondham and his men on her chaplain James Gloys, exemplifies the tone:

And Jamys Gloys come wyth his hatte on his hede betwen bothe his men as he was wont of custome to do. And whanne Gloys was a yenst Wymondham, he seid þus: 'Couere thy heed.' And Gloys seid ageyn, 'So I shall for the.' And whanne Gloys was forther passed by þe space of iij or iiij strede Wymondham drew owt his dagger and seid, 'Shalt þow so, knave?'[42]

[39] The variation of spelling and form discussed in 'A Scribal Problem ...' (note 9 above) is now seen to be paralleled in the undoubted autographs of single writers—though it remains an extreme case by reason of the speed of the changes.

[40] A. Hanham, *The Cely Letters 1472–1488* (E.E.T.S. 273 (1975)), nos. 11, 12, 13, 23, 24.

[41] Ibid. no. 126.

[42] no. 129.

The youngest John, in 1472, writes of a quarrel he had with the same Gloys: 'We fyll owght be for my modyr wyth "thow prowd prest" and "thow prowd sqwyer".'[43] And in 1469 he reports Edward IV as rebuking Sir William Brandon in these words: 'Brandon, thow thou can begyll the dwk of Norffolk and bryng hym abow[t] the thombe as thow lyst,[44] I let the wet thow shalt not do me so; for I vndyrstand thy fals delyng well j now.'[45]

In letters written by Norfolk men and women, who all, even when they lived elsewhere for a time, retained a strong interest in the county, we should expect to find regional usage not only in spelling and forms but perhaps even more plainly in vocabulary. The distribution of words in the fifteenth century is very imperfectly known, and most of what can be said of it is provisional; yet some attempt is worth making.

We cannot often hope to match the precision of the younger Edmond Paston's note on the strange phrase of abuse or contempt, '*calkestokke* on hys hed', of which he tells his brother: 'yat is schoryle [*sc.* churl] in Englyshe; yt is a terme new browthe vp wyth my marschandys of Norwyche.'[46] The word is 'kale-stock', which as *castock*, *calstock* and the like is well enough recorded from Trevisa onwards, mainly in the north. The spelling *calkestokke*, with an intrusive -*k*-, looks like a mere blunder, until we find that it is not unique, but that exactly the same form appears in the Harleian manuscript, and *calkstoke* in the Winchester manu-

---

[43] no. 353.

[44] no. 333. *O.E.D.* under *Thumb* sb.5.b gives '*To bring* (a person) *above the thumb, to turn over the thumb,* to get or have under one's control', comparing 'to twist round one's finger' (not recorded until 1855) and quoting the present passage. But there is no other example with *above*, and the two with *over* are not quite parallel. Professor Kihlbom, in 'Notes on some words in NED', *Studia Germanica tillägnade Ernst Albin Kock* (Lund, 1934), p. 105, compares *O.E.D.* under *Thumb* 5.i, '*Above one's thumb* (Sc.) beyond one's reach or ability', and suggests that the speaker may have mixed his metaphors; she does not notice the entry under 5.b. But John III does not use *w* for *v* (as some of the correspondents do), and he probably meant to write *abowt*, but left off the -*t* before the following *t*-. The likeliest explanation of the phrase is that it is simply an early variant of 'to twist round one's finger'.

[45] Cf. also Agnes's report of her husband's words during his last illness to his son John, who was dissatisfied with his father's will: '... askyng him the question wheder he held hym not content, so seying to hym in these termes: "Sir, and thow do not, I doo; for I will not geve so mekyll to on that the remenaunt xal haue to littill to leve on." ' no. 31.

[46] no. 394.

script,[47] of the *Promptorium Parvulorum*—the compiler of which says, 'Comitatus tamen Northfolchie modum loquendi solum sum secutus.' The *Promptorium* similarly is the only text I know which throws light on a word used by Margaret in an early letter (1448) to her husband: 'I pray ȝw be ware hw ȝe walkyn jf he be þere, for he js ful cursyd hertyd and *lwmysch*.'[48] The *Promptorium* glosses *lowmysh(e)* 'canicus' (Harl.) and 'arduliosus' (Win.), that is 'malicious',[49] and gives also the compounds *lowmysman* and *lowmyshnesse*. Several other unusual words used by the Pastons appear in the *Promptorium*, though not uniquely there. *Morkyn*, a new formation serving as the past participle of 'mark', which is used in letters of both the younger Johns and in Margaret's will,[50] is duly glossed 'signatus'. Agnes, writing of the death of a neighbour in 1453, says: 'And forth wyth he felt afeyntyng in hese legge and *syyd* doun'; and *cyynge downe or swoownynge* is glossed 'sincopacio'.[51] The *Promptorium* entry is the latest quotation under the verb *Sye* in this sense in *O.E.D.* Margaret writes, probably in 1441: 'Elysabet Peverel hath leye seke xv or xvj wekys of þe seyetyka, but sche sent my modyr word be Kate þat sche xuld come hedyr wanne God sent tyme, þoov sche xuld be *crod* in a barwe.'[52] The verb *crowd* in the particular sense of 'wheel in a barrow' appears in the *Promptorium*, earlier in *Amis and Amiloun*, and later in the modern dialect of East Anglia. The *Promptorium* has *breyel*, evidently for *breþel* ('good-for-nothing'), glossed 'brollus, miserculus'; *brethel* is used twice by Margaret, and by her husband, and appears also in the York plays, the Macro plays, the *Ludus Coventriae*—probably from Norwich—and in the works of John Bale, who was born in Suffolk and educated at Norwich. Margaret also uses *boy* in the sense 'male child' about 1454, not

[47] In both manuscripts the word follows *calme*, as if without the *-k-*.

[48] no. 129.

[49] *Ardulio* is recorded by Du Cange, from glosses in which it evidently means 'malignant': *actus cum malignitate, acutus cum malignitate*. It is used again in the *Promptorium* to gloss *slyman and doggyd*, and *doggyd, malicyows* is glossed 'maliciosus, perversus, bilosus'. *M.E.D.* glosses *loumish*, in a fascicle published in 1973, 'meddling'. The *Dictionary of Medieval Latin from British Sources* (British Academy, fasc. I (1975)) glosses *ardaliosus* 'crafty, deceitful', citing only *PP lowmysh*.

[50] nos. 320, 313 (these two both in *O.E.D.* under *Mark* v.2 and 13); 230. The form is frequent in *The Brewers' First Book* in Chambers and Daunt, *A Book of London English* (Oxford, 1931), pp. 182–3.

[51] no. 26.

[52] no. 125. This letter is attributed by Fenn and Gairdner to Margery, and dated 1477. For the attribution to Margaret and the date 1441 see the index to the manuscript, and *Medium Ævum*, xviii (1949), 15 n.2.

long after its first certain occurrence in the *Promptorium*.[53] *Sweme-full* 'grievous', which *O.E.D.* quotes last from Margaret, is recorded only from the fifteenth century, including the *Ludus Coventriae*; the noun *sweam* seems to be characteristic of the eastern counties, and the *Promptorium* has *swemyng or mornyng* 'tristitia'. Other words of the Pastons in the *Promptorium*, as well as in other eastern and northern texts, are Margaret's *plawncher* 'floor', *quethword* 'last will',[54] and *reder* 'thatcher',[55] the second John's *pedde* 'basket', and the youngest John's *scrat* 'scrape'.[56]

Some other more or less technical words are dialectal. When Margaret writes to her husband, 'It is tyme to *crone* your old officere',[57] she means to discharge him. The noun *crone* 'old ewe' is recorded from Norfolk, Suffolk, and Essex, and the verb, meaning 'to pick out and reject (from the flock)', seems to be characteristic of the same region. The first John Paston twice writes of *shakke* (*chacke*) *tyme*,[58] the season when animals were turned into stubble fields to feed on the shaken-out grain. This is mainly East Anglian.

A number of words have more generally northern connexions. The first John and his eldest son both use *pratte* 'trick',[59] which, recorded several times in Old English as *prætt*, occurs earlier in Middle English only in Laȝamon, and later is only Scottish. The second John once uses *thyre* 'these'.[60] Margaret has *ripple* 'scratch, graze',[61] the youngest John *spere* 'ask',[62] and the younger Edmond *skyft* 'move'.[63]

There are also one or two peculiar forms of words. 'World' appears as *werd*, a well-known northern and eastern form, in letters written by the youngest John for Margaret, and as *word* in Clement. 'Enemies' is often *elmyes*, *elmyse*, once in the second John's earliest letter, at least nine times in letters written by James Gloys for Margaret, and in an autograph letter of the bailiff Richard Calle.[64]

These examples by no means exhaust the list of words of doubtful distribution; but certainly the number of clearly or

---

[53] The date may be a year earlier (*English and Germanic Studies*, iv (1951–2), 61). See E. J. Dobson, 'The Etymology and Meaning of *Boy*', *Medium Ævum*, ix (1940), 121–54, esp. 143–4.

[54] no. 208.   [55] no. 144.   [56] no. 326 (misread in G. 569/661).

[57] no. 166.   [58] nos. 66, 73.   [59] nos. 77, 312.   [60] no. 282.

[61] no. 129.   [62] no. 332.   [63] no. 400.

[64] Neither *O.E.D.* nor *M.E.D.* (Part E 2, 1953, p. 134) quotes such forms from any other text. But *elmys* occurs in *The York Plays*, ed. R. Beadle (1982), xxxiv, 121.

probably regional words is remarkably small for so great a volume of correspondence. It may well be significant that most of those that do occur are in the letters of Margaret, who was born and brought up at Mautby, near Yarmouth, and seldom moved far from Norwich and the family estates. The vocabulary as a whole shows less affinity with the north than might have been expected. William the judge, for example, who is the first recorded user, about 1430, of 'new-laid' applied to eggs, used the word *ey*, not *egg*.[65] But this again conforms to the vocabulary of the *Promptorium*. The Brewers' Company of London, on the occasion of a dinner on the Feast of the Decollation of St. John Baptist 'yn þe ȝere of kynge Henry þe vj^te þe seconde ȝere' (*sc.* 29 August 1424) spent eightpence on *c. of egges*.[66]

So voluble a company of letter-writers naturally left their mark on the dictionaries by using many words and phrases and more or less proverbial expressions which have escaped earlier record; and some that they used have been missed. Their contributions are as varied as the topics of the letters. The judge uses *chippe* as an intransitive verb applied to stone in 1425,[67] and it is not recorded until 1753. His son William provides the first quotations of *jantyllmanly* and *a folis paradyce*, the first John of *in hoder-moder* 'secretly'. Margaret has *hert-brennyng* in 1449,[68] and it does not otherwise appear until More in 1513. She gives the first examples of *captenesse*, *doggebolt* 'one who is the tool of another', and the expressive compound *schyttyl-wyttyd*; and she anticipates by a few years the first records of the coin *riale*[69] and the phrase *sche hath no fantesy þer inne*.[70] The second John is first with *what-calle-ye-hym*: 'Nowe bere the cuppe euyn, as what-calle-ye-hym seyde to Aslake.' He is a few years ahead of Caxton with *prenostik* as a verb,[71] and of Rastell with *contraryaunt* as an adjective.[72] He

---

[65] no. 7.
[66] Chambers and Daunt, op. cit., p. 179.   [67] no. 1.   [68] no. 132.
[69] no. 209, 1471. *O.E.D.* first Warkworth 1473. An example possibly earlier still is in no. 210. Gairdner dated this tentatively 1466, the year of John Paston I's death, on the ground that the contents show that administration of his will had not yet been obtained. But in no. 279, of 30 July 1473, Sir John tells his mother, 'I have provyd my fadres wyll and testament'; so that the date of no. 210 might be at any time before that. 1470 is possible.
[70] no. 145, perhaps of 1453; also *swyche . . . as the pepyll hathe a fantsy in*, no. 168, 1462. *O.E.D.* first *I have non fansey with some of the felechipp*, no. 193, 1465.
[71] no. 304, 1477. *O.E.D.* quotes the form, as *pronostikyth*, under *Prognostic* v.; but the abbreviation in the first syllable is that for -*re*, not -*ro*. *Prenostic* is quoted from 1480.
[72] no. 279, 1473. *O.E.D.* 1530.

uses *in preente* of *The Game and Playe of the Chesse* in an inventory of indeterminable date, but certainly—since he died in 1479—very soon after Caxton's first printed English book of 1475. (*O.E.D.* follows the editors here in wrongly attributing the inventory to the youngest John, and dating it 1482.)[73] But perhaps his most interesting word is *toy*. Writing to his mother, probably in 1479, of an interview he had had with his uncle's widow, in which she kept from him certain deeds he was anxious to see, he says, '. . . and ther com iiij. off her neyborys and wer ther present, whyche as I conseyuyd wer but shewyd and browte vppe for þat I sholde thynke þat she lakked noon helpe; and many suche soleyn toyes she hathe.'[74] *Soleyn toyes* must mean 'strange tricks'. This reinforces the evidence for this early sense of *toy*, hitherto recorded from 'before 1500'; and it raises new doubt about the validity of basing etymological conjecture about this difficult word on the sense 'amorous sport', which is known earlier only from a single occurrence in Robert Manning.[75] The youngest John anticipates the Dictionary records of *bend* 'band',[76] *mysfacyon*,[77] and *thanklesse*,[78] and has *befor the hand* in a sense of 'beforehand' not quoted until fifty years later.[79] A few words and phrases are not recorded at all. The second John has *encomfort*,[80] and *goo balke* in 'Bothe [my moodre] and Playtere haue promysed me so largely þat it is shame for them to goo balke wyth it.'[81] The youngest John has *chaseueleyns*, apparently instruments of war of some kind.[82]

[73] no. 316. The handwriting is unquestionably John II's, as the manuscript index says.

[74] no. 313.

[75] So most recently A. J. Bliss, 'Three Etymological Notes', *English and Germanic Studies*, iv (1951–2), 27–9.

[76] no. 330, 1468. *O.E.D.* quotes first Caxton 1475, and attributes to him the introduction of the word from French. *M.E.D.* does not record it, perhaps because Fenn, and consequently Gairdner, misread it *bands*.

[77] no. 331. *O.E.D.* Levins 1570.

[78] no. 361, 1473 ('. . . þat ye tweyne may fynd the meane to get hym owght of þat *thanklesse* offyce'). *O.E.D.* in this sense Surrey *a.* 1547.

[79] no. 360, 1473. *O.E.D. Beforehand* l.d 1526.

[80] no. 243, 1469.

[81] no. 276, 1473.

[82] no. 325, 1467. Gairdner prints *chafeveleyns* and glosses 'javelins'. The fourth letter is a long *s*, written over another letter (apparently an unfinished round *s*), and so not perfectly distinct; but there is no cross-stroke. If the word were 'javelins' it would be the earliest recorded example in English. *M.E.D.* accepts Gairdner's reading, but its only other quotation is spelt *Gauelongis*, which can hardly be the same word. *O.E.D.* quotes first Douglas 1513. The present form cannot be accepted as a possible spelling of 'javelins' by John

Both the eldest and the second John use a catch-phrase which I have not come upon elsewhere. 'He can as good skyll theron as Bernard can on his sheld' is the father's form,[83] and the son writes to his brother, 'Master Lacy, an other Rome rennere heere ... knowyth my seyde proctore theere, as he seythe, as weell as Bernard knewe hys sheeld.'[84] Margaret writes: 'Yf he do oght therin he doyth it closely as he ys wont to doo, and *wayshyth his hondys therof* as Pylate dyde',[85] a phrase which *O.E.D.* records only from 1554. She often shows an effective command of apt metaphor and proverb: 'It is to myn hart a very spere'; 'He and alle his olde felaweship put owt their fynnes and arn right flygge and mery'; 'Men cut large thonges here of othere men's lethere'; 'We bette þe busschysse and haue þe losse and þe dysworschuppe, and othere men haue þe byrdys.'[86] She provides the last quotation of 'oftyn rape rewith', which she uses twice.[87] And her sons, especially the two eldest, enliven their letters with much popular simile and 'sentence'. Sir John recommends four 'sadde and wel advysed men' to his brother to help in the defence of Caister: 'Ye schall fynde them gentylmanly comfortable felawes, and that they wol and dare *abyde be there takelyng*'[88]—an expression first quoted from More in 1529. He urges him, 'I pray yow wynne yowre sporys in thys mater';[89] and dismisses the loss of one of his inherited estates to his rivals with, 'Farweell Drayton, the devyll doytt them!'[90] Maxims of his are: 'Men may nott lure

Paston III. The context ('they ryd and go dayly ... in ther trossyng dowblettys wyth bombardys and kanonys and *chaseueleyns*') strongly suggests that some kind of ordnance is meant. But Godefroy records *chassevilain* only in the sense 'hod'.

[83] no. 77, 1465.

[84] no. 282, 1473. B. J. and H. W. Whiting, *Proverbs, Sentences, and Proverbial Phrases* (Cambridge, Mass., 1968), B256, cites only this case.

[85] no.185, 1465. *O.E.D.* under *Wash* v.3.e, Lady Jane Grey. Whiting H87 has no earlier quotations except the Biblical original.

[86] *The Oxford Dictionary of English Proverbs* (3rd edn. 1970) gives both these proverbs from 1300 onwards. See also Whiting F147, T217, B604.

[87] no. 200, 1469: 'oftyn tyme rape rueth'; no. 220, probably 1473: 'oftyn rape rewith'; the latter quoted in *O.D.E.P.*, both in Whiting R32.

[88] no. 238, 1468. Whiting T6 first More 1532.

[89] no. 282, 1473. *O.E.D.* and *O.E.D.P.* first Lydgate *c.* 1425; Whiting S643.

[90] no. 277, 1473. *O.E.D.* has *Doited* (Sc.) 'Having the faculties impaired, especially by age', from Wyntoun *c.* 1425 onwards. Craigie, *Dictionary of the Older Scottish Tongue*, besides this (and *Doitit, Doytit*), gives examples of *Doit, Doyt*, v. intr., from Lyndsay. Neither records a transitive use with object. Neither *M.E.D.* nor Whiting notices the word, probably because Fenn and Gairdner misread it *do ytt*.

none hawkys with empty handys'; 'Late men deme whatt they wylle, grettest clerkys are nott alweye wysest men'; 'It shall neuer neede to prykk nor threte a free horse'.[91] The youngest John adds, among many: 'Who comyth fyrst to the mylle fyrst must grynd';[92] 'Fere fro Iee, fer fro hert';[93] 'I eete lyek an horse of purpose to eete yow owte at the dorys';[94] and Edmond: 'I may sey pouerte partys feleschepe.'[95]

Sir John anticipates the first *O.E.D.* quotation of *now or never* (cited first from Shakespeare),[96] *to play the fool*,[97] *to dance attendance*,[98] *for good and all*,[99] *to harp on*, and *to lead (someone) a dance*.[100] He has one or two amusing or tantalizing references to tales, or catch-phrases: 'I haue kepyd hym thys iij yere *to pleye seynt Jorge and Robynhod and the shryff off Notyngham*;[101] 'Raff Blaundrehasset were a name to styrte an hare. I warant ther shall come no suche name in owre bokys nere in owre howse; it myght per case styrt xx[ti] harys at onys. "*Ware that*", *quod Perse*'[102]—recalling ' "Ware þat", quod Ser Wyly' in the play of *Wisdom*;[103] and, when he was left with only one servant, 'I am as he that seythe, "Com hyddre John, my men".'[104] The youngest John, telling his brother how he had upset a load of their adversaries' barley into a pond, is reminded of a drinking song: 'I let slype a sertyn of whelpys, that gaue the cart and the barly syche a torn þat it was fayne to tak couert in your bakhous systern at Caster Halle, and it was wet wythin an owyr after þat it cam hom, and is nye redy to mak off *good malt ale, ho ho*!'[105]

---

[91] These three proverbs are all in *O.D.E.P.* and Whiting, sometimes in slightly different form.

[92] *O.D.E.P.* under *First come, first served*; Whiting M558.

[93] no. 355, 1472. *O.D.E.P.* last *c.* 1400; Whiting E213.

[94] no. 332, 1469. *O.E.D.* under *Horse* sb.25 quotes *He eats like a Horse* from 1707; *O.D.E.P.* and Whiting *To eat (a person) out of house (and home)* from the Towneley plays onwards. The present form of words is exemplified in *O.E.D.* under *Door* 6 in 1659.

[95] no. 394, 1471. *O.D.E.P.* quotes first in these words from Heywood 1546, but Whiting P334 quotes Rylands MS. 394 *c.* 1450.

[96] no. 292, 1475.

[97] no. 282. *O.E.D. c.* 1532.

[98] no.291, 1475. *O.E.D.* Skelton 1522. This example was pointed out by Professor Kihlbom in *Studia Germanica*, p. 101 (See note 44 above.)

[99] no. 296, 1476. *O.E.D. The Parlament of Byrdes* ?1550.

[100] The last two both in no. 301, probably 1476. *O.E.D.* quotes from 1562 and *c.* 1529 respectively.

[101] no. 275, 1473.   [102] no. 273, 1473.

[103] *Wisdom* in *The Macro Plays*, ed. M. Eccles (E.E.T.S. 262 (1969)), line 604.

[104] no. 277, 1473.   [105] no. 325, 1467.

Nor is this light-hearted vigour of narrative the only quality that raises the letters above the commonplace. Most of the writers now and again show a real sense of style, and can turn a graceful or a telling phrase. Young John is perhaps the best of them: 'Now thynk on me, good lord, for jf I haue not an hawke I shall wax fatt for default of labor and ded for defawlt of company';[106] or again, 'He is on the lyghtest, delyuerst, best spokyn, fayirest archer; deuowghtest, most perfyght, and trewest to hys lady of all the knyghtys that euer I was aqweyntyd wyth; so wold God my lady lyekyd me as well as I do hys person and most knyghtly condycyon.'[107] But Agnes, his grandmother, can achieve something of the simple dignity of the Bible translations of the next century: 'Geffreie axid Palmere why the rentte was notte axid in myn husbonddis tyme; and Palmere seyde, "For he was a grete man, and a wyse man of the lawe, and that was the cawse men wolde not axe hym the rentte".'[108] And again, 'Be my counseyle, dyspose ʒoure selfe as myche as ʒe may to haue lesse to do in þe worlde. ʒoure fadyr sayde, "In lityl bysynes lyeth myche reste." Þis worlde is but a þorugh fare and ful of woo, and whan we departe þer fro, riʒth nouʒght bere wyth vs but oure good dedys and ylle.'[109] The eldest John, writing to his wife about their son, follows a more formal and intricate rhythm with a stern monosyllabic conclusion: 'I lete yow wete I wold he dede wel; but I vnderstand in hym no dispocicion of polecy ne of gouernance, as man of the werld owt to do; but only leuith, and euer hath, as man disolut, with owt any prouicion. ... Ne I vnderstond nothing of what dispocicion he porposith to be; but only I kan thynk he wold dwell ageyn in yowr hows and myn, and ther ete, and drink, and slepe.'[110] And the touching words of Margery to young John, when it seemed that her dowry would not content him, may even now bear repetition:

Yf þat ʒe cowde be content wyth þat good, and my por persone, I wold be þe meryest mayden on grounde. And yf ʒe thynke not ʒowr selfe so satysfyed, or þat ʒe myght hafe mech more good—as I hafe vndyrstonde be ʒowe afor—good, trewe, and lovying volentyne, þat ʒe take no such labure vppon ʒowe as to com more for þat mater. But let i[t] passe, and neuer more to be spokyn of, as I may be ʒowr trewe louer and bedewoman duryng my lyfe.[111]

It is evident that most of these people were highly literate, and even those who could not write were thoroughly articulate.

---

[106] no. 354, 1472.   [107] no. 352, 1472.   [108] no. 14.
[109] no. 30.   [110] no. 73.   [111] no. 416.

Though we may hear the tones of the pulpit in some of the graver cadences of Agnes's and Margaret's injunctions, for the most part the language is manifestly the speech of the time, plain and direct, only organized and sometimes heightened a little for the written page. This is an element in the history of English prose that should not be lost sight of.[112] We need not look to devotional treatises for the models of all competent narrative or lucid exposition, or of the simple, moving expression of true feeling, when men and women of no extraordinary talents could so skilfully command 'the comyn termes that be dayli vsed'.

[112] See also H. S. Bennett, 'Fifteenth Century Secular Prose', *R.E.S.*, xxi (1945), 257–63.

THE ORCHERD OF SYON AND THE ENGLISH MYSTICAL TRADITION

By PHYLLIS HODGSON

Read 1 July 1964

Habent sua fata libelli

*T*HE ORCHERD OF SYON has suffered the ups and downs of circumstance, after periods of esteem long centuries of neglect, yet its fate has not been inglorious, and its contribution to late Middle English spiritual writings claims recognition on three scores: what it is in itself; when it was introduced; how it enriched the native stock.

The high regard for this work in the fifteenth century is shown by the three large extant manuscripts, all finely written and elaborate—Harleian MS. 3432, St. John's College, Cambridge, MS. 75, and Pierpont Morgan Library MS. 162. But within a century it was to lie neglected even in its original home. From the colophon of Wynkyn de Worde's printed edition of 1519 we learn that Sir Richard Sutton,[1] Steward of Syon Abbey from 1513, had found a manuscript there, 'in a corner by itselfe. Wyllynge of his greate charyte it sholde come to lyghte, that many relygyous and deuoute soules myght be releued and haue conforte therby, he hathe caused at his greate coste this booke to be prynted.' As Hodnett says,[2] it is 'a rather striking production', with red letter titles and chapter headings, two founts of black letters, one 'a primer of great beauty' (117 mm.), eight large and fairly elaborate woodcuts representing the visions of St. Catherine of Siena, the set freshly copied, appearing in England for the first time, so that, to quote from Warton's description given to Churton[3]: 'in point of ornament and other respects, it is the most superb and curious specimen of ancient English typography I remember.'

---

[1] One of the founders of Brasenose College, Oxford. See R. Churton, *The Lives of William Smyth, Bishop of Lincoln, and Sir Richard Sutton*, Oxford, 1800.

[2] See E. Hodnett, *English Woodcuts, 1480–1535*, London, 1935, pp. 253–5.

[3] Op. cit., p. 421. See also William Herbert, the earlier editor and augmentor of Ames, *Typographical Antiquities*, London, 1785–90, pp. 158–60.

Copies[1] of this edition are frequent exhibits in library show-cases, but modern admiration has been limited chiefly to external appearance. The contents have been generally ignored. The rapidly multiplying studies of the English mystical tradition are silent about the *Orcherd*, or at the most give it bare mention, while essays proliferate on Richard Rolle, *The Cloud of Unknowing*, Walter Hilton, Julian of Norwich, Margery Kempe of Lynne.

The *Orcherd* contains a full and faithful version of St. Catherine's dictated composition, she called it her *Book*, about 130,000 words, with no major omissions, not even of the terrible chapters on the corruptions within the Church. The account of her original dictation in Tuscan to her three secretaries, Barduccio Canigiani, Stefano Maconi, Neri di Landoccio, is well known. We can learn the whereabouts of the early manuscripts from editions of modernized Italian versions.[2] There are, in fact, at least twenty-five manuscripts containing an Italian version of the *Book*, and fifteen a Latin translation. The earliest major manuscripts[3] of the Italian were originally transcribed without division into treatises or chapters; these divisions were added later to an official redaction, of which many copies were made. Twice the *Book* was fully translated into Latin in order to ensure wide circulation, first by Cristofano Guidini, a Sienese notary, and one of her early disciples who had been actually present at the original dictation, and later by Stefano Maconi, one of the original scribes. When a third translator, Raymund of Capua, her spiritual director and biographer,[4] died, he had completed his Latin version of only the first five chapters and the last two of her *Book*.

The search for the source of the Middle English translation is severely handicapped by the fact that there is still no critical edition of either the Italian or the Latin versions. Their inter-relationship remains unknown. Preliminary comparisons of passages from the *Orcherd* with their corresponding parts in early

[1] Copies are known to exist in the British Museum, the University Libraries of London, Cambridge, Glasgow, the Bodleian Library, Peterborough Cathedral Library, Winchester College Library, Blackburn Public Library, Sion College Library, in the collections of Sir R. C. Harmsworth, and at Longleat House, New York Public Library, Folger Shakespeare Library, Washington, D.C.

[2] M. Fiorilli, *Libro della Divina Dottrina*, Bari, 1928, pp. 409–34; I. Taurisano, *Dialogo della Divina Provvidenza*, Rome, 1947, pp. liii–lix.

[3] Codici maggiori—Senese t. II. 9, Estense t. 6. 5, Casanatense 292.

[4] He completed her biography, *Legenda Major*, in 1395.

printed editions and manuscripts give warning of likely complications. For example, Wynkyn de Worde's text of 1519 prints
also a translation from the Preface of Marcus Civilis which
occurs in the early printed edition of a Latin text, Brescia, 1496,
attributed then and until recently to Raymund of Capua. The
frequent attribution of the Latin translation to Raymund is
clearly mistaken. The Brescia version proves to be basically that
of Maconi.[1] One would expect the *Orcherd* too to be based on
Maconi's Latin version.[2] Most Middle English translations of
continental mystical writings were made from Latin versions,
and a frequent channel of transmission was Carthusian. After the
saint's death, Maconi joined the Carthusian Order, and in 1398
was elected Prior General. Manuscripts of his version certainly
reached France and the Netherlands. The manuscripts of the
Middle English text contain no information as to their source.
But there is no doubt that the English printer in 1519 had before
him a manuscript very close indeed to Harleian 3432, and a
text based probably on the Latin translation of Guidini, or less
probably on the original Italian. The Guidini text is much closer
to the Italian than Maconi's.

Until Fr. Benedict Hackett proves me wrong in his forth-
coming publications on William Flete and the activities of St.
Catherine's immediate circle in England, I shall not relinquish
the idea of the possibility of Dominican provenance. Raymund
of Capua himself, as Master General of the Dominican Order,
between 1393 and his death in 1399, was in close touch with
William Bakthorpe, the Prior of Lynne, that active centre of
English mysticism.[3] Or again, another Dominican channel—
Guidini's well-known story in his *Memoriale* might itself ultimately prove relevant. After many years of hard work Guidini
finished his version, sent it off to Maconi, probably in 1389 or
before,[4] for correction, and had a fair copy made. This had not

[1] A fairly extensive comparison has been made between the Guidini
version in MS. t. II. 4 in the Biblioteca Comunale of Siena and the Maconi
version in MS. AD. IX. 36 in the Biblioteca Nazionale of Milan.

[2] I am indebted to Fr. B. Hackett for the information that Maconi,
according to Caffarini, sent Catherinian material to King Henry (?IV),
though not apparently his version of the *Book*.

[3] At the end of the fourteenth century the Dominicans in England were
badly split through disaffection against Raymund. The English party on his
side was headed by the Prior of Lynne.

[4] According to R. Fawtier, *Sainte Catherine de Sienne*, ii, Paris, 1930, p. 341,
the version was sent to Maconi at the Carthusian House at Pontignano, which
he left in 1389.

been in his house twenty-four hours before he was visited by a venerable French bishop belonging to the Dominican Order, who was collecting information about Catherine and was accompanied by Raymund. Naturally Guidini brought out his beautiful manuscript for inspection, and once in the bishop's hands it stayed there. He wished to make it known in his own country, he said, where it would do more good than in Siena, where it was already known. The bishop begged so hard that Guidini finally gave him it. The bishop later wrote to Raymund of its great influence, and Raymund repeated his words. Perhaps we owe the *Orcherd* to this act of generosity. How far did that little candle throw his beams? We do not yet know, but a manuscript[1] now in the Edinburgh University Library certainly contains Guidini's Latin version.

St. Catherine's *Book* later became known under various titles, *The Dialogue*, *The Book of Divine Doctrine*, *The Book of Divine Providence*. The Middle English sub-title adopts *The Book of Divine Doctrine* and repeats her contemporaries' description of the circumstances of composition:

Here begynneþ þe Boke of Diuine Doctrine, þat is to seie, of Goddis techinge, ȝouen bi þe persone of God þe Fader to þe intellecte of þe glorious virgyn, Seint Katerine of Seene, of þe Ordre of Seint Dominike, whiche was write as sche endited in her moder tunge when sche was in contemplacioun inrapt of spirit, and sche heringe actueli and in þe same tyme tellinge tofore meny what oure Lord God spake in her.[2]

It is beside the present task to pursue the implications of this statement, or to set St. Catherine's colloquies against such admittedly fictional dialogues as St. Augustine's soliloquies or Suso's in the *Book of Eternal Wisdom*. The extraordinary nature of her dictation is well attested—in Raymund's biography, and in the depositions of her friends and disciples in the Process of Venice, 1411–13, whose claim anticipated that in the Bull of Canonization of 1461 (*Misericordias Domini*): 'Doctrina eius infusa, non acquisita fuit.' Suffice it now to say that the earliest

[1] Edinburgh University MS. D. b. IV. 18 (Bowland 87). This is probably an English manuscript, but unfortunately its early history is not yet known.

[2] Unless otherwise stated, the quotations from the *Orcherd* are taken from MS. Harleian 3432 (H). Where this is defective, the Pierpont Morgan Library MS. (M) is used. Here, M, f. 9ʳ. Cf. the Guidini version in the Edinburgh MS.: 'Incipit liber diuine doctrine date per personam dei patris intellectui loquentis gloriose & sancte virginis katerine de Senis ordinis sancti dominici de mantellatis conscriptus ipsa dictante licet vulgariter et stante in raptu & audiente actualiter quid in ea loquaretur dominus deus & coram pluribus referente.'

text extant was edited. It contains third person narrative, and lists in the beginning the four petitions which were to shape the rest. St. Catherine appears to take the initiative, and there is little likeness to any spontaneous interchange. The truths revealed are those of the Scriptures and dogma of the Church, with many echoes of literary sources and references to the saint's earlier visions. One wonders, with her great modern biographer, Edmund G. Gardner,[1] whether Catherine herself would have made any claim of supernatural authorship.

The Prologue of the *Orcherd* is explicit that this Middle English translation was prepared for the benefit of the Bridgettine nuns of Syon Abbey. None of the three extant manuscripts gives any indication for whom it was copied; none contains the translator's holograph. The only manuscript certainly at Syon was that rescued by Sir Richard Sutton. A consensus of expert opinion has attributed both the Harley and the Cambridge manuscripts to the early decades of the fifteenth century; the Pierpont Morgan manuscript has been dated *c.* 1470.

According to their marginalia, after that 'sorry 25 dai of November 1539' when 'the house of Syon was suppressed into the kinges hand, and the ladies and brethren put out, the landes and goods to the kinges use', the Harley and Cambridge manuscripts were in the Salop area, where loyalty to the Catholic faith long persisted. Subsequent ownership *is* traceable,[2] but if we are to avoid the giddiness of unfocused vision, we must

---

[1] *St. Catherine of Siena*, London, 1907, p. 354.

[2] MS. Harleian 3432 passed from William Tarboxe (Tarboke) of Kidderminster to George Horde, of a Bridgnorth family. Four other names appear in this manuscript in a large formal sixteenth-century hand: Roland Gosenell (of an ancient Salop family living at Condover); Walterus de Evereux, Miles, possibly the grandson of Walter Baron Ferrers and Viscount Hereford, whom he succeeded in 1558, becoming a Knight of the Garter and the first Devereux Earl of Essex in 1572; Ebor, ? Archbishop Heath of York 1555–9, Queen Mary's Chancellor who proclaimed Elizabeth's accession in the House of Lords, yet led the other bishops in their refusal to take the Oath of Supremacy; Norwycensis, ? Hopton of Norwich, (1554–8), a merciless persecutor of Protestants.

In the seventeenth century this same manuscript came into the possession of John Battely (1647–1706), the Kentish antiquary and Archdeacon of Canterbury, from whose nephew Wanley bought it on 5 Nov. 1723 for the Earl of Oxford.

In the sixteenth century the Cambridge MS. was in the possession of Robert Baxter of Kidderminster. *C.* 1615, along with much of William Crashaw's collection, it came into the possession of Henry Wriothesley, Earl of Southampton, the friend and patron of Shakespeare.

concentrate on the early history of the English text. One digression might be permitted. In the early seventeenth century the Cambridge MS. rested on the well-filled bookshelves of William Crashaw, the north-country divine, chiefly remembered for his virulent attacks on the papacy, but who also collected *A Handful, or rather a Heartful, of Holy Meditations and Prayers*, translating Catholic devotions for Protestant edification and use. His son was the poet Richard Crashaw, whose devotion to St. Theresa might not have been wholly uninfluenced by the images of blood and fire, the teaching on the Sacrament of the Altar, the 'large draughts of intellectual day' to be found also within the folios of the Cambridge *Orcherd*.

The translator's Prologue is directed to the 'Religyous modir & deuoute sustren clepid & chosen bisily to laboure at the hous of Syon' (f. 2ra). Since both the Harleian and the Cambridge manuscripts belong to the early fifteenth century, the temptation to look for the original recipients proved irresistible. The foundation-stone of the Bridgettine monastery was laid by Henry V on 22 February 1415, and the Foundation Charter granted in March, which designated Matilda Newton, a recluse of Barking, as provisional abbess, and William Alnwick, a recluse of Westminster, as Confessor General. The community began to assemble, but it was not until 1 April 1420 that the first professions were made.[1] What happened between 1415 and 1420 remains confused,[2] but Matilda Newton, never regularly elected, resigned in 1417, to retire to an anchorage at Barking, and was succeeded by Joan North, a nun of Markyate near St. Albans, who ruled until her death in 1433. John of Amundesham records that Wiliam Alnwick also retired in the course of a year, worn out and old, and was followed by Thomas Fyschborn, who had been an anchorite at St. Albans and who died in 1428.[3]

---

[1] According to British Museum MS., Add. 22285, f. 14, there were 27 sisters, 5 priests, 2 deacons, 4 lay brothers.

[2] Detailed accounts of the foundation of Syon Abbey are to be found in M. Deanesly, *The Incendium Amoris of Richard Rolle*, Manchester, 1915, pp. 91–130, D. Knowles, *The Religious Orders in England*, ii, Cambridge, 1955, pp. 177–80.

[3] MS. Harleian 3775, f. 109: 'Willelmus Alnewyk, reclusus monachus Westmonasterii, cum aliis monachis diuersorum locorum, in custodiam feminarum prefectus est: set post anni circulum, tedio et senio confectus, ad cellam suam unde egressus fuerat reuersus est... (f. 110^v). In tempore vero Willelmi Alnewyk, prima Abbatissa monialis de Berkyng a dignitate sua per Regem exonerata est.' Edited by H. T. Riley, *Annales Monasterii S. Albani a Johanne Amundesham, Monacho*, i, London, 1870, p. 27.

'Religyous modir...clepid and chosen.' 'Clepid and chosen' is a collocation familiar enough in the body of a text, with its scriptural associations, and as a translation of Latin *electi*, but here its unusually emphatic position in the actual address is arresting. Might it not possibly imply here 'titular', 'designate', but not yet actually professed? That is, before 1420. The dating of the manuscripts does not preclude the guess that the abbess could have been Matilda Newton of Barking, the abbey which had a leading position among English nunneries for its books, and prefigured Syon itself in the encouragement of learning. Two other books, near contemporaries with the *Orcherd*, are also associated with Barking, *The Chastising of God's Children* (dated before 1408)[1] and *The Cleansing of Man's Soul*. There might be a significant clue to authorship in the fact that the *Chastising* is further linked to the *Orcherd*, however tenuously, by Bridgettine influence and a similar ending. The *Chastising* ends: 'And as I am wonte to seie or to write, so heere I seie of al my defautis. A Iesu mercy.' Cf. *Orcherd*, f. 192rb: 'And for my neclygence & ignoraunce, as I am wont to seye so I now write. A Ihesu mercy.' This does not appear to be a common ending, though one comparable occurs in *The Revelations of St. Maud* (Mechthild),[2] a text which also has Syon associations.[3]

The translator tells us nothing about himself, unless we take his words in the Prologue to be more than a convention, and remember the frail and failing William Alnwick: 'Grete laborer was I neuer, bodili ne gostli. I had neuer grete strengþe my3tli to laboure wiþ spade ne wiþ schouel. Þerfore now, deuoute sustern, helpeþ me wiþ preiers...a3ens my grete febelnes.'[4]

The last heading in the early printed edition, *Lenuoye of Dane James the translator*, gave rise to an error perpetuated in most accounts of the *Orcherd*,[5] including Gardner's and Hodnett's, but which a careful reading of the following passage will correct: 'In 3oure deuoute praieris haueþ myn helper recomendid, 3oure broþir, Dan Iamys, which for þe mooste partye haþ laborid it to þe eende of þis goostly orcherd.'[6] Wynkyn de Worde's

---

[1] See J. Bazire and E. Colledge, *The Chastising of God's Children*, Oxford, 1957, pp. 34–37.

[2] Cf. Egerton MS., f. 212: 'Ande for alle my negligence in þis werke and alle othere, als I seyde in the begynnynge so I saye in the endynge. A Iesu mercy. Amen.'

[3] See *Myroure of Oure Ladye*, E.E.T.S. e.s. xix, 1873, pp. 276–7.

[4] M., f. 7v.

[5] e.g. Gardner, p. xv; Hodnett, loc. cit.

[6] f. 192ra–b.

title, *The Orcherd of Syon*, occurs only once in the manuscripts, in the Explicit of the early Harleian MS. 3432. The double significance of Syon would escape no medieval reader. The rest of the figure is explained in the translator's Prologue and Epilogue. This book of revelations he calls a 'fruytful orcherd'. 'In þis orcherd, whanne ȝe wolen be conforted, ȝe mowe walke & se boþe fruyt and herbis. And al be it þat sum fruyt or herbis seeme to summe scharpe, hard, or bitter, ȝit to purgynge of þe soule, þei ben ful speedful and profitable, whanne þei ben discreetly take and resceyued by counceil' (f. 2^{ra-b}).

This allegorical framework supplied by the Middle English translator is particularly appropriate for what it encloses, for St. Catherine herself frequently used the same image, e.g. God told her: 'Þan made I resonable creature to þe ymage and liknesse of me and sente him into þe orcherd, which orcherd by þe synne of Adam haþ brouȝt forþ þornes, where first it brouȝte forþ flouris of swete smyllynge innocencie' (f. 155ra). And again, man is a 'maner of orcherd…maad wiþ swete fruyt. Naþelees þe gardener of þis orcherd, which is fre chois, may make þis orcherd wielde if he wille…if he sowe þereynne venym of his owne propre loue' (f. 155^{rb-vb}).[1] Incidentally, this framework is appropriate too for Syon Abbey, for a comparable vision—'I will plant a new vineyard and will surround it with the hedge of my grace'— had inspired St. Bridget to found her Order.[2]

The Middle English translator ends with: 'Now, reuerent modir & deuoute sustren, ȝoure orcherd is plauntid & sett, and, at my symple deuyes, apparaylid' (f. 192ra). The apparelling must refer to his division into seven parts, five chapters in each part, thirty-five alleys in the orchard in which the sisters might walk. Despite the sevens and fives, numbers of mystical significance, the Middle English divisions are no more arbitrary than those in the Italian and Latin versions, and correspond about equally loosely to changes in dominant imagery and tone. Within the Middle English divisions, the chapter headings inserted by the early editors of the Italian and Latin versions are traceable.

[1] Cf. also God's revelation of Himself through His Son: 'I schewide me to þee in a figure of a tre: of þe which tre þou say neiþer bigynnyng ne eendyng, but oonli þou parceyuedist þat þe roote of þe tre was ioyned wiþ þe erþe' (f. 46ra); 'þe erþe of mekenes…where þis…tre of discrecioun is sett and plauntid' (f. 16ra); 'þe tre of charyte…norischid in mekenes' (f. 17ra); 'men… fayre trees of loue wiþ þe liif of a special grace' (f. 35va); and many others.

[2] See *A Royal Foundation. Syon Abbey Past and Present*. Syon Abbey, South Brent, Devon, 1946.

The choice of one of the first books to be made especially for the new Bridgettine foundation at Syon has indeed great significance. Its suitability is clear for a community strictly enclosed and partly composed of former anchorites and contemplatives. Moreover, there was a strong spiritual kinship[1] between St. Catherine and St. Bridget, not only in their mystical experiences, for both in ecstasy held long and intimate colloquies with God, but also in their practical concern with the reform of the Church. One may conjecture that it was more feasible to translate St. Catherine's Book than St. Bridget's. The vast compilation in MS. Harleian 612, made for Syon and dated 1427, contains fourteen books of St. Bridget's revelations in Latin, hundreds of chapters, many of which have been described as 'occasional, repetitive and monotonous', with 'frequent lack of cohesion and unity of thought'.[2]

Comparison between the *Orcherd* and some of the early vernacular translations[3] of the *Revelations* will show that St. Bridget's work lacks the powerful unity and magisterial authority of St. Catherine's pronouncedly orthodox dogma on the mysteries of Holy Church, the Trinity, the Redemption, the Eucharist, man's innate potentiality, Divine Providence, the unitive way. St. Catherine's Book, though never so colourful and graphic as St. Bridget's could be, was yet more immediate for the needs of Syon abbey.

But the *Orcherd* reflects more widely still current interests and tastes. For instance, the growing interest in continental mysticism and in women mystics in particular.[4] Before the late fourteenth

---

[1] There were also personal connexions. In 1374 Bishop Alphonse of Pecha, St. Bridget's confessor and the editor of her *Revelations*, sought out St. Catherine. In 1378, though there is no evidence of direct association, the Pope was minded to send St. Catherine with St. Bridget's daughter on a mission to the Queen of Naples. At least two witnesses who urged the canonization of St. Catherine in 1412, Stephen of Siena and Bartholomew of Ravenna, had testified to the authenticity of St. Bridget's visions in the Process which led to her canonization by Pope Boniface IX in 1391. It is to be noted that in MS. Harleian 612, col. 755, Bishop Reginald in his *Primum Defensorium* associates St. Bridget and St. Catherine.

[2] W. P. Cumming, *The Revelations of Saint Birgitta*, E.E.T.S. 178, London, 1929, p. xxviii.

[3] See Cumming, loc. cit.; Cotton Claudius MS. B. I, c. 1425; Cotton Julius MS. F. II, c. 1475.

[4] The many fifteenth-century translations include Egerton MS. 2006 and Bodleian MS. 220 of St. Maud (Mechthild of Hackborn). The Egerton MS. belonged to Richard of Gloucester and Anne Warwick. A 'Mauldebuke' was owned by Eleanor Ros of York in 1438. Douce MS. 114 contains the Lives

century I know of no records of women visionaries on English soil apart from the twelfth-century Christina of Markyate[1] and an anonymous Gilbertine nun[2]—in striking contrast to the situation along the Rhine described by Christine Ebner, who knew of only one woman in her convent who never experienced ecstasy, and yet she was a very holy person. The typically English attitude of Walter Hilton and the author of the *Cloud* towards Rolle's descriptions of sensory experience establishes that visions in England were more likely to be discredited than believed. Shortly before the *Orcherd*, the *Chastising of God's Children* had borrowed Bishop Alphonse's proofs of the sanctity of St. Bridget, but only to demonstrate that all revelations may be of diabolical origin, unless they satisfy certain tests. Margery Kempe herself described the rough handling she received when, according to Miss Allen's learned notes, she was but following in the steps of St. Bridget, St. Dorothy of Prussia, St. Mechthild, St. Gertrude, and St. Elizabeth of Hungary.

The new interest in women mystics was to remain a matter of controversy. The very year of the foundation of Syon (1415) and only seven months after the canonization of St. Bridget was confirmed at the Council of Constance, Gerson was to assert that 'All words and works of women must be held suspect'.[3] St. Bridget's cause was first stated by Bishop Alphonse before 1379, when he set out to prove that her 'glorious book...was wretyn in þe herte of the forseid lady with the fynger of all-myghty god'.[4] It was still being disputed a century later,[5] and many notable Englishmen had risen to her defence.[6] The mighty translation of St. Catherine's Book no less than the royal foundation of Syon can be regarded as an English affirmation of credence.

Monographs could be drawn from the *Orcherd* on favourite

of 'Seint Elizabeth of Spalbeck, Seinte Cristin the marvelus, Seint Mary of Oegines, a letter touchynge the lyfe of Seint Kateryn of Sennys, the which letter endyted in Latyn dan Stephen of Senys'; The Life of St. Elizabeth of Hungary is to be found in Cam. Univ. Lib. MS. Hh I. 11.

[1] C. H. Talbot, *Christina of Markyate*, Oxford, 1959. Her visions are to be found in MS. Cotton Tiberius E1, belonging to the second quarter of the fourteenth century.

[2] Sermo III, *Sermones de Oneribus B Aelredi*, Migne, *P.L.* 195, col. 370–2.

[3] *De Probatione Spirituum*, i. 15.

[4] Quoted from Cotton Julius MS. F II, f. 247.

[5] See E. Colledge '*Epistola solitarii ad reges*: Alphonse of Pecha as Organizer of Birgittine and Urbanist Propaganda', *Medieval Studies*, vol. xviii (1956).

[6] See D. Knowles *Religious Orders*, ii, p. 277.

late medieval topics such as the gift of tears, discretion, the *via triplex* of contemplation, the Sacrament of the Altar. We are justified in asking what the translation of St. Catherine's Book added to mystical literature in England. The framework of reference is clear. Passages from or about St. Catherine keep company with those by the key writers of the wholly English tradition, Rolle, the author of the *Cloud*, Walter Hilton; we find them together in manuscript compilations,[1] Carthusian records of gifts and loans,[2] medieval libraries.[3] At least three scholars recently have mentioned investigations into a possible connexion between St. Catherine and Julian of Norwich,[4] between Hilton and the circulation of Catherinian literature in England.[5] With the obvious confluence of native and continental traditions in the fifteenth century one may surmise that there were others before the Duchess of York, mother of Edward IV and Richard III, who during the time of dinner had a 'reading of holy matter, either Hilton on active and contemplative life, Bonaventure, St. Maud, St. Katerine of Siena or the Revelations of St. Bridget'.[6]

Paradoxically, where St. Catherine would seem in her choice of themes to belong most to her age, she is most strikingly individual. Let us take, for example, the favourite late medieval subject for religious art and literature, the Passion. In English writings we have Rolle's brooding *Meditations*, Margery Kempe's noisier sensibility, the 'showings' of Julian which started in

[1] e.g. University College, Oxford, MS. 14, Royal MS. 17 D v.

[2] See E. M. Thompson, *The Carthusian Order in England*, London, 1930, p. 321; D. Knowles, op. cit., p. 343.

[3] Some manuscripts of fourteenth-century English mystical writings probably connected with Syon: (i) Rolle Emmanuel Coll. 35
          Addit. 24661
          Brasenose 15
          Trin. Coll. 792.
   (ii) Hilton *Scale* Harleian 2387
          All Souls 25
          ? Laud. Misc. 602
          Uppsala U.L. C 159
          ? Columbia U.L. Plimpton 257.
  (iii) *Cloud* Harleian 993.

For the number and nature of Rolle MSS. at Syon, see H. E. Allen, *Writings Ascribed to Richard Rolle*, London, 1927, pp. 47–49, 411–12. See also N. R. Ker, *Medieval Libraries of Great Britain*, R.H.S., 1941.

[4] A. Levasti, Sister Anna M. Reynolds.

[5] Father B. Hackett.

[6] Quoted from W. A. Pantin, *The English Church in the Fourteenth Century*, Cambridge, 1955, p. 37.

pictorial visions of Christ's flowing blood, physical sufferings, and death, to set beside Hilton's claim that 'a man schal nouȝt comen to gostli delit in contemplacioun of cristes godhede. bute he come furst in ymaginacioun bi bitternes and be compassioun & be stedfast thinkeng of his manhede' (f. 22ʳ).[1] Sometimes in lyrics and prose treatises there is the soul's response of contrition or of rapturous love-longing; more often we find preoccupation with all the stark horror of torture, grief, suffering, and death. Mâle commented that from the wounds of the Crucified ran great rivers of blood in which St. Bridget and many other continental mystics wished to bathe.[2] The great English mystics stand apart in their restraint. Even Julian herself understood later that her graphic physical images were only means of instruction on the Godhead, 'as it were þe begynnyng of an A.B.C.' (f. 36ᵛ).[3] No saint was more inebriated, 'oonyd & whalwyd in the blessid blood' (f. 73ᵛᵃ) than St. Catherine. But in the *Orcherd* there is a fundamental intellectual and emotional austerity comparable to that of the *Cloud* or the *Scale*. Hilton said: 'Þe gostly biholdynge of þe godhed in Iesu man is more worþi more gostly & more medful þan þe beholdynge of þe manhode alone' (f. 103ᵛ).[4] St. Catherine goes further. She pre-supposes the historical life and death of our Lord, not as the author of the *Cloud* presupposes it, in order to still the working of reason and imagination, but rather to concentrate on the eternal redemptive purpose of the Trinity in the Incarnation. Like the doctors of the eleventh and twelfth centuries, she translates this ineffable reality into intellectual symbols. The one which spans the whole *Orcherd* and gives its unity is the great apocalyptic symbol of the Bridge. The like of this recurrent imagery is not to be found earlier in English mystical writings. The opening vision of *Piers Plowman* has comparable vastness and sublimity, but it is surpassed in dynamic force by the Bridge, which through its manifold interpretation is essentially a symbol of movement— the Way, the Truth, the Life. This is the Bridge of God's mercy. 'Þe greetnes of þat brigge...streccheþ fro þe heiȝt of heuene down to þe erþe' (f. 27ʳᵇ). The Bridge, God's son and His doctrine are 'al oone and þe same' (f. 34ʳᵃ). After man had broken up the road to heaven, 'of trespas and synne cam forþ

---

[1] *Scale*, i. 35. Quotations are from MS. Harleian 6579.
[2] E. Mâle, *L'Art religieux de la fin du Moyen Age*, Paris, 1931, pp. 108 sqq.
[3] Unless otherwise stated, the quotations from Julian's *Revelations* are from MS. Sloane 2499.
[4] *Scale*, ii. 30; cf. i. 35, 36.

an unrestful flood which smoot him alwey of hise watris'
(f. 27ʳᵃ), 'which flood is a feruent see of þis wrecchid liif'
(f. 27ʳᵃ). 'No man may passe ouer þat flood wiþ þe liif, but needis
he moste be drenchid' (f. 32ʳᵃ). Before this Bridge was 'areisid up',
'heuene was not til þat tyme undo wiþ þe keye of his precious
blood, and þe reyn of riȝtwiisnes wolde suffre no man to passe'
(f. 31ʳᵇ). There are three steps to this Bridge, 'tweyne weren
maad in þe tre of þe holy cros', the third 'ful greet peyne of
bittirnes whanne þei ȝauen hym boþe galle and aysel to drinke'
(f. 30ʳᵇ). This Bridge is walled with stones, 'soþfaste vertues'
(f. 31ʳᵇ). 'He plauntid hem as lyuynge stoones wiþ His holy
blood, þat alle feiþful men mowen frely passe þat brigge withoute
ony dreede of greet reyn of þe riȝtwiisnes of þe Godheed' (f.
31ᵛᵃ). By this Bridge men come to 'þe gate of sothefastnes. Þanne
comen þei to me, which am þe pesable se' (ff. 31ᵛᵇ–32ʳᵃ). The
three steps have become the *via triplex* of perfection. The
traditional three stages of contemplation, for the beginner, the pro-
ficient, the perfect, are worked out in terms of the feet, the side,
the mouth of Christ crucified,[1] in imagery that in its spirituality
recalls St. Bernard's Threefold Kiss.[2]

Only the barest reference is made to the instruments of the
Passion in the *Orcherd*, as when Christ is 'fast held' to the cross
'wiþ naylis of loue'.[3] The blood shed is inseparable from
St. Catherine's thought, but it is identified in the sacraments,
in Baptism,[4] in Confession,[5] but most often in the Sacrament of
the Altar.[6] Upon the Bridge 'þe viridarye of myn holy chirche
stondeþ in batel and fiȝteþ. Which chirche haþ breed of liif and

---

[1] 'In þe first gree þei han spoilid þe foot of affeccioun fro delectacioun of
vices. In þe secounde gree þei han taastid þe secreet affeccioun of herte,
wherby þei han conceyued deliit in vertu. In þe þridde gree, þat is, in pees
and tranquillyte of soule...þei fynden reste in þe doctryn of my sooþfast-
nesse ...þou maist se and knowe þat to hem I am a mete table, and my
Sone is to hem mete, and þe Holy Gost is to hem a seruitour' (f. 78ʳᵃ⁻ᵇ,
f. 78ᵛᵃ).

'Þei ben al brennyd in þe furneyse of my charite. Wherfore þere may noon
take hem out fro me, for þei ben imaad oon with me and I with hem'
(f. 79ʳᵃ⁻ᵇ).

[2] *Sermons on the Canticles*, III. iv.

[3] f. 76ᵛᵇ.

[4] f. 74ᵛᵇ.

[5] f. 74ʳᵃ.

[6] 'Þe which charite is maad to ȝou visible of my oonli sooþfast Sone
Ihesu whanne he made it open in his blood. Þe which blood makeþ a soule
goostly drunke & araieth it rialy wiþ þe fier of dyuyne charite & ȝeueþ to
hir þe blessid goostly mete of þe sacrament of þe auter' (f. 65ᵛᵃ).

ʒeueþ þe drynk þat is mynystrid, … þe holy blood, þat by þat, my creaturis, whiche ben pilgrymes & goon in þe weye, faylen not in þe weye' (f. 31ᵛᵃ).

Though there are many separate treatises on the sacraments in Middle English, it has often been remarked that on the Mass the fourteenth-century English mystical writers are inexplicably reticent. May we not see in the *Orcherd* a forerunner in England of such later devotional writers as Sir Thomas More who explicitly integrated their devotion to the Person of our Lord with the Mass, and were constantly aware of the mystical Body of the Church?

There is a comparable distinction, a touch of intellectual splendour, in St. Catherine's eight chapters on the gift of tears.[1] *The Book of Margery Kempe* with Miss Allen's commentary describes Margery's 'plentyous teerys & booystous sobbynges', and recalls continental women mystics who in the intensity of devotion had so great a gift of tears that at length their cheeks were furrowed by continual weeping: the bibliographical notes also give guidance to the long and sober literary tradition going back to the early Church and ultimately to the scriptures, associating tears with penitence and prayer, and systematizing them according to their spiritual sources or their fruits. The methodical and comprehensive chapters of the *Orcherd* have the same essential control. St. Catherine's revelations, made, as she repeatedly says, 'to þe iʒe of intellect', lead almost invariably to the working of the Trinity and the way to perfection. She abstracts all the diverse states of tears, imperfect and perfect, with their fruits, and shows how the soul can rise in succession from the wholly self-centred tears of death, the tears for 'dreede of peyne' (f. 87ᵛᵇ), the sensible 'teeris of goostly loue' (f. 88ʳᵃ), the selfless tears wept for 'hertly loue in me (God), and for compassioun of þe offence þat is doon to me' (f. 88ʳᵇ), to the 'teeris of swetnesse by þe feelyng of myn eendelees godheed' (f. 88ᵛᵃ). The perfect weep with the tears of heaven. 'How glorious is sich a soule þat so rialy can passe out of þis troublous see of þe world & come to me, þat am þe greet peesable see, & fille þe vessel of þe herte in þe see of myn euerlastynge souereyn Godheed' (f. 88ᵛᵃ). She includes further the tears of those perfect souls who desire to weep and are not able. Theirs are tears of fire, 'mental teris, ful of fier of dyuyne unspecable charite . . . in þe whiche teris of fier þe Holy Goost waylyth & wepiþ for hem' (f. 91ʳᵃ⁻ᵇ).

---

[1] ff. 87ʳᵃ sqq.

The contribution of the *Orcherd* may perhaps best be assessed by close reference to two of the key figures of the wholly English tradition, Walter Hilton and Julian.[1]

There is promise of a rewarding comparison between the writings of St. Catherine and Hilton, both spiritual directors providing a *summa* which met the needs of all,[2] concerned with the growth in spiritual life from the state of fallen man to the highest sanctification possible on earth. The teaching of neither is esoteric. Both regarded the attainment of contemplation as the goal for all, and progress towards this as a continuous and gradual development of the life of grace begun at baptism. Their end is the same, to come, by degrees of love and enlightenment, 'to þe gostli felyng of God... þat þou miȝtist knowe þe wisdom of God, þe endles miȝte..., & þe grete goodnes of hym in himself and in his creatures' (f. 8ʳ).[3]

The idea behind St. Catherine's recurrent figure of the spiritual cell of self-knowledge which the would-be contemplative must enter and never again leave is fundamental of the *Scale*, and indeed controls the whole plan of Book I.[4] God is best known in the soul made according to the scriptures in His image. The echoes of St. Augustine and the Victorines are clear. This self-knowing must be bifocal, both self-knowing and God-knowing, an equilibrium of humility and love, a realization of one's own present nothingness matched against the perfection of God and the dignity for which one was originally created. Like Moses, St. Catherine had heard the voice of God: 'I am He who is; you are she who is not' (cf. f. 25ʳᵇ). Hilton's password for his pilgrim to perfection (ii. 21) signifies the same: 'I am noȝt. I haue noȝt. I coueite noȝt bot on' (f. 85ʳ). To seek refuge in this cell of self-knowledge is to flee the ephemeral things of the world, and to persevere in this cell is the only effective discipline to 'reende up þe þornes of deedly synnes and... plaunte þe hiȝenes of vertues' (f. 28ʳᵇ).

Both describe mystical experience in terms of understanding

---

[1] The thirteenth-century group (*Ancrene Wisse*, *Wohunge*, &c.) and *Piers Plowman* are most concerned with the stage of Purgation; Rolle is thought not to have progressed beyond that of Illumination; the *Cloud* is esoteric in its concentration on a special exercise of unitive prayer.

[2] This is true of much of the *Scale*, even though Book I was written for a recluse.

[3] *Scale*, i. 12; cf. Eph. iii. 17–19.

[4] This 'Christian Socratism', as Gilson terms it, is the only basis of contemplative life. It is 'an hiȝe pleyn weye as mekil as may ben in mannes werke to contemplacioun'. *Scale*, i. 42, f. 25ᵛ.

and in imagery of true light.[1] 'I haue tastid & seen wiþ þe liȝt of intellecte,' cried St. Catherine, 'wiþ þi liȝt, þe depþe of þin eendelees trinite...þou art þat fier þat illumynest, & wiþ þi liȝt þou hast maad me knowe þi truþe' (f. 191ʳᵇ⁻ᵛᵃ).

There are many other arresting points of comparison. Both writers show a deep knowledge of the human soul in its operations. They see its nature, its faculties and their mutual relations and interactions under influences both human and divine, and the effect of the soul's action upon the body and the body's upon the soul. The proportions and the emphases are, of course, different, but there are few fundamental ideas in the *Scale* not also in the *Orcherd*, excepting of course the advice on the technique of prayer, which Hilton introduced because the *Scale* was primarily a manual of direction. The *Orcherd* too will serve as a handbook, but, first and foremost, it is a personal spiritual testament. Hilton frequently disclaimed any attainment of unitive prayer,[2] and when he would appear to be writing from personal experience he dreads 'mikel to speke ouȝt of it' (f. 123ʳ).[3] In her descriptions of herself 'goostly dronke wiþ þat blessid blood' and 'brennyd in þe fier of love' (f. 79ᵛᵃ), 'abouen hersilf wiþ a greet longynge desier out of coorse of þe bodily feelynge' (f. 87ʳᵇ), 'þe ponderous body...maad liȝt...lift up fro þe erþe' (f. 79ᵛᵃ), St. Catherine directs our gaze to the sublimest heights.[4] As Gardner says: 'We feel that we have almost passed behind the veil that shields the Holy of Holies, and that we are in very truth hearing Catherine's rendering into finite words of the ineffable things that she had learned by intuition in that half hour during which there is silence in Heaven.'[5]

---

[1] Herein lies the great difference between the *Scale* and the *Cloud*. Cf. *Scale*, ii. 46: 'for luf & liȝt goon boþe togidir in a clene soule' (f. 139ᵛ); ibid. i. 8: 'he...bi þe grace of þe holy gost is illumined for to see bi undirstandynge soþfastnesse whilk is god, & gostli þinges, with a soufte swete brenninde luf in him' (f. 5ʳ); ibid. ii. 46: 'þan is it opned soþfastly to þe eiȝe of þe soule þe onhed in substance & distinccioun of persons in þe blissid trinitee' (f. 139ʳ).

[2] See *Scale*, i. 33, 93.

[3] Ibid. ii. 40.

[4] Cf. *Orcherd*: 'Euery place is to hem a place, and euery tyme is to hem a tyme of preyer, for her conuersacioun is lift up fro þe erþe and areisid up to heuene' (f. 78ʳᵃ).

Cf. also: 'And aftir tyme þei ben so goostly dronke wiþ þat blessid blood and be brennyd in þe fier of my loue, anoon þei taste in me þe eendelees Godheed, þe which is to hem as a pesible see, in þe which see þe soule haþ cauȝt sich an vnyoun and oonheed þat sich a soule haþ no maner of mouyng but in me' (f. 79ᵛᵃ).

[5] Op. cit., p. 355.

In this she is more comparable with Julian. Not primarily concerned with growth in the spiritual life, Julian gave no 'map and general information for those setting out to explore a country for themselves', but, as Father Sitwell says,[1] 'as a traveller returned with a first-hand description of what she has seen there'. Julian also was pronounced *theodidacta, profunda, ecstatica*.[2] Indeed the two are somewhat alike both in their kind of enlightenment and in the circumstances of literary composition. Both had imaginative visions and divine locutions, sensible manifestations which were accidental compared with the knowledge received in infused contemplation, when their minds, directly and supernaturally impressed, were flooded, not so much with new knowledge as with new light on basic theological truths. Both found in their revelations the nucleus of their books, and both reflected long, Julian for twenty years or more, before setting them down in writing. Both described God exhorting, affirming, revealing, and expounding in answer to petition, and both in turn gave thanks in outpourings of devotion. And if St. Catherine suffers more, hopes, demands, implores more fervidly—'al brennynge in loue and goostly drunke...wondirly woundid in herte of so grete bittirnesse' (f. 146ʳᵃ)—the differences lie in personality, intensity, and amplitude, and, of course, national temperament, rather than in kind.

For example of this difference in amplitude let us take their intellectual visions of the operations of the Trinity. Theirs is the mystics' apprehension of the Trinity which Hilton described, though he declined to enlarge upon the theme.[3] Both women bring all things into focus with the Trinity, writing with a profundity of feeling and intimacy that recalls St. Theresa's description of 'that mysterious manifestation of the truth... when all three Persons communicate Themselves to the soul and explain the Lord's words that He and the Father and the Holy Spirit will come to dwell with the soul which loves Him and keeps His commandments. What a difference there is between hearing and believing these words and being led in this way to realise how true they are.'[4]

St. Catherine, like St. Francis before her and Dante, uses in

---

[1] G. Sitwell, *Medieval Spiritual Writers*, London, 1961, p. 100.

[2] The judgment of a seventeenth-century French Protestant. Quoted from E. I. Watkin, *The English Way*, London, 1933, p. 130.

[3] *Scale*, ii. 46.

[4] *Interior Castle*. Mansion vii, c. 4.

explanation the favourite medieval image of the sun with its light, heat, and fire. God the Father is the 'verry sonne' (f. 111ᵛᵇ), of whom 'gooþ out boþe þe Sone and þe Holy Goost' (f. 112ʳᵃ). 'My myȝt is neuere departid fro his wisdom, ne þe heete of þe fier of þe Holy Goost is neuere departid fro me, þe fadir, ne fro my sone, for he is oon wiþ us' (f. 112ʳᵃ). 'Þe toon of us may not be departid fro þat oþire no moore þan may þe heete of þe sonne fro þe liȝt ne þe liȝt fro þe heete. That sonne is neuere dyuydid, and ȝit to al þe world and to ony creature þat wil be maad warm by hym it ȝeueþ liȝt' (f. 111ᵛᵇ).

In her initial revelation the Trinity filled Julian's heart with the utmost joy. 'The trinite is our Maker & keeper. the trinite is our everlasting lover, everlasting ioy & blisse...where Iesus appereith the blissid trinite is vnderstond' (f. 3ᵛ).[1] The Trinitarian providence manifested in the Creation, the Incarnation, the Redemption, is the main motif of the *Orcherd*. St. Catherine is far more detailed than any of the English mystics as to how man is made in the image of the Trinity in the three powers of his soul, mind, reason, and will, that he might participate in everything belonging to God. This belief overflows into her view of all the soul's activities as within the Trinity, and conditions her description of the soul's mystical progress, its shortcomings, its highest achievement, or its ultimate perdition.

Þei þat ben slayen in þe wickid flood of þe worldly mysgouernyd loue ben dede as to grace. And bycause þei ben deede, her mynde haþ forȝete þe greet benefeete of my large mercy. Also her iȝen of intellecte seen not and knowen not my sooþfastnes, for his witt and feelyng is deed... his wil is deed as fro my resonable wil, for his wil loueþ not but þingis þat ben deed (f. 35ʳᵇ).

The title given by modern editors to Julian's Book, *The Revelations of Divine Love*, would serve equally well for the *Orcherd*. St. Catherine's keywords are love and mercy. Both women, in the apostolic degree of the contemplative way, were motivated by the same wish: to communicate the deep knowledge of the love of God revealed to them, that their fellow Christians might be sped in the way of salvation. Both counterbalanced a horror of sin with boundless trust, though their reasoning differs. Both wrote repeatedly that 'sin is right nought',[2]

---

[1] See also *Revelations of Divine Love*, trans. by James Walsh, London, 1961, ch. 4, p. 51.

[2] *Orcherd*, f. 160ʳᵇ; Julian, Add. MS. 37790 (Shorter version), f. 101ᵛ; Sloane MS. 2499 'synne is no dede' (f. 10ʳ).

'it hath no maner of substance ne no party of being'.[1] Neither ignored the paradox of only too obvious evil in a world created and held in being by an all-powerful, all-knowing, all-loving, unalterable God. Julian sought to resolve this paradox chiefly by metaphysical argument; St. Catherine, perhaps more disturbed by the reality of the human wilful and sinful soul, is more militant in exhortation. But her understanding that 'from the nouȝt of synne which is a þorn þat prickeþ þe soule' God has 'drawn out a rose' (f. 160ʳᵇ⁻ᵛᵃ) is no less comforting than Julian's celebrated conclusion that 'Synne is behovabil, but al shal be wel, & al shal be wel, & al manner of thyng shal be wele' (f. 18ᵛ). Julian's speculations on sin drew her to faith in 'a mervelous hey privitye hid in God' (f. 19ʳ), and to the often challenged conviction that 'in every soule that shal be savid is a godly wil þat never assentid to synne ne never shal' (f. 24ᵛ). St. Catherine's answer likewise was a doctrine of the will, but one more orthodox and more easily comprehensible:

þat fredom of wil þat a man haþ is so myche, and maad so strong by vertu of þis precious blood þat þe feend may not compelle hym to do þe leeste synne, and no creature moore þan he wole hymsilf (f. 23ʳᵃ).[2]

I am he þat is iocunde and myrie, which kepiþ a soule in greet goostly gladnesse þat arayeþ hersilf wiþ my wille (f. 156ᵛᵃ).

The radiant confidence of both springs from their awareness that the Redemption realized the desire of God. The *Orcherd* reiterates the theme: 'myn owne loue constreyneþ me, for I louede ȝou eer þan ȝe loueden me, & eer þan ȝe myȝt loue I louede ȝou meruelously' (f. 160ᵛᵃ). God has a thirst and love-longing for us here, says Julian, 'lestyng in hym as long as we be in nede. us drawing up to his blis' (f. 20ᵛ). And St. Catherine:

Al woundid in loue, me semeþ þat þou hast nede of us wrecchide creaturis...þou canst not lyue wiþoute us, notwiþstondynge þou art eendelees liif, of whom alle þinges taken liif, & wiþout whom may noþing lyue (f. 173ʳᵇ).

I knowe wel, lord, þat first þou openest þe gate eer þanne we knocke þerate, for wiþ þe affeccioun and loue þat þou hast ȝoue to þi ser-uauntis, þey knocke to þee (f. 148ʳᵇ).

Apart from the vivid 'showings' of the agony of the Passion and the somewhat unorthodox speculations on sin, there is little matter in the *Revelations* not also to be found in the *Orcherd*. And

[1] Sloane MS. f. 19ʳ.

[2] Cf. 'þis gate of wille which is fre I wil not suffre goostly enemyes to vndo it' (f. 161ʳᵇ).

one might add that apart from the passages on the Sacrament of the Altar there are few mystical themes in the *Orcherd* to which Julian or Hilton do not give some prominence. The differences are almost always those of magnitude and personality. One last, but essential, example must suffice—their treatment of the second great commandment, to love one's neighbour as oneself. St. Catherine felt herself far more involved in the evil of the world than either, 'þe moost cause and þe instrument of alle mennys synnes' (f. 21ʳᵃ), for which she would take punishment upon herself: 'I praie þi dyuyn charyte þat þou take veniaunce of me, but spare þi peple. I schal neuere go fro þi presence til I se þee haue mercy on þat peple. What were it to me to haue liif & se þi peple haue deeþ?' (f. 21ʳᵃ). The beginning of Julian's experience lay in a threefold petition for herself, for mind of the Passion, for a purifying bodily sickness, for the three wounds of true contrition, kind compassion, and earnest longing for God. St. Catherine's initial petition was for mercy for herself that she might be worthy to help others, the second for the reformation of Holy Church, the third for mercy for the whole world, and the fourth for Divine Providence in things general and particular. Such dimensions and such a combination of the practical and sublime are characteristic of the whole *Orcherd*.

'For the honour of God and the salvation of souls' was her watchword throughout. God declared all these things to her, he told her, 'þat þe fier of holy desier myȝte encreesse in þee, and compassioun and sorowe of dampnacioun of soules' (f. 86ʳᵇ), that she and others 'togyderis schulen preye and in maner constreyne me for to schewe mercy to al þe world, and to þe mysterial body of holy chirche' (f. 86ᵛᵃ). Holy Church should be reformed, not 'by werre or by cruelte...but by pees and reste, and by weilynge and wepynge of my seruauntis' (f. 86ᵛᵃ); 'ȝit schulen ȝe not ceesse to ȝeue me encense of ȝoure wel smyllynge and riȝt swete prayeris for heelþe of soulis, for I wil do mercy to þe world and to holy chirche' (f. 86ᵛᵃ⁻ᵇ). Hunger for the salvation of souls must accompany the stages of spiritual ascent of beginners and proficients, of purgation and illumination. The English mystics in their decriptions stop short before the highest degree of contemplation. St. Catherine passes beyond the peace and joy of union to a fourth degree which comprehends the mystery of vicarious suffering:

Siche ben so ful of loue, and fro hemsilf, for þe worschip & honour of my name, and so hungry upon þe mete of soulis heelþe, þat þei renne to þe mete table of my sones cros, and þere desiringe to suffre myche

greuous peyne, þerby for to wynne and purchace vertues, to edifica-
cioun and profiȝt of her neiȝboris, berynge contynuely þe blessid
[prentis] of þe woundis of my sone ... þat is, þe ynly loue þat þei han for
heelþe of her neiȝboris soulis, crucifiinge hem so in her bodies, and
schewynge by schynyng to oþire, insomyche þat þei sett riȝt nouȝt by
her owne bodyes, but raþir desyren with greet delyte for to suffre
repreuys, heuynes and peynes, reckynge neuere in what wise þei ben
ȝeue to hem, for heelþe of her neiȝboris soulis (f. 77ᵛᵃ⁻ᵇ).

I have been able to indicate only a part of the *Orcherd*'s claim
to recognition. The prose of the translation merits attention in its
own right, as I hope the illustrations have shown. Those interested in Syon Abbey will find in the *Orcherd* strong proof of
the intellectual and spiritual attainment of its early days. After
reading the *Orcherd* those studying the English mystical tradition
will return to the great fourteenth-century writers with fuller
understanding. Rolle, Hilton, the author of the *Cloud*, Julian,
are all very different. The *Orcherd* speaks of divine love as
passionately as Rolle; elsewhere it has the austerity and restraint
of the *Cloud*, the wide embrace of Hilton, the immediacy of
personal rapture and the profundity of meditation found in
Julian. In addition, it offers us the first version in English of the
revelations of a unique saint.

The *Orcherd* was first rescued from neglect in the twentieth
century by Miss H. E. Allen[1] in her researches into the contemporary world of Margery Kempe. It will soon be given fitting
dress for publication again, this time by the Early English Text
Society.[2] The Middle English translator's counsel might once
again be followed: 'clerely to assaye & serche þe hool orcherd,
and taste of sich fruyt and herbis resonably aftir ȝoure affeccioun,
& what ȝou likeþ best, aftirward chewe it wel' (f. 2ʳᵇ).

---

[1] This article owes much to Miss Allen's notes and correspondence.

[2] A critical edition has been prepared by the present writer in collaboration
with Dr. G. M. Liegey. [Now E.E.T.S. 258, 1966].

THE DATE AND COMPOSITION OF
ANCRENE WISSE

By E. J. DOBSON

Read 25 May 1966

THE date of the *Ancrene Riwle* or, as I prefer to call it, *Ancrene Wisse*, has been so long and so often debated by scholars that it may seem superfluous to return to it yet again. My reason must be that the work concerns an unusual variety of medieval disciplines, some of which require as precise a date as we can assign; moreover, the consideration of its date involves questions of its genesis and authorship of even greater importance.

I do not propose to go over all the familiar ground. During the last forty years it has come to be generally agreed that *Ancrene Wisse* cannot have been written much before 1200. The study of its literary sources by R. W. Chambers and others has shown that it is influenced by books written in the mid twelfth century and indeed later.[1] Professor J. R. R. Tolkien, in a fundamental discussion of the language of the Corpus MS.,[2] demonstrated that it was so pure that one must assume that the scribe wrote and spoke the same dialect as the original author; and it is now generally accepted that this was a West Midland dialect, probably of north Herefordshire or south Cheshire. Tolkien also argued that, in a time of rapid linguistic change, so uniform and unmixed a language could not have been produced if any great interval of time had separated composition from copying; he was disposed to limit the interval to some twenty years, and as the Corpus MS. cannot be earlier than 1224 this would mean that the date of composition could hardly be before 1200. Tolkien's views have been challenged,[3] though

---

[1] See G. Shepherd, *Ancrene Wisse*: Parts Six and Seven (1959), pp. xxii–xxiii; A. Zettersten, *Studies in the Dialect and Vocabulary of the Ancrene Riwle* (1965), pp. 13–14; and the references there given.

[2] J. R. R. Tolkien, '*Ancrene Wisse* and *Hali Meiðhad*', *Essays and Studies*, xiv (1929), 104–26.

[3] See J. R. Hulbert, 'A Thirteenth Century Literary Standard', *JEGPh*, xlv (1946), 411–14; Dickens and Wilson, *Early Middle English Texts* (1951), p. 91.

not to my mind convincingly: it has been argued that (i) accurate translation from one ME. dialect into another, which Tolkien dismissed as inconceivable, has to be reckoned with (I do not think that this is at all likely), and (ii) if, as Tolkien held and everyone would agree, the language in question was a cultivated literary one, then it would of its nature be conservative and a greater interval of time might have elapsed between composition and copying, without leaving traces on the language of the Corpus MS., than he had allowed. In theory this argument has some validity, but in practice Tolkien was certainly right. It was also argued that his assumption that Corpus preserved the original dialect was itself dubious, since more archaic forms occurred in other manuscripts, and it was assumed that these forms, being more archaic, must be more original; but this is in fact a false assumption, for collation proves that the more archaic forms are introduced by the scribes of the manuscripts in question (mostly the Nero MS.) and are not original.[1] The author's dialect was more modern than that of some of the scribes, and it would not be easy (in view especially of its accidence, syntax, and vocabulary) to date it before 1200.

In 1945 Miss Beatrice White added an argument of a different sort.[2] Pointing to the passage[3] which describes Christ on the cross as having 'the one foot, according to the opinion of many, set upon the other', she argued that it reflected a new style of iconography in which Christ's feet were portrayed as transfixed by a single nail, and that no examples were to be found before 1200. But subsequent investigation has shown that this feature, though more likely to be met with in the thirteenth century, is not inconsistent with a date in the late twelfth; in particular Mr. Shepherd[4] cites a literary reference in a meditation of which the earliest known manuscript is dated to the end of the twelfth or the beginning of the thirteenth century.

Mr. Shepherd's[5] is the most compact recent discussion of the problem. Without relying on Tolkien's linguistic argument, he accepts a date about 1200, 'and on the whole probably after,

[1] See C. A. Ladd, 'A Note on the Language of the *Ancrene Riwle*', *N. & Q.*, ccvi (1961), 288–90; E. J. Dobson, 'The Affiliations of the Manuscripts of *Ancrene Wisse*', *English and Medieval Studies presented to J. R. R. Tolkien* (1962), ed. N. Davis and C. L. Wrenn, pp. 133–4.

[2] Beatrice White, 'The Date of the *Ancrene Riwle*', *MLR*, xl (1945), 206–7.

[3] Corpus MS., ed. J. R. R. Tolkien (E.E.T.S. 249, 1962), f. 106a/2–3.

[4] Shepherd, op. cit., p. 57 (note to p. 22, l. 13).

[5] Ibid., pp. xxi–xxiv. See also Zettersten, op. cit., pp. 12–18, for a fuller but less incisive account.

rather than before 1200'. He rejects the view that the correspondences between the Rule and later twelfth-century writings might be due to the influence of the Rule on them (and not vice versa), and says that if the passages concerned are later interpolations into the original Rule 'then we need not be much concerned with the original Rule, for it must have been completely recast and reformed'. He goes on to say that the material of latest date as yet discovered which has been incorporated into the Rule is a salutation *Ave principium nostrae creationis* which is stated by an early thirteenth-century writer to have been composed by 'dominus P. Cancellarius Parisiensis', i.e. either Peter of Poitiers, who was chancellor of the University of Paris from 1193 to 1204, or Praepositinus, chancellor from 1206 to 1210.[1] And more generally Mr. Shepherd remarks that the liturgical background of the Rule 'cannot be earlier than the late twelfth century, and may well be that of the early thirteenth'.

I rehearse very summarily these arguments, because they seem to me to be in accordance with all informed recent thinking on the subject. But Shepherd's attempt to set up a *terminus ante quem* of about 1215 is less happy. He has two arguments. The first is that, if he had been writing much after that date, the author, if he 'was knowledgeable about contemporary affairs, as he appears to have been, . . . would not have referred to the tournament as he has done';[2] and he cross-refers to one of his textual notes, which discusses love-tourneys and the presence of ladies at tournaments.[3] In the note, as I understand it, the line of thought is this: (i) the author refers to knights performing in love-tourneys, but only as something that happened in days gone by (*sumhwile* 'at one time, formerly'); (ii) in fact ladies were only just beginning to attend tournaments in the early thirteenth century, so the allusion must relate to an ideal past and be based on passages in Geoffrey of Monmouth; (iii) the earliest reference to a tournament in England 'at which ladies

---

[1] Shepherd refers to V. L. Kennedy, 'The Handbook of Master Peter Chancellor of Chartres', *Medieval Studies*, v (1943), 9; but it was C. H. Talbot, 'Some Notes on the Dating of the *Ancrene Riwle*', *Neophilologus*, xl (1956), 49–50, who pointed out the significance of the fact briefly recorded by Kennedy. There is no explicit evidence that the salutation was composed during P's chancellorship, and Shepherd points out that Peter of Poitiers was active in the learned world by 1175; Zettersten, op. cit., p. 19, goes too far in saying that the salutation establishes 1193 as a *terminus a quo* for the composition of *Ancrene Wisse*.

[2] Shepherd, op. cit., p. xxiii.

[3] Op. cit., pp. 56–57 (note to p. 22, ll. 8 f.).

were present, i.e. [to] something which can plausibly be described as a love-tourney, is in 1215 at Staines, where the prize
of a bear was presented by a lady'. So the note: but the Introduction seems to turn the argument round slightly, to the
proposition that since ladies were present at tournaments in
England as early as 1215, whereas the author does not know of
it as a contemporary practice, therefore he must have written
before 1215 (or at least not long after).

I must say that I think the argument mistaken. In the first
place, a *terminus ante quem* which depends on the assumption that
the author must have known almost immediately of a new
fashion seems insecure. Tournaments were under papal ban and
royal prohibition; a religious living in the Welsh marches might
not have known, for years afterwards, that ladies had started
attending them in France and the east of England. Secondly,
the reference in the text of *Ancrene Wisse* does not explicitly refer
to love-tourneys or the presence of ladies, and to take it in this
sense is probably to read into it something more definite than
the author intended. What he says is that Christ, like a noble
wooer,

after many messengers and many good deeds came to prove his love
and showed through knightliness that he was worthy of love, as knights
were at one time accustomed to do; he engaged himself in a tournament
and for the love of his dear one had his shield pierced on both sides in
the fight, like a bold knight.[1]

The reference is plainly to knights engaging in deeds of valour
and in tourneys to show that they are manly and worthy of love
(here indeed the author is almost certainly thinking of Arthurian
material, either in early romances or in Geoffrey of Monmouth),
but it is not necessarily to formal love-tourneys, nor does it
necessarily imply the presence of ladies to watch. And finally
and most important, Mr. Shepherd seems to have got his
historical facts wrong; the very historians to whom he refers
(Lady Stenton and Mr. Denholm-Young) contradict him. Some
misunderstanding seems to be involved in the belief that at
Staines in 1215 ladies were present and the prize was 'presented
by a lady'. Lady Stenton[2] translates the relevant sentence as

[1] Corpus MS., f. 105b/21–27.
[2] Doris M. Stenton, *English Society in the Early Middle Ages* (1951), p. 82.
The Latin text is 'Qui melius ibi faciet, habebit ursum, quem domina
quædam mittet ad torneamentum' (Roger of Wendover, *Flores Historiarum*,
ed. H. G. Hewlett (Rolls Series, 1887), ii. 138). The ambiguous phrase,
'prize . . . presented by a lady', used by Shepherd, p. 57, comes from a

'He who shall do best there will have the bear which a certain lady will send to the tournament.' The lady 'presented' the prize in the sense that she donated it, not that she handed it to the winner; she need not have attended at all, and indeed the word used (*mittet* 'will send') implies that she intended to keep well away from both tournament and bear. Clearly the discreetly anonymous lady was encouraging this tournament (doubtless because she was a political supporter of the barons in rebellion against King John, who were arranging it), but this seems a slender basis for assuming that 'ladies' (in the plural) 'were present' and that the occasion was 'something which can plausibly be described as a love-tourney'. The participants were not fighting for the lady, but the bear; and that is not my idea of a love-tourney. The tournament at Staines seems indeed to have been the ordinary early type, a mass engagement in open country between two teams; and Mr. Denholm-Young assumes, as is surely obvious, that the occasion was political. Denholm-Young[1] himself says that apart from this lady in 1215, 'the ladies at Kenilworth [in 1279] are the first heard of in connexion with an English tournament'. After referring to *Ancrene Wisse* and the romances, he observes that in the romance of *Fulk FitzWarin* (which he dates about 1258), the men 'are specifically stated to have tourneyed for love (*pur amurs*)'; but in his next sentence he coldly remarks, 'We have no actual records of this in thirteenth-century England.' The whole notion of knights tourneying for the love of ladies seems to have originated as a romantic literary fiction; and when eventually they did begin to joust for ladies' favours, it was a case of fact trying to catch up with fiction. The *Ancrene Wisse* author's use of the word *sumhwile* is therefore not at all surprising; he was doubtless very well aware that though 'Gawain with his olde courtesie' may have tourneyed for the love of ladies, real knights in his own day fought, often in deadly earnest, for horses and arms, and sometimes for all that they owned. Certainly, if there are no records of love-tourneys in thirteenth-century England, there is no case for using the author's ignorance of them as an argument for dating his work.

footnote of Denholm-Young's (on his p. 245) which refers for details to Kate Norgate, *John Lackland*, p. 239. Only Miss Norgate gives a reference to Roger of Wendover, without quoting him.

[1] N. Denholm-Young, 'The Tournament in the Thirteenth Century', *Studies in Medieval History presented to F. M. Powicke* (1948), ed. R. W. Hunt, W. A. Pantin, and R. W. Southern, p. 265.

Mr. Shepherd's second reason for preferring a date early in the thirteenth century is that the author's

devotional interests belong to the twelfth rather than the thirteenth century. His treatment of confession, his apparent aversion from mysticism, his insistence on the usefulness of reading as against overmuch prayer, all point in the same direction. The Fourth Lateran Council of 1215 insisted upon a stricter ecclesiastical control of unattached religious, and it is reasonable to assume that the original Rule, even the Rule as presented in N[ero], is somewhat less concerned with institutional religion than is *AW* [i.e. the Corpus text], and considerably less concerned with it than the Lateran Council expected spiritual directors to be. Most of the insertions peculiar to [the Corpus text] attempt to inject into the Rule a slightly more formalistic spirit.[1]

I do not understand what is meant by the contrast thus drawn (or rather, considered as 'reasonable to assume') between the original Rule and the Corpus text, for I cannot think of any Corpus addition or alteration (let alone 'most' of them) which in any way modifies the attitude to 'institutional religion'. One of the most characteristic additions, which occurs both in Cleopatra and in Corpus, is the passage in Part VIII which reads:

Understand always concerning all these things that none is a command or a prohibition which is comprised in the Outer Rule, which matters little; for when the Inner is well kept, as I said in the beginning, this can be changed wheresoever any necessity or any reason requires it, according as she may best serve the Lady Rule as her humble handmaid. But assuredly without her the Lady comes to disaster.[2]

This, so far from 'injecting' any more formalistic spirit, is repeating and re-emphasizing the author's teaching that the outward observances are secondary, and matter little compared with the spiritual life; and it is expressed in terms of a metaphor used in the Preface which is undoubtedly an integral part of the original text.

The belief that the 'original Rule' did not show the influence of the Lateran Council of 1215 is in any case to be set against the views expressed in 1955 by Dom Gerard Sitwell in his Introduction and Appendix to Miss Salu's translation of the Corpus text.[3] This important discussion seems to me not to have received sufficient attention, perhaps because, being published in this

---

[1] Shepherd, op. cit., pp. xxiii–xxiv.
[2] Corpus MS., f. 115a/15–21; cf. Cleopatra MS., f. 193 foot.
[3] *The Ancrene Riwle* translated into Modern English by M. B. Salu (1955).

context, it is thought to refer only to the Corpus text, and not to the original work; but in fact Mr. Sitwell's arguments are not in any way based on the Corpus modifications. His major point is that *Ancrene Wisse* shows the influence of the manuals for confession that began to appear in the early years of the thirteenth century, but received a 'great impetus' from the decrees of the Lateran Council of 1215; and he draws attention to particular activity in this matter in England in the years immediately before the Council of Oxford in 1222.[1] He also remarks on certain features of the devotions prescribed for the anchoresses, especially the comparative modernity of the purely private devotions, which he says might be regarded as typical of a fifteenth-century book of hours;[2] he comments, as others had done, on the significance of the devotions for the Elevation of the Host,[3] and says that *Ancrene Wisse* 'seems to give the earliest known example of the devotion to the Five Joys of Mary set out in an elaborate form'.[4] In the following year Professor C. H. Talbot independently discussed, in rather closer detail, certain of these liturgical and devotional questions.[5] Of the Hours of the Holy Ghost he concluded that 'it seems safe to say that the end of the twelfth or the beginning of the thirteenth century saw the beginning of this new devotion'.[6] Of the Elevation of the Host, he argues that no writer could have referred to the consecrated host as 'godes licome' and suggested prayers as an expression of adoration until the theological controversy about the precise moment at which the host became the Corpus Christi had been settled and the ecclesiastical legislation had been completed, and that 'this would have been 1207 at the earliest and may well have been some time after 1215'.[7] He points out that the Constitutions of London (1215–22) warn priests not to raise the host above the head until the words of consecration have been uttered, and that Pope Honorius II in 1219 decreed that all parish priests should bow reverently at the elevation; he might have added that the Constitutions (1216–22) of Bishop Richard Poore of Salisbury have an article *De reverentia habenda in elevatione hostiae*.[8] The link in this matter

---

[1] Op. cit., pp. xviii–xxi. [2] Op. cit., p. xxii.
[3] Op. cit., pp. 193–4. [4] Op. cit., p. 196.
[5] C. H. Talbot, 'Some Notes on the Dating of the *Ancrene Riwle*', *Neophilologus*, xl (1956), 38–51. [6] Op. cit., p. 46. [7] Op. cit., p. 48.
[8] W. Rich Jones and W. D. Macray, *Sarum Charters and Documents* (Rolls Series, 1891), p. 147. The text of the article (§ 56) reads: 'Moneantur laici quod reverenter se habeant in consecratione eucharistae, et flectant genua, maxime in tempore illo quando post elevationem hostia sacra dimittitur.'

between *Ancrene Wisse* and English synodal legislation in the period after 1215 seems to me especially significant, in view of evidence to be cited later.

There are a few minor points, all concerned with the Outer Rule, which may reinforce the argument for a date after rather than before the Lateran Council. But first I should like to glance at one which has nothing to do with the Council. It concerns the practice of blood-letting or *minutio*, on which Professor Knowles has a section in *The Monastic Order in England*.[1] He tells us that originally blood-letting took place only when supposedly necessary: so in Lanfranc's *Statuta*, which provide that the individual concerned 'stays away from choir until chapter on the following day and for two days takes the anticipated light meal or *mixtum;* there is no mention of recreative talking'. But in the next century blood-letting had become 'a regular event treated in effect as a kind of vacation. The earliest detailed enactments are those of Abbot Warin of St. Albans (1183–95), who was himself a master of the medical university of Salerno.' Abbot Warin expressly permitted two periods of talking, and provided that if the permitted two days of relaxation were interrupted by the occurrence of a great feast, then the day lost should be made up on the day following (i.e. the two days of relaxation had become a vacation to which the monk had a right). Finally, says Knowles, the *minutio* ceased to be a matter depending on 'personal initiative or the abbot's judgement', but a matter of routine, and the whole community went in batches to be bled 'four or five times a year'; at Peterborough this practice seems to have been introduced as 'one of the first acts of Abbot Robert in 1214', though 'it may possibly have been introduced somewhat earlier elsewhere'. It is obvious, from this account, that the system prescribed in *Ancrene Wisse*[2] is the fully developed one of the thirteenth century: the anchoresses are to be bled four times a year and if need is oftener (though if anyone can do without it, the author can well allow it); and when they are bled, they are to do nothing for the *three* days that they feel ill, but are to talk with their maidens and entertain themselves with virtuous stories. The two days of relaxation have become three, and have passed even beyond the stage of being a recognized holiday; rest is *commanded* as something necessary and prudent, and so is the conversation.

Professor Knowles also has much to say about meals in religious

[1] David Knowles, *The Monastic Order in England* (1940), pp. 453–6.
[2] Corpus MS., f. 115a/1–5, 8–12.

communities. Originally the winter fast, during which a single meal was taken, began on 14 September and continued until the end of Lent. But the monks whittled this away, first by making exceptions for the major feasts as well as for Sundays, and then by putting off the beginning of the winter fast; by the early thirteenth century it had become customary to have two meals a day until 1 November, and for a period of two or three weeks at Christmas.[1] The monks also found various means of avoiding the prohibition on the eating of meat. By 1216, says Knowles, these practices were almost universal, though 'a few monasteries . . . held for long to the original observance and may have preserved it unimpaired'.[2] The Lateran Council of 1215 set out to reform the abuses, but its decrees were only reluctantly accepted by the English Benedictines; it was not until their second General Chapter of September 1219 that the strict rules of the winter fast were accepted, and even then a relaxation, whereby monks might eat meat in a separate room, was continued until a special visitation ordered by Gregory IX took place a few years later.[3] Now *Ancrene Wisse* is notable for its strictness in these matters. Twice the author says that the winter fast is to start on 14 September—once in Part VIII, where it is altogether appropriate,[4] and once in Part I, which deals with the anchoresses' devotions;[5] here it comes in as a rather inappropriate parenthesis, which suggests that it may be something much in the author's mind. During the winter fast, two meals are to be eaten on Sundays only; there is no mention of feast-days or of the Christmas period. They are never to eat meat or fat (*seim*) except in great sickness or if anyone is over-feeble; and they are not to eat dairy products (*hwit*) in Advent (this seems an extension of the Lenten régime to Advent). This is obviously a very strict régime, and not the lax practice described by Knowles as typical of the beginning of the thirteenth century. It is true that the author is simply reasserting traditional rules,

---

[1] David Knowles, *The Religious Orders in England* (1948), i. 17–18.

[2] Knowles, *Mon. Order*, p. 462.

[3] Knowles, *Relig. Orders*, i. 19. The final article of the decrees of the Council of Oxford of 1222 forbids monks to receive special food either in refectory or elsewhere, or when dining with abbot or prior or almoner, and to eat meat in refectories in which it is not customary to do so; this is obviously aimed at the continuing attempts to avoid conformity to the strict rule. (D. Wilkins, *Concilia*, i. 593.)

[4] Corpus MS., f. 111b/9–19. There is the usual exception for those who are ill or have been bled.

[5] Corpus MS., f. 6a/6–7.

as any rigorist might have done at any time; but in a book which lays down so few rules of external observance, and which normally treats the external rules as comparatively unimportant and capable of variation, the insistence on strict dietary rules is striking and somewhat surprising. It would be easier to understand if these matters had been the subject of recent discussion, as they obviously were in England after 1215.

There are other details of the same sort. Bishop Poore's Salisbury Constitutions, which served as a model for those of other dioceses,[1] forbade clerics to engage in secular business or trade, as did Archbishop Langton's Council of Oxford in 1222; *Ancrene Wisse* forbids trade to the anchoresses.[2] Poore orders all clerics to wear dress appropriate to their order, and priests to wear 'clausa desuper indumenta', Langton that they shall wear clerical dress, 'et cappis clausis utantur'; *Ancrene Wisse* refers to 'a wid hod ant a loke cape' as distinctively clerical dress.[3] Poore and Langton both forbid clerics to let their hair grow and order them to be properly tonsured; *Ancrene Wisse* modifies this for women, but retains a shaven head as one of its alternatives.[4] Poore forbids clerics all ostentation in dress, instancing masculine vanities (long sleeves, embroidered or painted shoes, gilded riding-gear); *Ancrene Wisse* condemns feminine vanities, especially wimples.[5] Poore and Langton both qualify their prohibition of non-clerical attire by the phrase 'unless a matter of justified *fear* shall have demanded a change of clothing'; *Ancrene Wisse* twice uses a similar qualifying phrase, saying that an anchoress shall not change her place of abode 'except for necessity alone, as force and *fear* of death', and that the anchoresses shall not guard other men's possessions 'unless necessity or force bring it about, or great *fear*'.[6] Langton, after observing that among other vices gluttony is liable to attack religious in no

[1] Marion Gibbs and Jane Lang, *The Bishops and Reform 1215–1272* (1934), pp. 116–17.

[2] Poore in *Sarum Charters*, p. 134; Langton in Wilkins, *Concilia*, i. 586; *A.W.* (Corpus MS.), f. 113a/8–10 (the sentence is slightly expanded in Corpus and Cleopatra but is part of the original text).

[3] Poore in op. cit., p. 133; Langton in op. cit., i. 589; *A.W.* (Corpus MS.), f. 14b/7–8.

[4] Poore and Langton, loc. cit.; *A.W.* (Corpus MS.), ff. 114b/26–115a/1.

[5] Poore, loc. cit.; *A.W.* (Corpus MS.), ff. 113b/18–114a/15.

[6] Poore, loc. cit. ('nisi justi causa timoris exegerit habitum transformari', after a reference to clothing); Langton, loc. cit. ('nisi forte justa causa timoris exegerit habitum transformari', immediately after the reference to tonsure); *A.W.* (Corpus MS.), f. 2a/23–24 and f. 113a/16.

mean way (*non mediocriter*), forbids monks or canons regular to presume to take time off for eating or drinking except at the appointed times and places, unless someone is really thirsty, when he may after getting permission go in a proper way into the refectory to supply his need; *Ancrene Wisse* forbids eating and drinking between meals, except with permission, to the servants and *a fortiori*, we may assume, to the anchoresses themselves.[1] Finally, and perhaps not least, Poore provides by his article 75 that

> every priest, if he has anchorites in his parish, shall admonish them that they shall not receive a young woman by night in their house, and likewise that a woman shall not receive a male; nor shall they receive articles for deposit without the knowledge of the priest and of trustworthy living persons.[2]

The first part of this is repeated, in almost identical words, in Constitutions believed to have been issued either by Alexander Stavensby, Bishop of Coventry and Lichfield 1224–38, or by his predecessor.[3] The passage in *Ancrene Wisse* forbidding the anchoresses to guard other men's possessions and legal documents in their house, or to let any man sleep in their dwellings, might have been written in direct obedience to such an injunction.[4] It is not easy to believe that these correspondences between *Ancrene Wisse* and the episcopal legislation after 1215 are fortuitous; and it would be unreasonable to suppose that the bishops were the debtors.[5]

[1] Langton in op. cit., i. 593; *A.W.* (Corpus MS.), f. 116b/3–5. But there is a textual difficulty at this point in Corpus; see Appendix A on pp. 206–207 below.

[2] *Sarum Charters*, p. 153.

[3] Gibbs and Lang, op. cit., pp. 108–9, 119–20 on Stavensby's Constitutions; text of the article referred to in Wilkins, op. cit., i. 661. The Constitutions undoubtedly issued by Stavensby himself (Wilkins, op. cit., i. 640 f.) contain what has been described as the most explicit treatment of the devotions for the Elevation of the Host after *A.W.* (Talbot, op. cit., p. 48), and a fairly elaborate exposition of the Seven Deadly Sins, with the English names of some of them (somewhat mangled by Wilkins; they include *iiscinge* for Avarice, which he gratuitously and fancifully emends).

[4] Corpus MS., f. 113a/13–19.

[5] One might add, as a further less easily demonstrable instance, the fact that the author in his Preface tells the anchoresses that they are to vow obedience only to the bishop 'or to his superior' (*oðer of his herre*, Corpus MS., f. 2a/25, and so Cleopatra; the Nero-Vernon *hire* for *his* is an error). The addition of the latter phrase may reflect the attempt, after the Lateran Council, to extend the powers of supervision of the metropolitans—an attempt much resented, during the thirteenth century, by English diocesan bishops and religious houses (Knowles, *Relig. Orders*, i. 80–81).

For such reasons of detail, and for the more general one suggested by Mr. Sitwell—the interest in penance and confession—it seems that *Ancrene Wisse* might well have been written in or shortly after the period, between 1215 and 1222, when the bishops and abbots were promulgating the Lateran decrees in England. Certainly the attempt to set up 1215 as a *terminus ante quem* must fail. There is in fact no later limit that can be set other than the dates of the manuscripts. The Cleopatra MS. is I think the earliest, though only perhaps by a year or two;[1] but there is no way of dating it otherwise than by the inexact estimates of palaeography and philology. Strictly speaking there is no better means of dating the Corpus MS., but we know that the revision of which Corpus is a copy must have been made after 1224; for a passage peculiar to Corpus, but containing textual errors, refers to the friars, both Dominican and Franciscan, as men of such a way of life that they may be trusted, and received whenever any of them comes to instruct and comfort the anchoresses—indeed, if he is a priest, the anchoresses should make confession to him.[2] There is also a briefer reference added in Part VIII to friars of both orders as men whom the anchoresses might allow to eat in their presence by general leave of their director (in contrast to the special leave required for all other men).[3] The Dominicans came to England in 1221, the Franciscans in 1224, but plainly the two passages were not written immediately after their arrival; the Franciscan house in Hereford is believed to have been set up about 1227,[4] but we should probably allow a year or two more before their visits to the anchoresses could become as regular as the passages imply. This is still merely a *terminus a quo* for the revision, but on linguistic grounds (particularly some of the conservative features of the orthography) it would be difficult to regard the Corpus MS. as

[1] This view depends on the assumptions (*a*) that the additions in the Cleopatra MS. were first drafted in its margins and were not transferred to it from any other manuscript, (*b*) that some of them are earlier drafts of the related but slightly different versions of Corpus. Cf. E. J. Dobson in *English and Medieval Studies*, pp. 158–62, and see further below.

[2] Corpus MS., ff. 16b/13–17a/2.

[3] Corpus MS., f. 112b/10–14. This is part of an addition to the basic text which is shared by the Latin version, though in an abbreviated form which omits the reference to the friars; but the Latin version in Part VIII follows the expanded text, as in Corpus, and is not independent. Cleopatra lacks both additions, as does the Vitellius French version.

[4] Knowles, *Relig. Orders*, i. 132. According to Knowles (ibid., i. 182) few of the first friars were priests, but this situation appears to have changed by 1230; hence perhaps the author's qualification *ȝef he is preost*.

much later than 1230; and indeed 'about 1230' is the date that is usually accepted.[1]

I turn from these attempts to date *Ancrene Wisse* by reference to external evidence to matters concerned with the internal history of the text itself. Anyone who reads any discussion of its composition will soon find himself faced with the concept of an 'original Rule' different from any of the texts that survive. This concept obtrudes itself twice even in Shepherd's brief discussion of the date. In its more extreme form, with which he wisely refuses to concern himself, it is of a text so different from what survives that it contained none of the passages referring to or based on later twelfth-century writers. This notion of an '*ur*-text', it may fairly be said, exists solely in order to accommodate those who wish to believe in an earlier date for the origin of the Rule than the extant text allows; it is strictly beyond reason; and it is impossible. *Ancrene Wisse* is a most carefully and explicitly planned work. The division into parts, and their order, is explained in the Preface and is kept constantly in view throughout, and the individual parts are equally carefully planned internally—sometimes indeed their arrangement is explicit, and always it is revealed by analysis. Despite the liveliness of the style and the ease with which the transitions are managed, *Ancrene Wisse* is from first to last an ordered book, conceived and written as a unity. It has not just grown by successive additions and amplifications by various hands. Moreover, it is unified in style and language. Take away any substantial part—in particular take away the parts that show the influence of St. Bernard and his disciples—and one would not be left with an *ur*-text; no book at all would remain. Such an 'original Rule' is not merely a thing with which we need not concern ourselves; it can never have existed.

The other form of the concept of an 'original Rule' is very different; it is simply an original text contrasted with the admittedly revised version of the Corpus MS., and differing to some degree (though not so much) from any other surviving early manuscript. Shepherd (like many others) speaks of this 'original text' as if it too were somewhat hypothetical, though he implies (as is generally and rightly held) that the Nero MS. is closer to it, in content, than is Corpus;[2] but in fact it need not

---

[1] Shepherd, op. cit., p. xxi, says 'after 1225 and probably before 1235' and Zettersten, op. cit., p. 19, says '1225–1230', but for the reasons given 1225 is several years too early.   [2] Op. cit., p. xxiv.

be at all hypothetical, for it is the archetype from which the extant manuscripts descend and can therefore be reconstructed by the ordinary processes of collation and textual criticism. It is the 'basic text' common to all the extant manuscripts and versions; for there is no reason at all, in text, language, style, or thought, to suppose that this 'basic text' was itself an alteration or a rewriting of any earlier version—on the contrary, it was the text as originally written. But, of course, by the same processes of collation and criticism the additions and deletions and alterations are revealed. We are not here concerned with the extensive rewriting of some later redactions (the Trinity French version, or the Pepys and Royal versions) or with the mere extracts, in rearranged order, of the Gonville and Caius MS., but with revisions found in texts which remain generally faithful to the original, i.e. the early English manuscripts (including Caius as far as wording is concerned in the extracts which it gives), the French version of the Vitellius MS., the Latin version (with some reservations, as it tends to compress), and the Vernon MS. (which, though late, is very faithful). In these manuscripts and versions one may distinguish three types of alterations:

1. Deliberate changes obviously not by the original author nor intended for the original audience: so especially in the Titus MS. and its group, where the text is generalized as part of the process of making it suitable for a male audience (as Caius also does, to a lesser degree).

2. Purely scribal changes, mostly mere errors of the ordinary sort, but also deliberate attempts to improve on the original (e.g. in details of grammar or word-order, or by more serious alteration when the scribe failed to understand his exemplar and attempted emendation). The Nero MS., though in content closest to the original text, is a particular offender in this way, and the original Cleopatra scribe was also too ready to emend and rewrite when he did not understand.

3. Alterations, omissions, and additions which belong to neither of these categories, i.e. are neither plainly by a different author and/or intended for a different audience, nor plainly merely scribal. They are by a redactor or redactors (to use a neutral term), not by a mere scribe, but are still addressed to an audience of women religious and either develop the thought of the original or else (to put it at the lowest) are not evidently inconsistent with it. Such changes occur in all early manuscripts, even in Nero, which contains a few passages (two peculiar to itself) which are not part of the basic text; but above all they

occur in Corpus, which not only contains all the more important additions found in one or more of the other manuscripts (sometimes in revised form), but also many peculiar to itself. Corpus is in a special sense the revised text of the Rule, which is why some scholars reserve to it the distinct name *Ancrene Wisse*, in contrast to the title *Ancrene Riwle* used of all the rest.

Now there are two contrasting attitudes to this last class of alterations, and one's view of the problem of dating is inevitably affected by one's attitude to the revisions. Some hold that the revisions are not, or are not necessarily, by the original author, and are not, or are not necessarily, intended for the original community. In this case one can well envisage quite a long gap —as long as the external evidence will allow—between the date of original composition and the date of the Corpus MS.; indeed, one may try to extend the gap as much as one can, to allow time for the 'original Rule' to fall into the hands of revisers who were not its author. But others hold that the revisions are by the original author and intended for the original community, and merely show that the community had grown in numbers and to that extent somewhat changed in nature. In this case one will not wish to separate by any great length of time the original composition from the Corpus revision; both must come within the working life of a single author, though time must be allowed for the growth of the community.

I myself am entirely committed to this second view. I can see no reason at all to suppose that the revisions were by a different hand. They are identical in language and style, and are most skilfully fitted into the original text; for the most part their purpose is simply to elaborate or make clearer, or sometimes to qualify, the original thought, or to deal with points that had been overlooked or too lightly treated; others can be explained by altered circumstances either within the community or without (e.g. the coming of the friars). It may be that it cannot be definitely proved that the Corpus revision is by the original author,[1] but I do not see why it should really need to be proved. When two or more states of a text transmitted in writing, and not orally, are known to have arisen at an early stage of its history—as is the case here, for only a few years at most can separate the Cleopatra MS., which as originally written was essentially the 'unrevised' text, and the Corpus MS., with its

[1] Dr. Zettersten observes of my view that the Corpus version is 'the author's own final and definitive version of his work' that it is 'very likely but cannot be definitely proved' (op. cit., p. 287).

'revised' text—there is a presumption that they are due to the original author. We do not ask for proof that Chaucer was responsible for the various states of the text of *Troilus and Criseyde*, or Gower for those of the *Confessio Amantis*; we assume it, and leave the onus of proof to anyone who wishes, against the evidence of language and style, to assert the contrary.[1] If the Corpus MS. alone had survived, so that we could not demonstrate its revisions and additions by comparison with other texts, no one would dream of denying its unity of authorship.[2] Nevertheless I accept the obligation, if not of giving strict proof of the identity of reviser and author, at least of indicating some of the difficulties that lie in the way of those who doubt it.

It will I think be found, when the work of collation and recension is complete, that the archetype of the surviving manuscripts and versions was a most unusually correct text. I do not mean that its readings can never be improved; there are places where they obviously could be, and where the medieval scribes themselves succeeded in improving them. But a text is not corrupt merely because it contains an anomaly that can easily be got rid of; the author may have written the anomalous form or sentence. There are a number of such cases in the archetypal text of *Ancrene Wisse*.[3] Again there are places where no satisfactory explanation has yet been found for what was evidently the archetypal reading, but where, I am convinced, the fault is in our knowledge or understanding, not in the text.[4] So far as my work has gone, I know of only one case where the archetypal

---

[1] It may be pointed out that Gower does not name himself in the revised passages of the Prologue and conclusion of the *Confessio*, and that Chaucer does not name himself at all in *T. & C.* As far as the evidence of the texts is concerned, the revisions of both works are anonymous; but no one doubts their authenticity.

[2] The discrepancy remaining in the Corpus MS. between the reference to 'three women' and that to 'twenty now or more' would no doubt be rationalized by saying that the author's concern was with three women in particular who lived in a larger community.

[3] Thus at Corpus f. 3a/6, the false syntactical sequence *openlukest descriue⟨t⟩ . . . þen is* (superlative followed by 'than') is apparently the archetypal reading; it is easy to correct and was indeed corrected early (it is not in Cleopatra or the Vitellius French version), but is a blend-construction that an author might well fall into. At Corpus f. 83a/3 *subtra* for the correct *subtus* (used by Anselm, who is being quoted) is an analogical form suggested by the preceding *supra*; Mr. Peter Dronke kindly informs me that one other instance is known in Medieval Latin.

[4] For an example, see Appendix B on pp. 207–208 below.

text must be regarded as corrupt, in the sense that the author cannot possibly have intended to write what it represents him as writing, and that is where, in a description of a warrior-ascetic, there is applied to him the ludicrous phrase *wiuene sarest* 'most grief-stricken of wives'.[1] We should emend, in my view, to *wiuene sune sarest* 'most grief-stricken of the sons of women', an alliterative phrase entirely in the author's style; the tag *wiues* (*wiuene*) *sunen* 'sons of women' occurs earlier in the text,[2] and it is only in this traditional phrase that the author uses *wif* in its old generic sense of 'woman' as distinct from 'wife'. But if so, the error (the omission of a word from a conventional phrase), though it is one to which copyists are very liable, is also one which an author himself can easily commit; we have all done it in letters or lecture-notes, or even in typescript sent to press.[3] When we consider the length and complexity of the text—for it is often difficult, in style or syntax or vocabulary—and the number of errors committed even by the meticulous Corpus scribe, the almost complete freedom from error of the archetype can only reasonably be explained by the assumption that it was the author's autograph. Otherwise we should be confronted with the phenomenon in which textual criticism

[1] Corpus MS., f. 103b/15. For further details, see Appendix C on p. 208 below.

[2] Corpus MS., f. 43a/4 (*wiues sunen*); Nero MS., ed. Mabel Day, 70/7 (*wiuene sunes*).

[3] Another probable but not certain case of the accidental omission of a word occurs at Corpus f. 13a/13, where *cla ð* must be supplied or understood after *parlures*; Nero and Cleopatra (as originally written) agree with Corpus, but scribe B of Cleopatra (on whom see below) adds *cla ð* between the lines, to give a reading shared (or adopted) by Titus, Vernon, and the Trinity French version. (But the Vitellius French version has *louerture del parler*, supplying the omission in a different way.) The Corpus reading must be that of the archetype; what is doubtful is whether the omission of *cla ð* was an accidental error, as the word could be understood from the previous sentence.

At Corpus f. 33b/13, the reading *seinte stefne þ te stanes* is an error for *seinte stefne þolede þe stanes*. The other manuscripts running agree with Corpus in having *þ* or *þet* or its translation (so Cleopatra, Caius, Nero, Vernon, Titus, Vitellius French version, Latin version), except for the Trinity French version, which inserts *ausint soffri* before *ke*, and Pepys and Royal, which rewrite. On the face of it, the error goes back to the archetype. But I think it more likely that the author used the *ad hoc* abbreviation *þ.* for *þolede*, as he used similar abbreviations elsewhere for repeated words (e.g. *m. b.* for *muchele blisse* at Corpus f. 9b/20, f. 10a/2), and that this was independently miscopied as *þ* both in *β* and in Corpus (or alternatively, the author himself wrote *þ* though intending an *ad hoc* abbreviation for *þolede*).

refuses, with good reason, to believe: the perfect or near-perfect copy of a long and difficult text.[1]

This in itself does not affect our consideration of the date, for an archetype may long antedate the earliest surviving copy. But it does have relevance to another textual fact. The Corpus text, though very good, has not infrequent errors, often revealed only by collation; but they are always simple, and never require the assumption of more than a single process of copying. And if we again bear in mind the length and complexity of the text, we must conclude that if it is only necessary to assume a single process of copying, it would be wrong to assume more; for error begets error, and in particular omissions which obviously destroy grammar or the continuity of sense (and Corpus has such omissions) provoke rewriting in the attempt to restore coherence. But in Corpus there is no difference at all between the state of the unrevised parts of the text (which are the overwhelming bulk of it) and that of the added passages; indeed the only complex error, where for once the Corpus scribe attempted to rewrite a sentence he did not understand, comes in one of the additional passages.[2] Textually, Corpus is no more remote from the original in the basic text than in the additional passages, and it must follow that the reviser who produced the Corpus version used, as the physical basis of his revision, the archetype; the exemplar from which the Corpus scribe copied was the archetype as altered and added to by the reviser. But if, as I believe,

[1] On a parallel case of errors in a text which are attributable either to the author's autograph or to a master-copy used in his own scriptorium see G. C. Macaulay, *The Works of John Gower*, vol. **, pp. cxxx–cxxxi.

[2] Dobson, op. cit., pp. 154–5. The argument that the Corpus MS. is a direct copy of the revised version is unaffected by the fact that for this long addition (Corpus f. 28b/21–29b/25), which occurs also in the Vitellius French version and in the Vernon MS., it is necessary to assume that in two respects Corpus and Vernon descend from a common antecedent distinct from that represented by the French version (Dobson, op. cit., pp. 153–5, especially p. 155). It is clear that this addition was originally written and circulated on separate sheets of vellum, for both the French version and Vernon misplace it; and we must suppose at least three copies of the addition, (i) that inserted into the ancestor of the French version, (ii) that inserted into the exemplar of Corpus, (iii) that inserted into the ancestor of Vernon. The author of the addition may well have sent his first draft to the anchoresses, to be inserted eventually in the ancestor of the French version, and have kept for his own use (and insertion into the exemplar of Corpus) a second copy in which (a) the phrase *leafdi of londes* had been changed to *leafdi of hames*, (b) a desirable though not essential clause had been omitted (probably by accident, but perhaps by design). The third copy, inserted into Vernon, derived from the second, but not by way of the Corpus MS. itself.

the archetype was the autograph, this means that the reviser possessed the author's own manuscript and used it to make the revised text. This need not surprise us, since Middle English literature provides one exact and one close parallel among surviving manuscripts. The exact parallel is the *Ormulum* MS., an admitted autograph in which one can still see the revisions and additions; the close one is the Fairfax MS. of the *Confessio Amantis*, which Macaulay held to have been used as an exemplar in Gower's own scriptorium and which was altered from the first state of the text to the third.[1] But if we ask, as we must, how it came about that the reviser of the Corpus version owned and used the autograph, there are two possible answers, one simple and the other complex; and I take it that simple answers are always to be preferred unless there is positive evidence to the contrary. The simple answer (suggested by the parallels I have cited) is, of course, that the reviser was the author, and therefore naturally used his own manuscript. The complex answer is that he was some friend or literary executor or successor in function of the author, who had therefore been given the autograph; who wrote the same language and style, and thought the same thoughts; and who so perfectly understood the original text, despite its difficulties, that his revisions and additions were made in a way that the author himself could not have bettered. I can imagine such a man, but I cannot believe in him.

No discussion of the genesis of *Ancrene Wisse* can afford to neglect the evidence of the Cleopatra MS. It has been corrected or annotated by a variety of hands, of which two stand out. One is that of an early fourteenth-century north-east Midland scribe, whose interventions are notable—apart from the damage they do to the text—chiefly for the fact that he had access to a lost manuscript of the Rule, not (it would seem) very accurate. The other is an early thirteenth-century scribe who used the pure form of the 'AB language', and whom I call scribe B. I have spent much of the last three years or more in preparing an edition of the Cleopatra MS., and I have recently reviewed in detail the changes made by scribe B.[2] He makes numerous alterations to the original scribe's punctuation, converting it into the same system as that of the Corpus MS.—in all but a couple of

---

[1] Macaulay, vol. cit., p. cxxx.

[2] Scribe B works on ff. 3–25^v, 123^v–29^v, 149^v–50 (corrections by erasure), 190–97^v. For a brief preliminary account of his work see Dobson, op. cit., pp. 158–62; but the detailed evidence must await my edition of the Cleopatra MS. for the Early English Text Society. [Now E.E.T.S. 267, 1972].

cases (where he blunders) as the intended sense requires; he corrects spellings or grammatical forms, especially but not only when to do so aids the understanding; he corrects the text when it is miscopied, and sometimes revises it, especially if an error of the first scribe's was obviously due to some difficulty in the original text; and he makes many additions to the original text, some peculiar to the Cleopatra MS., others shared with one or more other manuscripts, especially, in Part VIII, with Corpus. He is an extremely skilful corrector, and the great majority of his textual alterations exactly restore the original text, often in small details; such corrections could obviously be transferred from another manuscript, providing that we assumed that it was one in the original dialect and at least as good as, but not identical with, Corpus. Similarly many of his additions could be regarded as transferred to the Cleopatra MS. from some revised and expanded text[1]—though it would have to be one different from Corpus or any other surviving manuscript. But there is a substantial and significant minority of cases where such an explanation will not do at all: where a correction restores the original sense but not the original wording or word-order, or a faulty piece of text is corrected into an acceptable sense which is not the original sense, or a revision is plainly occasioned by an error of the first scribe, or a good addition which clarifies the original sense is based on and grows out of an unauthorized

[1] So G. C. Macaulay, 'The *Ancren Riwle*', *M.L.R.*, ix (1914), 146, followed by Shepherd, op. cit., p. xi. But Macaulay's can hardly be thought a considered opinion; his inspection of Cleopatra was obviously very superficial (his main concern having been with Corpus). He did not distinguish the hands of the correctors of Cleopatra, and in particular appears not to have noticed the very obvious difference between hand B and the early fourteenth-century hand D; 'alterations for the worse' and 'the substitution of a more modern or familiar form' are a correct description of D's usual activities, but are phrases quite inapplicable to B's. Macaulay does not mention, and presumably did not notice, the additions and alterations by hand B which are peculiar to Cleopatra, including those that obviously originated in it (cf. p. 201, note 1, below for two examples).

Such an explanation as Macaulay's assumes that scribe B worked by careful comparison of Cleopatra as originally written with his superior copy of the expanded text, so that he was able to detect passages not included in Cleopatra and to supply them. But this was plainly not his regular method of working; he often misses errors or omissions in Cleopatra, especially if the sense remains acceptable. He obviously tended to read the manuscript through for sense, and to intervene if he noticed that the sense was broken or unsatisfactory. He would be unlikely to observe the lack of added passages unless he were specially looking for them (as, in Part VIII, he might have been, if he knew that it had been revised and expanded).

and nonsensical rewriting and expansion by the first scribe.[1] Such corrections, revisions, and additions are plainly made for the first time for the Cleopatra MS. and in it, and the same is probably true of other additions in hand B which Cleopatra shares with other manuscripts; indeed in one case it can be proved that another manuscript must have got the addition from Cleopatra.[2] The work of scribe B, all in all, resembles nothing so much as a modern author correcting and revising a bad set of proofs, and concerned not always to restore the text into agreement with copy, but sometimes to take what the compositor has been pleased to supply and to make something acceptable out of it with the minimum of change. Again two explanations are possible, one simple and the other complex. The simple one is that scribe B was indeed the author, correcting and revising parts of a copy of his own work and holding himself free to alter it if he wished, and naturally enough not always bothering to look up his own original autograph to discover exactly what he had said, or exactly how he had said it, in the first place; if so, here in the Cleopatra MS. is the author's hand preserved for our inspection. The complex explanation is to suppose some friend or colleague of the author's, using the same

[1] Sometimes one can see the first scribe change in mid-sentence from copying the true text to rewriting it. Such a case is at Cleopatra ff. 127ᵛ–8, where the true text (as at Corpus f. 77b/15) is *lime is þe frensch of file*. The Cleopatra scribe began to write *lime is þe* but then interlined *þ* and continued so as to read *lime is ⟨þ⟩ þe | þe file fret of þeiren* 'lime is that which the file rubs from the iron' (the last six words being at the top of f. 128). Scribe B erased the interlined *þ* and altered the words at the foot of f. 127ᵛ to *lime is þe frencs of file* (the true text, but for the form of *frencs*). At the top of f. 128 he adopted the original scribe's unauthorized phrase (but rewrote *þeiren* as *þe irn*) and added to it to give the sentence *þe file fret of þe irn þe rust & tet rugget & Makeð hit hwit & smeðe*, an addition found in no other manuscript. On f. 129, after the phrase *to freo of hire seluen* (corresponding to Corpus f. 78a/26–27), the first Cleopatra scribe had added a line of text for which no other manuscript offers any parallel; scribe B erased it so completely that it is now illegible, but wrote over the erasure *þ is. in hire ahne bodi large towart lechur þurh hire gestninges*. This is a meaningful explanation of the preceding sentence, and again occurs in no other manuscript; it was obviously occasioned by the first scribe's unauthorized addition, whatever it may have been.

[2] The first marginal addition in Cleopatra (f. 3) is also found in Vernon, but misplaced in a way directly explicable from the facts of Cleopatra's text; for at this point in Cleopatra there is a long omission, and Vernon brings in the addition so as to follow the omitted passage when it ought to precede it, i.e. Vernon inserts the addition *before* the sentence which it happens to *precede* in Cleopatra (owing to the omission), when it belongs *after* the sentence which it *follows* in Cleopatra. Only in Cleopatra is there precisely this omission.

literary dialect and commanding the same style; possessed of
an excellent manuscript which he nevertheless did not always
bother to consult, though he was not correcting his own composition, even when he detected an error; possessed also of a
remarkable understanding of the intended sense, a keen eye for
detail, great self-confidence, and a willingness to revise and add
to what his friend had written. Again I can imagine such a man,
but I cannot believe in him.

It does not seem credible that the skilful and tactful corrector
of the Cleopatra MS., who had access to an excellent text in the
original dialect, understood it so well, and was himself capable
of writing in the original style and dialect, should be a different
man from the skilful and tactful reviser of the Corpus version,
who used the archetype as the basis of his revision, understood it well, and was also capable of writing in the original
style and (unless the Corpus scribe has completely translated
him) in the original dialect. Moreover, there is an obvious relationship between some of the additions made by scribe B in the
Cleopatra MS. and some of those of the Corpus version; if
scribe B and the Corpus reviser were different men, we should
have to explain how one of them got to know of the other's work.
We could perhaps suppose that the two revisers (more than two
could be imagined, but I confine myself to two) were members
of a close-knit religious community which possessed the autograph of *Ancrene Wisse* and had a uniform literary language and
a common style; but then the question would arise why the
community, instead of leaving the work of revision to a single
person, should have put it, as it were, into commission. For such
an improbable process definite evidence would be required. And
since on the evidence of language and style we should have to
suppose that the original author was or had been a member of
the same community, we should also have to explain why he was
not left to revise his own work. At all points explanation is easy
if one accepts the obvious and simple hypothesis of an author
who continued to revise copies of his work for the benefit of those
for whom it was written; but difficulties, improbabilities, and
complications multiply if one rejects it.

That the obvious answer is the right one is in any case strongly
suggested by the use in additions of the pronoun *I*. An addition
to the Preface which is peculiar to hand B of the Cleopatra MS.
reads: 'You shall not, I say, make any greater use of firm
promises.'[1] The 'Understand ever' addition, which is shared by

[1] Cleopatra MS., f. 4ᵛ (to follow *herre*, corresponding to Corpus, f. 2a/25).

hand B and the Corpus version, not only picks up the metaphor used by the original author in his Preface, but also uses the phrase 'as I said in the beginning'.[1] The reviser could easily have written here 'as was said in the beginning', using the passive turn of expression which is so common in this work in references back; but he did not. Similarly the last of scribe B's modifications of the Cleopatra MS., which seems certainly to be an addition to the basic text in spite of its occurrence in Nero as well as in Corpus, is the closing sentence 'I am moderate enough who ask for so little'.[2] In a modern work it might just be possible, though by no means easy, to explain this use of 'I' in added passages as a dramatic device, the deliberate assumption by a reviser of the personality of the original author; in a medieval work it is much more difficult.[3]

If then a single man was responsible for the composition of *Ancrene Wisse*, for the correction and revision of the Cleopatra MS., and for the making of the Corpus version (including the additions which it shares with other texts, notably the Vitellius French version), the whole process must fall within a comparatively short span of years. But we have still to allow for an evident change in the numbers of the community for which the work was written. Three passages are relevant. The first is a passing reference to 'all three of you, my dear sisters, the women dearest to me', which, presumably because it was unobtrusive, escaped revision; the numeral could easily have been deleted without other change in the sentence, but was not, even in the Corpus version.[4] The second is a longer passage which refers in some detail to the personal circumstances of three well-born anchoresses, sisters born of one father and one mother, for whom it is generally and rightly accepted, from this and the previous reference, that the Rule was originally written. This second passage occurs in full only in the Nero MS.,[5] where it consists of two paragraphs. In the Titus group[6] the passage is generalized

---

[1] Corpus MS., f. 115a/17–18; Cleopatra MS., f. 193 foot.

[2] Corpus MS., f. 117b/14–15; Cleopatra MS., f. 197ᵛ; Nero MS., ed. Day, 196/20–21.

[3] Since even in works of fiction, and even in the fourteenth century, the concept of the wholly fictitious first-person narrator seems to have been unknown; to a medieval author 'I' meant himself, even if what he represented himself as doing or as being was fictitious. Cf. George Kane, *Piers Plowman: The Evidence for Authorship* (1965), pp. 53–58.

[4] Corpus MS., f. 31b/15. But Titus (30/23) excises the reference.

[5] Nero MS., ed. Day, 85/8–86/5.

[6] Titus MS., ed. Frances M. Mack, 61/1–19; Pepys MS., ed. (as *The Recluse*)

and depersonalized, but it seems clear that the redactor who was responsible (presumably the same man as generalized the text elsewhere in the ancestor of this group) had the full text of the two paragraphs before him, i.e. his exemplar had the same text as Nero's. This is consistent with the textual affiliations, for the Titus group and Nero are related.[1] Their text at this point must go back to a very early and quite unrevised manuscript. But in the Cleopatra MS.,[2] despite its early date, the two paragraphs are already truncated in the text as written by the original scribe: of the first only the opening sentence, which is entirely general, is left, and the rest, containing the personal allusions, is cut; so is the first sentence of the second paragraph, which refers back to the excised matter, but the rest of the second paragraph remains. The result is unsatisfactory, for what is left is pointless. But the cut is significant, for it shows that already, before the Corpus version had been made, the personal details had become inappropriate and therefore had to be deleted; and they had obviously been deleted (or marked for deletion) in Cleopatra's exemplar, for the scribe writes straight on. In the Corpus version[3] the whole of the two paragraphs is removed, which is much more satisfactory; and the same is true of the Vernon MS.,[4] which, despite its close textual affiliation with Nero, here as elsewhere follows the revised text of Corpus.

The third passage was first added in the Corpus version.[5] It begins

> You are the anchoresses of England so many together—twenty now or more; God increase you in good—that most peace is among, most singleness and unity, and community of a united life according to one rule

and continues that their manner of life is 'as though you were a community (*cuuent*) of London or of Oxford, of Shrewsbury or of Chester'. As throughout the passage the writer makes use of the word *cuuent*, though not in any technical sense (it evidently

---

by J. Påhlsson, 91/20–25; Latin version, ed. Charlotte D'Evelyn, 66/2–15; Trinity French version, ed. W. H. Trethewey, 266/28–267/32.

[1] See the stemma given by Dobson, op. cit., p. 137.

[2] Cleopatra MS., f. 80, l. 11–f. 80ᵛ, l. 8. The omission is from the words (in Nero's spellings) *vor mid more eise* (Nero 85/10) to *of ower mede* (Nero 85/29) inclusive.

[3] Corpus MS., f. 51b/1.   [4] Vernon MS., f. 380ᵛ, col. 2, l. 34.

[5] Corpus MS., ff. 69a/12–69b/11.

means no more than 'community'), and speaks of their fame as having recently (*nunan*) become widely known,

> so that your community begins to spread towards the extremity of England; you are as the mother-house from which they are begotten,

some have taken the passage as referring to a larger community of a different sort. But its beginning makes it clear that the persons addressed are still anchoresses, not nuns, and that the community is not in fact a convent in our sense, and the phrase 'twenty *now* or more' clearly implies growth from a smaller number; the whole passage is dealing with an increase in numbers and reputation, with some allusion to the consequent risk of loss of unity. The addition of this passage in Corpus, and the omission of the one dealing with the personal circumstances of the three sisters, are perfectly well accounted for by the supposition that the community had outgrown its origins in such a way that revision was forced on the author himself. It is significant that the Cleopatra MS. was made by some form of *pecia* system,[1] and for that there can be only one probable explanation—that more copies than one were being made simultaneously from a single exemplar; evidently there was some urgent need for additional copies. And in the exemplar of Cleopatra, as we have seen, the main reference to the original three anchoresses had already been cut.

Plainly we must allow some years for the growth of the community, but at this period, when the eremitical movement was strong and there was much renewed enthusiasm for the religious life (one need only cite the extraordinarily rapid development of the orders of friars), we need not allow very many. Moreover, though obviously there were still only three anchoresses when the author first wrote, their community was not newly founded; they had for many a day begged him for a Rule,[2] and he spent

---

[1] This is shown (to summarize very briefly) by the fact that the manuscript subdivides into six unequal sections, the end of each section being marked by (i) a break in the regular collation in quires of eight leaves, (ii) the failure of the text, on the last leaf of each section except the fifth, exactly to fill the writing-space (at the end of the first section the text was a few words too long, which necessitated an extra but only part-filled line, at the end of the second, third, and fourth it was too short). The last two sections (fifth and sixth) were probably copied continuously, i.e. are really one continuous section; but each of the first four had evidently to be returned by the scribe to his employer before he was issued with the exemplar of the next section, so that he was unable to make the text run continuously, without blank spaces, from the end of one section to the beginning of the next.

[2] Corpus MS., f. 1a/11-12.

a great deal of time writing it.[1] The increase in numbers may have begun soon afterwards. The sort of time-scheme that I have in mind is that the work was first written after the Lateran decrees had become known in England, even possibly after the Council of Oxford of 1222; and that there soon began a process of progressive revision of the text, culminating in the correction and revision of the Cleopatra MS. and the making of the Corpus version about 1228–30, followed almost immediately by the writing of the Corpus MS. itself as a fair copy of the revised text. Such an assumption seems best to satisfy the requirements. It is true that it means that the latest of the identified literary sources is a good deal earlier than the date of composition, and I do not doubt that it is true that the purely intellectual interests of the author are those of the late twelfth rather than the thirteenth century. But some allowance must be made for an author living and working in a remote situation in the Welsh marches; and if, as is probable, he was a man of some authority and seniority, his days in the schools were probably far behind him. It would not be the first time that a middle-aged man was more up to date in such matters as liturgical practice, pastoral theology, and ecclesiastical legislation than in his intellectual interests. Nor should much be made of his indifference to mysticism; not all men are of a mystical temper. The later date that I suggest would suit well the iconography; the advanced liturgical and devotional practices; the general nature of the work, and its concern with confession and penance; the minor but I think significant details of the Outer Rule; and more importantly, the uniformity of the language of the Corpus MS. and the virtual identity of the language of scribe B of the Cleopatra MS. Above all it enables us to regard the unity of style and thought of the Corpus version not as some miracle performed by a tactful redactor, but as the normal consequence of single authorship, of a man revising his own work before he has had time to alter his view or forget what he meant.

APPENDIX

A

At Corpus f. 116b/3–5, the manuscript now reads *ne gru[ch]esi ȝe naut*, but *gru[ch]esi* is an alteration of whatever the original scribe wrote (probably *grulesi*) and *ȝe*, though by the original scribe, is a false addition to the text which is shared by Nero and Titus. The Cleopatra MS.,

[1] Corpus MS., f. 117b/2–3.

f. 196, reads *ne gruuesi naut* (corresponding to *ne manguent* in the Vitellius French text), in which the subject of the subjunctive verb is understood. Corpus and Cleopatra together point to an archetypal form **grulesi* for normal *gruseli* (as Nero; cf. *O.E.D.*, s.v. *gruse, grusel,* and Tolkien's note ad loc., which are followed by Zettersten, op. cit., p. 225). We should restore the text as *ne grulesi* (or *gruseli*) *naut* 'let them not munch anything'. As Tolkien's note says, the context clearly requires 'they' as the subject; but the evidence of the manuscripts is better explained by the assumption that it was left to be understood than by treating the false *ȝe* as a substitution for an expressed *ha* or *heo.* The archetype obviously did not have the erroneous pronoun; Corpus and the original of the Nero–Titus group have independently supplied the wrong subject-pronoun, doubtless because they knew that religious were forbidden to eat or drink between meals and assumed wrongly that the injunction was directed to the anchoresses themselves.

It may be observed, in view of my argument that the archetype was the autograph, that if the assumed archetypal reading **grulesi* is to be regarded as an error and not as a genuine metathesized form, it is an error of a type which an author himself may make, and that hand B of Cleopatra has the similar error *wimlunþe* for *wimplunge* in an addition on f. 193ʳ.

B

At Corpus f. 26b/25–26, *Ga ut as dude dyna iacobes dohter to himmere heile, hire to wraðer heale,* where Corpus alone seems to preserve the archetypal text, no one has satisfactorily explained *himmere heile,* but I do not think it is corrupt; Cleopatra has *to himmere Heale* (omitting *heile hire to wraðer* by homeoteleuton), and the alliteration on *h* within the phrase and the jingle *to himmere heile / to wraðer heale* seem to be intended. The problem is to find an etymology for *himmere.* I would suggest OE. **hin-mǣre,* similar in formation and meaning to OE. *ūt-gemǣre* 'extreme boundary' (used to translate Latin *finis* and *terminus*) and to OE. *ūt-land* 'foreign land', *el-lende* sb. 'foreign parts'. For the prefix, cf. OE. *hinfūs, hingang, hinsīð,* OS. *hinfard* (beside OE. *ūtfūs, ūtgang, ūtsīð, ūtfaru*); and for the extension of the sense of *(ge)mǣre* from 'boundary' to 'boundary district' and (in the plural) 'territories' see especially Bosworth–Toller, Supplement, s.v. *gemǣre,* sense I (2). But *himmere* in *A.W.* probably represents not an OE. noun, but an OE. *jō*-stem adjective **hin-mǣre* 'foreign'; cf. OE. *ūt-lende* and *el-lende* adj. OE. **hinmǣre* could well become *himmere* in *A.W.* (i) by assimilation of *nm* to *mm* (cf. assimilation of *n* to *m* before *b* and *p* in OE. *hlimbed* < **hlin-bed,* ME. *hemp* < *henep*), (ii) by the change of secondarily-stressed OE. *ǣ²* to *e,* as in the suffix *-red(d)en* < OE. *-rǣden.* The sense of *to himmere heile* would then be 'to foreign fortune'. *O.E.D.* does not record the noun *hail* < ON. *heill* so early, but the verb occurs, in the sense 'to salute, to greet', in Orm and Laȝamon and implies the noun. This meaning for *to himmere heile* agrees (*a*) with the immediate context, in which the leading idea is of going or being driven into exile to seek abroad a transitory and illusory prosperity (cf. especially the phrase *Ga sech* wiðuten *þe worldes frakele froure*); (*b*) with the Biblical citation, 'ut uideret mulieres *alienigenas*' (Corpus MS., f. 14a/16–17) for the Vulgate's 'ut videret mulieres *regionis illius*' (Genesis xxxiv. 1); and (*c*) with the *Glossa Ordinaria*, which says that Dinah went out to see 'mulieres *extraneae* regionis' (marginal gloss) and interprets her as 'infirma anima quae postpositis propriis *aliena* negocia curat' (interlinear gloss) and as 'mens . . . actiones *alienas* curans [quae] extra ordinem proprium evagatur' (marginal gloss, which goes on to speak of 'spem ac securitatem vacuam'). I would translate the sentence, 'Go out as did Dinah Jacob's daughter to a foreign fortune, to her misfortune.'

C

Only Corpus and Titus preserve the reading *wiuene sarest* (Corpus MS., f. 103b/15). Cleopatra and Nero alter it to *monne sarest*, the two French translations omit *wiuene* and translate *sarest* as an adverb (*angoissousement* Vitellius, *mout tendrement* Trinity), and the Latin and Pepys versions omit the whole phrase. I agree with Mr. Shepherd (op. cit., p. 51) that *wiuene sarest* was the archetypal reading; only so can the variations of the manuscripts be explained. But I think him mistaken in saying that the reading *monne sarest* 'improved nothing but the gender', for it gives the required sense ('grief-stricken' being a well-established ME. sense of *sore*; cf. *O.E.D.*, sense 11); and his emendation, *wi[ð e]uene sarest*, seems to me improbable in method and result. It assumes that two meaningful words have been telescoped into a quite different meaningful word, which does not happen very often; and I doubt whether *wið euene sarest* is acceptable ME. idiom for 'in bitterest fashion'. Moreover, when the evidence so strongly suggests that the archetype was the autograph, an emendation which assumes a type of error unlikely to be committed by an author himself must be suspect. I am aware of the danger of circuity of reasoning; but what is required is proof of one or more undoubted errors, of a type which an author cannot reasonably be supposed himself to have committed, before we can entertain emendations which presuppose processes of error unlikely in an author. The case where the archetype may be suspected to be the autograph arises so seldom in classical and medieval studies that we all of us forget that it is, or ought to be, a principle of textual criticism that certain types of emendation are only acceptable *after* it has been proved that the archetype was not the autograph. Ordinarily we assume that it was not, and get away with the assumption; but it really always needs to be proved, for every copy must in the end descend from the autograph, and only chance—aided no doubt by a preference on the part of scribes for a fair copy as an exemplar—has decreed that in most cases the archetype is distinct from the autograph.

MEDIEVAL POETRY AND THE FIGURAL VIEW OF REALITY

By ELIZABETH SALTER

Read 24 January 1968

IN the Gollancz Memorial Lecture for 1944,[1] Professor Nevill Coghill gave new direction and impetus to our study of Langland's poetry. Without minimizing the difficulty, for the modern reader, of receiving the 'serial and simultaneous voices'[2] of an allegorical composition, he described the rewards of our effort with such exhilaration that many of us made our dedication to *Piers Plowman* largely on the strength of his assurances, and have never been disillusioned.

This paper is also offered as 'an investigation of poetry',[3] but less, perhaps, as a redirection of ideas and responses than as a redefinition. If it attempts to question and supplement our view of 'allegory' in some medieval English verse—and particularly in *Piers Plowman*—it is not prepared to question the truth of the observation that *Piers Plowman* is a 'great and single vision made of many visions, held and harmonized in the mind of the revising poet, and written down so that we can hold it in the same way'.[4] For by such large imaginative claims Professor Coghill ensured that the rich complexities of Langland's art and meaning would never long be ignored. The voices of those who might have been tempted to reinstate some of Isaac D'Israeli's opinions—

A voluminous allegory is the rudest and the most insupportable of all poetic fictions. . . . A genius of the highest order alone could lead us through a single perusal of such a poem, by the charm of vivifying details, which enables us to forget the allegory altogether . . .[5]

have sounded thinly since 1944. Recommendations of a literal rather than an allegorical reading of the poem can still be found[6]

[1] 'The Pardon of Piers Plowman', *Proceedings of the British Academy*, xxx (London, 1944), 303–57.　　　　　　　　[2] Ibid., p. 353.
[3] Ibid., p. 303.　　　　　　　　[4] Ibid., p. 355.
[5] I. D'Israeli, *Amenities of Literature* (London, 1884), p. 100.
[6] R. W. Frank, *Piers Plowman and the Scheme of Salvation*, Yale Studies in English, no. 136 (New Haven, 1957), p. 2.

and Langland's 'realism' is more often admired than precisely described.[1] There are few, however, who would now praise without qualification the 'veracious simplicity' of Langland's vision of the world.

But we have heard, over the past twenty years, the voices of the 'allegorists' strengthen and sharpen. 'Allegorical thinking needs practice', Professor Coghill told us:[2] he could hardly have foreseen how many supervisors would appear to guide our exploration of deeper meaning in texts vibrant with allegorical promise, and in others quite innocent of allegorical design. It is a matter for regret that invitations to 'practise allegorical thinking', first issued with such persuasive gaiety,[3] were accepted with such sobriety and followed by sterner prescriptions, ordering, for instance, the application of the techniques of biblical exegesis to the understanding of religious poetry.[4] It would be particularly regrettable if a process which originally involved the imagination and the sensibility were supplanted by a rigorous intellectual discipline, numbing to poetic response. Not surprisingly, the resistance to these methods has always been active. But there are dangers here, too, for resistance can lead to over-simplification. We may not, any longer, debate in overt terms 'realism or allegory', 'literal or spiritual': they are, however, issues which work powerfully in our critical discussions of medieval religious verse, and still affect our judgements.[5]

For the debate—whether open or concealed—is illusory. It hardly needs demonstrating that the 'realism' of Langland's presentation of his world—the beans and baked apples, the leaking church roofs, the quiet cloisters, the plague-ridden

[1] See, for instance, J. A. Yunck, *The Lineage of Lady Meed*, University of Notre Dame Publications in Medieval Studies, no. 17 (University of Notre Dame Press, 1963), pp. 303–6.

[2] 'The Pardon of Piers Plowman', op. cit., p. 313.

[3] Not only by Nevill Coghill, on behalf of *Piers Plowman*, but also by C. S. Lewis, on behalf of secular allegory, in *The Allegory of Love* (Oxford, 1936).

[4] See Chapter I, 'The Method', of *Piers Plowman and Scriptural Tradition*, by D. W. Robertson and B. F. Huppé (Princeton, 1951), which significantly equates (p. 5) 'the medieval student of theology' and 'the poet'.

[5] Determined resistance to the 'fourfold method' of interpretation seems to result in a narrow reading of *Piers Plowman*: see, for instance, some of the conclusions reached by Frank, op. cit., pp. 117–18, and, more recently, by D. R. Howard, in *The Three Temptations* (Princeton University Press, 1966), pp. 163 f. On the other hand, the exegetical approach is still not yielding *literary* fruit: see B. H. Smith, *Traditional Imagery of Charity in Piers Plowman* (The Hague, 1966).

cities—exists, so to speak, in spiritual solution. And so does the 'realism' of the *Pearl* poet's presentation of his world: the August heat, the precise, unnerving sounds of summer

Quen corne is coruen wyth croke3 kene[1]

press home a pain which, in its unbearable substance, demands spiritual resetting.

Neither does it need much demonstration that *Piers Plowman* and *Pearl* are badly served by subjection to precise and thorough-going analysis in terms of allegory, and especially in terms of fourfold allegory, the 'allegory of the theologians'.[2] The tissue of the poetry is torn by such clinical handling.

There is, of course, no reason why the choice of procedure should ever have been so difficult and so limited. As early as 1944, Erich Auerbach's brilliant essay, 'Figura',[3] illuminated what, indeed, had always been open to discovery in the writings of the Church Fathers: that, from the beginning, Christian ex-egetical tradition, drawing upon both Hebrew and Greek sources, recognized typology and allegory, or, in other words, figural and allegorical methods of interpretation. The allegorical method of handling the sacred text, with its revelation of successive and deepening levels of divine meaning, might well have encouraged a simple polarity of values for the literal and the spiritual: if not inimical to 'the letter' it could lead to the devaluation of the letter.[4] A divorce of history and faith, and of history and ethics is a risk that allegorical study of the Bible constantly took, and when we read some of the more extreme interpretations of early Alexandrian commentators, it is easy to understand why the most distinguished of Western medieval theologians were concerned to modify, compromise, and supplement. Allegorical

---

[1] *Pearl*, ed. E. V. Gordon (Oxford, 1958), l. 40.

[2] To support such analysis by Dante's famous *Letter to Can Grande* about the 'many meanings' of the *Divine Comedy* is to raise rather than solve problems. (See M. W. Bloomfield, 'Symbolism in Medieval Literature', *Modern Philology* lvi (1958), 73–81.) It is still worth stressing, however, that the *Letter* writes more sympathetically about 'alternate meanings' than we sometimes assume, describing their operation as 'play' or 'revolution' around the subject of the poem: 'circa quod currant alterni sensus', 'around which the alternate meanings play'.

[3] *Neue Dantestudien* (Istanbul, 1944), pp. 11–71: trans. R. Manheim, in *Scenes from the Drama of European Literature* (New York, 1959).

[4] See B. Smalley, *The Study of the Bible in the Middle Ages* (Oxford, 1952), p. 2: 'The spiritually minded commentator will accept the letter, but treat it ascetically, as the good religious treats his flesh, in order to devote himself to the spirit.'

procedures and attitudes were not undisputed or even dominant in the Western formulation of God's truth, as it was contained in the Scriptures.[1]

Much more continuously influential was the typological or figural method, which did not deal so much in distinctions and polarities as in relationships. Based firmly upon the stated connections between the Old and New Testaments, and, in essence, designed to illustrate prophecy and fulfilment of prophecy in the course of events from Creation to Last Judgement, it was convinced of the historicity of an act, or person, or speech and equally convinced of its larger significance, to be revealed within Christian history:

Figural interpretation establishes a connection between two events or persons, the first of which signifies not only itself but also the second, while the second encompasses or fulfills the first. . . . Both . . . are within time, within the stream of historical life . . . the understanding of the two persons or events is a spiritual act, but this spiritual act deals with concrete events whether past, present, or future, and not with concepts or abstractions; these are quite secondary, since promise and fulfillment are real historical events, which have either happened in the incarnation of the Word, or will happen in the second coming. . . . Figural interpretation . . . differs from most of the allegorical forms known to us by the historicity both of the sign and what it signifies.[2]

It would not be appropriate to discuss here the complex ways in which figural or typological and allegorical methods are opposed, interact, and are reconciled in the theory and practice of medieval exegesis. That they could be reconciled is important to accept, for this may clarify our understanding of the greatest of all medieval English poems, *Piers Plowman*, as it does our understanding of the *Divine Comedy*.[3] But it is also important to distinguish them, for their operation in medieval literature and in medieval art was sometimes as distinctive as it was strong.[4]

[1] See J. Daniélou, S.J., *From Shadows to Reality. Studies in the Biblical Typology of the Fathers*, trans. W. Hibberd (London, 1960).

[2] Auerbach, 'Figura', pp. 53–4.

[3] See A. C. Charity, *Events and their Afterlife* (Cambridge University Press, 1966), pp. 247–9.

[4] See Daniélou, op. cit., p. 64: 'typology is a legitimate extension of the literal sense, while moral allegory is something entirely alien. . . . Origen was the first to bring together these two interpretations in a forceful synthesis. But they are in reality two distinct approaches, artificially put side by side.' For a useful brief account of allegory and typology in medieval exegesis, see

In 'Figura', and, later, in *Mimesis*,[1] Auerbach proposed that, whatever the usefulness of allegory as a weapon for biblical scholars, and whatever the attractions of allegory as a descriptive mode for writers and artists, typological or figural attitudes permeated medieval thought. Medieval views of history, concepts of time and timelessness, concepts of reality were based figurally upon a philosophy of promise and fulfilment, most completely described and illustrated by the Scriptures, but discernible as a constant rhythm in every part of Christian experience, past, present, and to come. An awareness of its existence and its power is 'indispensable for an understanding of the mixture of spirituality and sense of reality which characterizes the European Middle Ages.'[2]

It is certainly indispensable for an understanding of medieval Christian literature, for here, I believe, typology offered richer rewards to the imagination than allegory. It accepted earthly life, in its concrete historical truth, but it saw that it was endlessly, and miraculously, capable of fulfilment—'endlessly', that is, until the end of time, and the coming of the kingdom of God. Nothing could, surely, be more stirring for the creative artist than the knowledge that 'the figural structure preserves the historical event while interpreting it as revelation; and must preserve it in order to interpret it'.[3]

Auerbach's treatment of figural composition in the *Divine Comedy* was exemplary, and it is all the more remarkable that we have taken so long to test the relevance of his theories and methods for medieval English poetry.[4] English poets of the fourteenth century were as familiar as Dante with that basic text of figural, typological truth—the Bible: some of them were also familiar

C. Donahue, in 'Patristic Exegesis: Summation', *Critical Approaches to Medieval Literature*, ed. D. Bethurum (Columbia University Press, 1960), pp. 61–82.

[1] *Mimesis*, trans. W. R. Trask (New York, 1957), pp. 169 ff.

[2] 'Figura', p. 61.

[3] Ibid., p. 68. Boccaccio's frequent association of Scriptural and poetic composition may be significant here: see, in particular, *De Casibus Illustrium Virorum*, facsimile reproduction of the 1520 edition, with introduction by L. B. Hall (Gainesville, Florida, 1962), Liber Tertius, fo. xxxii, in which Boccaccio claims that poetry 'sola quantum humane imbecillitati possibile est sancte pagine vestigia sequi conata. Nam prout illa divine mentis arcana prophetis futuraque sub figurato tegmine referavit: Sic et haec celsos suorum preceptus sub figmentorum velamine tradere orsa est.'

[4] A beginning was made in Charles Donahue's essay 'Patristic Exegesis: Summation', op. cit., p. 81, in which he suggested that typological forms of thought might 'turn imaginative writers to realism rather than allegory', and mentioned medieval drama as well as Langland.

with Dante. It is possible that many of the fiery critical arguments about literal or allegorical readings of *Pearl* and of *Piers Plowman* could have been quenched far earlier if we had been willing to work not simply with concepts of 'dramatic realism' and 'spiritual application', with 'drama' and 'allegory', but also with the far more flexible concept of typology, or the figural mode. *Piers Plowman* studies could have benefited much more than in fact they did from Auerbach's definitive statements about the comprehensive nature of a work such as the *Divine Comedy*, in which figural, allegorical, and symbolic forms occur— 'but . . . basically it is the figural forms which predominate and determine the whole structure of the poem'.[1] We could well have taken early note, when discussing the Pearl maiden, or Piers the Plowman, of Auerbach's remarks about Dante's characters— Cato, Virgil, and, above all, Beatrice: 'the historical reality is not annulled, but confirmed and fulfilled by the deeper meaning.'[2]

Perhaps it is understandable that the English Miracle Play cycles have been first to receive adequate treatment as examples of typological, figural literature. They demand such attention since their very principles of selection are typological. The basic structure of the cycles is dictated by the fulfilment of the events, characters, and words of the Old Testament in those of the New, and the promise of ultimate fulfilment beyond Judgement Day:

> All þat euere I saide schulde be
> Is nowe fulfillid thurgh prophicie,
> Ther-fore nowe is it tyme to me
> To make endyng of mannes folie.[3]

The formal satisfaction we derive from the arrangement of material in these cycles is comparable to our satisfaction with the typological art of the Middle Ages: the Kennet Ciborium, for instance, which completes or 'fulfils' the Old Testament scenes on the base of the cup by matching New Testament scenes on the lid, thus identifying functional and typological truth: or the Alton Tower Triptych, in which the Crucifixion, Resurrection, and Harrowing of Hell are flanked by parallel events from the Old Testament, and yet *all* events are grouped about the central act of Redemption, Christ crucified.[4] The structure of

---

[1] 'Figura', p. 64.   [2] Ibid., p. 73.
[3] 'The Judgement Play', *York Plays*, ed. L. T. Smith (Oxford, 1885), pp. 498–9.
[4] Both the Ciborium and the Triptych are in the Victoria and Albert Museum: see plates 447–50 and 423 in H. Swarzenski, *Monuments of Romanesque Art* (London, 1967).

this splendid example of twelfth-century art, equally rich in material substance and in meaning, recalls what has been written very recently about the Miracle Plays: 'the shape of the drama is a linear progression. . . but the metaphysic of its structure is centrifugal'.[1] For in all typological or figural art, the acts to which all else must be referred are the acts of Christ's life; while they do not in any sense destroy the linear narrative of history, they have the power to supersede it, by showing how that narrative can be reordered about Christ's birth, death, and resurrection.

We might be tempted to judge the English Miracle Plays a rather simple version of figural art, were it not that in the hands of the best dramatists the 'structural potential (of the figures) becomes real', and, 'like recurring chords in music, the figures and their fulfillment discover singleness in diversity. Form and meaning become one'.[2]

And this, surely, is the crux of the matter for our study of medieval poetry: the multifarious ways in which the 'potential' of the figural view of reality could be 'realized' by the creative mind. In the case of the Miracle Plays, what could have been only a somewhat mechanical exercise in forecast and recapitulation became a study in historical and spiritual resonance.

In the case of the dream-poem, *Pearl*, such 'potential' is realized in a strikingly different manner. It now seems extraordinary that critical comment upon this poem should have concerned itself so much with discussion of 'allegory or elegy', 'the spiritual manifesto, or the personal document'. Auerbach wrote, in a similar context, 'there is no reality in such a choice'. And, in almost every respect, his description of the nature and role of Beatrice in the *Divine Comedy* is directly applicable to the nature and role of the Pearl maiden:

she is no *intellectus separatus*, no angel, but a blessed human being who will rise again in the flesh at the Last Judgement . . . there is no dogmatic concept that would wholly describe her . . . she is precisely an incarnation of divine revelation and not revelation pure and simple.[3]

It may, however, be objected that in the *Divine Comedy*, as in the Miracle Plays and in the Scriptures, there is a very clear

[1] V. A. Kolve, *The Play Called Corpus Christi* (London, 1966), p. 119. I would suggest that 'centripetal' is a better term than 'centrifugal' for this passage, which describes how 'the relationship between Noah and Abraham exists in God.'

[2] Ibid., p. 84.

[3] 'Figura', pp. 74–5.

assurance of the historical truth in which the literal narrative is grounded. The figural demands, as starting-point, a belief in the historicity of the events and persons which it then proceeds to complete, in their fullest significance. The 'figures' of Abraham, Moses, and Jonah in the Old Testament, of Adam and Abel in the Miracle Plays, of Virgil and Cato in the *Divine Comedy* are acknowledged parts of a historical tradition: Beatrice herself is drawn first from the known 'history' of Dante's experience.

With poems such as *Pearl* and *Piers Plowman* we have no independent proof of the grounding of the literal narrative in historical truth. We have no means of knowing whether Pearl, in fact, lived, and was loved by the dreamer-poet, died, and was extravagantly lamented. So, too, we have only slender means of verifying the earthly, historical existence of a poet, William Langland, who lived on Cornhill, with a wife and daughter, and whose life is recorded, in his poetry, as a series of turbulent encounters with sin, temptation, love, and God.

And yet those earlier writers on *Pearl* and *Piers Plowman*, who eagerly set about reconstructing for us the 'real' biography, of which the poems are a version, were not so insensitive as later writers, who saw only literary projections of experience, or, even less, only allegorical inventions. For at least they discerned, though they certainly misused, what the poets were attempting to provide for us—an imitation of history, a construction of literal, historical truth, which can be accepted in its own right, like the literal, historical truth of the Scriptures.[1] This imitation was successful. But of course the poets envisaged that, like the Scriptures, like all recorded, continuing, and promised history, their literal narratives were *capable of*, and *in need of*, fulfilment.

So that here we have examples of figural composition of a secondary type, if we must make such distinctions: secondary, in that such poems invite us to accept as 'historical reality' what cannot ever be susceptible of total proof; but figural indeed, in that they combine a passionate belief in the reality of earthly life, the 'reality of the flesh into which the Logos entered',[2] with the strongest conviction of the divine reality which encompasses and completes it.

This is a crucial point for *Pearl*. The poem is lavish in expressive

---

[1] So Sir Israel Gollancz in his edition of *Pearl* (London, 1921), and A. H. Bright in *New Light on Piers Plowman* (Oxford, 1928) produced far-fetched 'biographies' for the *Pearl* poet and Langland: they were, however, responding to strong suggestions of personal identity and experience in the poetry itself.   [2] 'Figura', p. 72.

methods: its clustered symbolism of great visual splendour, its light but sophisticated allusions to the familiar medieval allegories of will, reason, and delight,[1] its dazzling display of verbal expertise, setting sound and meaning to ring insistent changes against each other. All these work towards the 'gret dyuersite of undirstondyng' which a medieval sermonist found in the language of the Scriptures, and described in an image most fitting for *Pearl*—that of refracted light: '. . . and if we taken heede of dyuerse preciouse stoones, how þei shinen, now with oo colour and now anoþer, we moun þe more liȝtli undirstonde þis gret vertu. . . .'[2]

But the central power of the poem draws upon essentially figural concepts: upon an acceptance of the reality of an earthly relationship between dreamer and Pearl maiden, which is not rejected but fulfilled in spiritual terms, as the fragile human emotions of love-longing, tenderness, and self-pity are subsumed and transformed into charity, compassion, and self-knowledge.

The *Pearl* poet very deliberately establishes for us the substance of the earthly situation: both dreamer and maiden refer to it, and we are right to react strongly to that moment in the vision when the dreamer *recognizes* his Pearl:

> I knew hyr wel, I hade sen hyr ere.
> As glysnande golde þat man con schere,
> So schon þat schene an-vnder shore.
> On lenghe I loked to hyr þere;
> þe lenger, I knew hyr more and more.[3]

The vision does not deny the earlier existence—it simply completes it. So the poem deals much in images of transformation and continuity. What was lost was a creature 'smal' and 'smothe' as a pearl: she reappears, fulfilled in nature as a heavenly pearl, but remains

> þat gracios gay wythouten galle,
> So smoþe, so smal, so seme slyȝt . . .[4]

Similarly, although Pearl describes her earthly self as

> . . . a rose
> þat flowred and fayled as kynde hyt gef,

she is still, in her transfigured state,

> . . . so ryche a reken rose, . . . that lufly flor.[5]

---

[1] *Pearl*, ll. 52–56, 1129, 1153, etc.
[2] British Museum Harleian MS. 2276, f. 122ᵇ.
[3] *Pearl*, ll. 164–8.
[4] Ibid., ll. 189–90. 　　　　　　　　[5] Ibid., ll. 269–70, 906, 962.

Certainly the dreamer's joy at recognition has to be freed from its earthly consequences, and redirected, but it is that same closeness of relationship, put into a different and spiritual context, which qualifies and enables him to see, to learn, and to accept.[1] Whatever her spiritual stature, Pearl is recognizably 'my littel quene' to the end of the vision.

To say that Pearl is *no more* than her transfigured self is not to limit the meaning of the whole poem: she is also *no less* than her transfigured self. As a figure or embodiment of revelation, she has the power to teach the dreamer all he needs to know about justice, fortitude, and love: she interprets death to life. But she is also the embodiment of a miracle—the miracle of grace 'whereby men are raised above other earthly creatures', and in the fulfilment of their natures, witness to salvation.

Our last sight of Pearl shows the spontaneous gaiety of a child transformed, but not destroyed—transformed into spiritual delight:

> Lorde, much of mirþe watȝ þat ho made
> Among her fereȝ þat watȝ so quyt![2]

The potential of the 'figure' has, in all senses, been realized.[3]

The latest study of *Pearl* strengthens the probability that 'the poet could have found in the *Divina Commedia* a precedent for the treatment of figures as part allegorical, part humanly individual. . .'. '. . . it is, indeed, hard to see where else he could have acquired this blend of the modes of realistic and symbolical writing'.[4]

We could, I think, use terms a little more precise than this, and describe these particular creations of Dante and the *Pearl* poet as 'figural', rather than 'part allegorical, part humanly individual'. For there is no division of functions, such as this might imply. The absolute authority of Pearl over her dreamer depends as much upon the fact that she had been, on earth, the 'ground of all his bliss', as it does upon the fact that, as bride of Christ, she is now fully 'grounded in bliss'.[5] Earthly love and pain are now fulfilled in that larger pattern of redemptive love which reconciled, once and for all, suffering and joy.

[1] See, for comparison, E. Gilson, *Dante and Philosophy*, trans. D. Moore (New York, 1963), p. 79: *'on the strength of the love that he bore her*, Beatrice is exclusively marked out to be his intercessor with God' (my italics).

[2] *Pearl*, ll. 1149–50.

[3] So also the poem displays the New Jerusalem as a 'fulfilment' of the Old: a striking piece of typological presentation. See ll. 937–60.

[4] P. M. Kean, *Pearl: An Interpretation* (London, 1967), pp. 120 and 138.

[5] *Pearl*, ll. 372, 408, and 420.

So the dreamer marvels at his vision of the Lamb, bleeding, but content:

> The Lombe delyt non lyste to wene.
> þaȝ he were hurt and wounde hade,
> In his sembelaunt watȝ neuer sene,
> So wern his glenteȝ gloryous glade.[1]

At the same time, we could widen our perspectives, and see *Pearl* indebted not only, in a special literary way, to the *Divine Comedy*, but also to the figural or typological view of reality, as it was presented to the Middle Ages, in the Bible itself, and as it was re-presented, by the Middle Ages, in varied forms of art and literature.

This widening of perspectives is certainly necessary for a whole view of *Piers Plowman*: we cannot be at all sure that Langland knew the *Divine Comedy*. We can be sure, however, that he knew the Bible, and that he was familiar with a great deal of learned and popular religious writing, which displayed to a receptive public how 'god schewed of olde tyme / be figuratif lyknesse'[2] his entire plan for the present and for the future of the world. Langland tells us, more than once, of this familiarity:

> Lawe of loue oure lorde wrot. longe er Crist were,
> And Crist cam and confermede...[3]

It has been rightly remarked that the setting of *Piers Plowman* as a 'dream-poem' has often led us to associate it, over-exclusively, with certain kinds of medieval poetry. So, although some of its early dream-prologues remind us of the *Romance of the Rose* and personification allegory, it is not a particularly helpful reminder when we come to reading *Piers Plowman* and judging Langland's intentions. We can, I hope, agree that personification is only one of the many methods which Langland adopts, first to pursue, and then to express, his meaning. By describing the poem as a 'personification allegory', we fail to capture some of Langland's most characteristic procedures and, even further, some of his most profound thoughts.[4]

---

[1] Ibid., ll. 1141–4.

[2] *The Miroure of Mans Saluacionne*, ed. A. H. Huth (Roxburghe Club, 1888), p. 2: a fifteenth-century translation of the very popular early four-teenth-century *Speculum Humanae Salvationis*, which presented, in visual and literary form, New Testament history with its Old Testament prefigurations (ed. J. Lutz and P. Perdrizet, Mulhouse, 1907, 2 vols.).

[3] *The Vision of William Concerning Piers the Plowman*, ed. W. W. Skeat (Oxford, 1886), repr. 1954: C. xv. 38–39. All quotations are made from this edition.

[4] For such reasons, the categories proposed by R. W. Frank, in 'The Art of Reading Medieval Personification-Allegory', *E.L.H.* xx (1953), 237–50, are

If, on the other hand, we take Langland's obviously wide knowledge of the Bible to mean that he was devoted to biblical exegesis of one particular sort—the fourfold 'allegory of the theologians'—and intended that his poetry should demonstrate this, then we are only partly in touch with medieval attitudes to the Bible, and with *Piers Plowman*. If *Piers Plowman* is an allegory, it is like no other extant literary allegory: comparisons with the *Romance of the Rose*, the *Desert of Religion*, the *Faery Queene*, and *Pilgrim's Progress* all miss the point of comparison. Again, if it is an allegory, it is quite unlike a theologian's exposition of multiple significance.

Since it is, I believe, the most comprehensive work of the English Middle Ages, it touches most literary forms and methods: like that most comprehensive work of the Italian Middle Ages, the *Divine Comedy*, it utilizes allegory (in many forms), symbolism (although not greatly), and typology, the figural mode. And it could be said that we have too often tried to describe as 'allegorical' features of *Piers Plowman* which are much better described as 'figural' or 'typological'. We have sometimes been at a disadvantage in our mappings of the poem, because our equipment has been deficient.

To suggest that in *Piers Plowman*, as in the *Divine Comedy*, it is the 'figural [or typological] forms which predominate'[1] is not to suggest that multiple meaning, personification allegory, and realism of a startling, dramatic quality are not all present in the poem. It is simply to say that Langland's understanding of his material was strongly—although not exclusively—figural, and that figural concepts bear rich and various fruit in his poetry.

We cannot restate too often the fact that the most pervasive single influence upon *Piers Plowman* was that of the Bible. And whatever Christian scholars have made of the biblical text, whatever systems they have devised as plummets to sound its truth, the Bible itself asks, explicitly, to be regarded as a figural or typological document. Its subject is 'those matters which have been fulfilled among us' (Luke 1:1)[2] and which will take their ultimate fulfilment in 'a new heaven, and a new earth'.

Typology is an integral and a practical element in biblical writing: it is not simply used as a way of elucidating the history

not entirely satisfactory. But the view of personification as the 'obvious technique' of *Piers Plowman* (Bloomfield, op. cit., p. 78) goes largely unquestioned.

[1] 'Figura', p. 64.
[2] 'Quae in nobis completae sunt rerum.'

of the world, and man's destiny, but also as a way of involving the particular Christian reader in the redemptive processes it describes. A great amount of New Testament teaching is concerned with relating the past and the future to the present life of the aspiring Christian. Christ is frequently called upon, as is Holy Church in *Piers Plowman*, to deal with the question 'how may I be saved?'.[1] And the lives of the apostles and saints give practical demonstration of the truth of his answers. In a very conscious, deliberate fashion, Christ's life is presented as the fulfilment of a divine purpose, dimly perceived and partially exemplified by Old Testament lives and words—

Lawe of loue oure lorde wrot . longe er Crist were. . .:

it is also presented as a model for all present and future lives, as we move on to the final revelation: 'typology stays with us even in the new dispensation, in the Church's and the believer's commitment to the "imitation" of Christ'.[2]

It is clear, I think, that, apart from providing Langland with a traditional framework of correspondences, a 'structural potential', the Bible also provided him with a vast, patterned, and creative view of history, as urgently relevant to the choices which faced fourteenth-century man as it had been to those facing Paul or Augustine, and as it would be to the choices of all men

Til the vendage valle . in the vale of Iosaphat . . .[3]

The essential messages of *Piers Plowman* are conveyed at their greatest intensity by figural or typological means, as are those of the Bible.

And here, because the figural must be set firmly into history ('it differs from most of the allegorical forms known to us by the historicity both of the sign and what it signifies'), we must reaffirm what was earlier said of *Pearl*: that Langland asks us to accept as 'historically real' what cannot be historically verified. *Piers Plowman* is a far more complex poem than *Pearl*, but it, too, draws a good deal of its power from its insistence upon a personal, historical, autobiographical grounding. The life of the poet-dreamer may, in fact, be illusion, but it is presented vividly, as if it were real. There is, on reflection, a vast difference between Langland and Chaucer in their treatment of the dreamer's life and its relevance to the dream-vision; if Langland's dreamer

---

[1] *Piers Plowman*, C. ii. 79–80.
[2] See Charity, op. cit., p. 152.
[3] *Piers Plowman*, C. xxi. 414.

is a fiction, a *persona* only, he plays a part more nearly comparable to that of the 'I' of Revelation than to that of the agreeably diverted narrator of the *Parliament of Fowls* or the *House of Fame*.

Much of the pressure we feel when reading *Piers Plowman*, our sense of close engagement with the meaning of the poem, is derived from a persuasion of the historical reality of the dreamer's own life—a life which was perhaps Langland's,[1] a frank record of aspiration, rejection, temptation, and reconciliation. From its uneven, often precarious, vantage points the reader is invited to view and compare the patterns of lives which are more, and less, satisfactory: the lives of Hawkin, *activa-vita*, of Trajan, of Piers Plowman, of the patriarchs and prophets, and of Christ himself. Or, to change the metaphor, another glass is held before us—one of many in *Piers Plowman*—in whose flawed and cloudy depths we glimpse, fleetingly, and 'darkly', the image of Christ.

A belief in the 'reality' of the dreamer is, of course, a belief in 'figural reality', for he functions in the poem as both living historical creature, and sign. His painful humiliation, within and without the dream, is set against his admission, as a witness, to Christ's death and resurrection:[2] this is not only humanly moving, but revelatory of the truth that 'the grace of God is great enough'. The message that he gasps out, with relief, to his wife and daughter, when he wakes in a peal of triumphant bells

> Arys, and go reuerence . godes resurreccioun,
> And creop on kneos to the croys . and cusse hit for a Iuwel . . .
> For godes blesside body . hit bar for oure bote,
> And hit a-fereth the feonde . for such is the myghte,
> May no grysliche gost . glyde ther hit shadeweth[3]

is a moment of great dramatic poignancy, but it is also, in single focus, a sign to be read, and understood, telling of the efficacy of the gospel in reforming the life of sinful man.[4]

---

[1] See the important chapter, 'Signatures', by G. Kane, *Piers Plowman: The Evidence for Authorship* (University of London, Athlone Press, 1965), in which the identification of poet and narrator in medieval dream narratives is discussed: '. . . the greater likelihood is that the concept of the wholly fictitious first-person narrator in a fourteenth-century poem is anachronistic' (p. 58).

[2] *Piers Plowman*, C. xxi 35 ff.

[3] Ibid., 474–5, 477–9.

[4] See Charity, op. cit., p. 168: '. . the biblical tradition of typology fastens on an event of conversion with the aim of effecting another.'

Similarly, 'characters' such as Piers the Plowman, and the Good Samaritan, are brought before us as if they existed in the same kind of historical tradition as Abraham, Moses, and Trajan: they are rooted in historical life, and in time. Fresh from the field, the plough, or from horseback, they break into the poem with as much dramatic force as the Canon and his Yeoman into the Canterbury Pilgrimage at 'Boghton under Blee'. And this is immensely important for Langland's purpose. Piers Plowman and the Good Samaritan, like Abraham, Moses, and Trajan, must be historically secure in the reader's mind, for they are to illustrate, even more significantly than the Old Testament prophets and the Roman Emperor, the working of divine providence in the actual earthly life of man. They must be 'thoroughly real, with the reality of the flesh into which the Logos entered'.

But this, again, is figural, not literal and limited realism. Both Piers Plowman and the Good Samaritan reveal themselves as 'figures', in the precise sense of the word, as well as recognizable dramatic 'characters': Piers, by his immediate and confident exposition of a spiritual mystery, which will only much later be fulfilled, in himself—the discovery of divinity within, 'Treuthe sytte in thy selue herte. . .':[1] the Good Samaritan, by an increasing number of interesting and, in a way, disturbing details, which gradually convince us that 'the situation is only in part perceptual'.[2]

So, the 'syttynge on a mule', the haste to reach Jerusalem, the 'wilde wildernesse'[3] of the setting remind us that this is not simply a story of a good human being, but a foreshadowing of the earthly journey of Christ. These indications of further meaning are not, however, indications of allegory: neither Piers nor the Good Samaritan are presented as allegorical characters— they are incarnations or figurations of charity, of divine truth immanent.

In reusing the parable of the Good Samaritan, Langland was of course fully aware of its traditional allegorical interpretation

---

[1] *Piers Plowman*, C. viii. 255. See E. Zeeman (Salter), 'Piers Plowman and the Pilgrimage to Truth', *Essays and Studies*, xi, N.S. (1958), 1–16.

[2] I. T. Ramsay, *Religious Language* (London, 1957), p. 147.

[3] *The Miroure of Mans Saluacionne*, p. 18, has 'and *in desert* commyng/ he fell in theves hande'. No doubt here we are meant to remember also Christ's temptation in the wilderness ('et agebatur a Spiritu in desertum diebus quadraginta et tentabatur a diabolo', Luke 4: 1–2), for this was, typologically, both a fulfilment and a prophecy of universal human experience. The echoic nature of typological presentation could not be better illustrated.

as the story of the redemption of man.[1] But he did not so much coalesce or overlay the allegorical interpretation with the figural, as choose, very deliberately, to allow the figural view fullest extension.[2] Thus what is predominant in our reading of the episode is the gradual, strengthening conviction of the 'imago Christi' in the Good Samaritan, a fulfilling of the man in the image of Christ, as he rides 'the righte wey to Jerusalem' (C. xx. 77) and expounds to the dreamer the meaning of the redemption and the operation of the Trinity.

There is, then, in *Piers Plowman*, a strong movement to establish a historical base for the 'characters' who are to carry the main messages of the poem. But this is no simple movement towards what is often spoken of as Langland's 'dramatic realism'. Abraham's human aspect, 'a man . on Mydlentens Soneday/As hor as a hawethorn', his conversational warmth as he talks to the dreamer:

'Hauest thow seyen this?' ich seide . 'alle thre, and o god?'
'In a somer ich seyh hym,' quath he . 'as ich sat in my porche,
Where god cam goynge a-thre . ryght by my gate',[3]

are not meant only to delight and relax us: familiar moments in a rare religious context. They are meant to bring before us, with some urgency, the substance and force of faith, as it sustained man before the days of Christ. Salvation by faith is solidly embodied for us in Abraham.

Even the structure and procedures of *Piers Plowman* can be more precisely described, if we admit the presence of typological, or figural elements. In 'The Pardon of Piers Plowman', Professor Coghill spoke of the 'levels of reality' in the poem, and of the 'parallel thinking' characteristic of allegory.[4] But he also pointed to 'foretastes and echoes', the 'technique of anticipation' in *Piers Plowman* as a part of allegorical thinking.[5] I should like to distinguish here particularly between allegorical and typological thinking: even if these foretastes and echoes were not 'placed where they are to suit an exact theory of composition',[6] they are a very clearly recognizable feature of typological or figural

[1] Clearly analysed by B. H. Smith, op. cit., pp. 74 f.
[2] Here, I believe, it is not quite accurate to say that 'Allegory has resolved argument' (Coghill, op. cit., p. 350): we are working in a figural mode.
[3] *Piers Plowman*, C. xix. 241–3.
[4] Coghill, op. cit., p. 351.
[5] Ibid., pp. 312 and 335 ff.
[6] Ibid., p. 312.

composition. The Bible is the prime example. It is not simply a matter of 'historical resonances', although these are important in the Bible and in *Piers Plowman*, as the particular moment is suffused with memories of the past, premonitions of the future. A speech such as that of Christ, after the Harrowing of Hell—

> For ich am lord of lyf . loue is my drynke,
> And for that drynke todaye . deyede, as hit semede[1]

is patterned with verbal 'foretastes and echoes'. This has been recognized,[2] but it cannot be stressed too emphatically that the verbal knitting of strands which occurs here is dependent upon an essentially figural or typological view of truth. Christ's speech fulfils, verbally, all the language of the poem which has hinted at this moment, and suggests language yet to be used, just as the Harrowing of Hell fulfils, doctrinally, the promise of redemption and looks forward to that final act of the drama, when Christ will 'haue out of helle . alle menne soules' (C. xxi. 417). There are many similar speeches in *Piers Plowman*, though none quite so centrally placed, nor so harmonious to the imagination.[3]

We can go further, and enlarge upon the idea of 'foretastes and echoes' as it applies to the typological structure of *Piers Plowman*. The poem has frequently been criticized for its failure to solve its formal problems: for its habit of loose repetition, the merging of one similar episode or character into another. But its incremental repetitions are not a sign of confusion. Like those of the biblical narratives, they are often deliberately set to recall each other, in a way which is allusive but not accidental. It is a way which is typological: 'one thing does not mean another in typology: it involves it, or has inferences for it, or suggests it.'[4]

This cannot be better illustrated than in Langland's use of the motif of travelling in *Piers Plowman*. The pilgrimage, the search and the journey are variations upon that great constant theme of the poem—movement towards a goal. The searches for St. Truth, for Dowel, for Charity, for Perfection, and for Piers Plowman unfold from each other, in a rhythm of repetition and change. There is a sense of perpetually renewed action, a driving

---

[1] *Piers Plowman*, C. xxi. 406 f.

[2] See A. C. Spearing, *Criticism and Medieval Poetry* (London, 1964), p. 90, and E. Salter, *Piers Plowman: An Introduction* (Oxford, 1963), pp. 49–52.

[3] So, the choice implied in the remark that 'the Jousting at Jerusalem and the Harrowing of Hell present themselves not as figure but as fact' (John Lawlor, *Piers Plowman: An Essay in Criticism*, London, 1962, p. 253) is really non-existent: both episodes are powerfully, and equally, 'figure' and 'fact'.

[4] Charity, p. 199.

forward to something infinitely desirable, which may be variously defined as a place, a state, an event, or a person, but which, over the course of the poem, is revealed as the attainment of salvation through Christ.

Thus the repetitiveness of the journeys, their overlapping and echoing nature are not due to indecision in Langland, but rather to a belief in divine repetitions—the continuous pattern of search and fulfilment traced for medieval man by the Bible itself.

The biblical—and typological—background is particularly evident in Langland's treatment of journeying at the climax of the poem, when Abraham, Moses, the Good Samaritan, and the dreamer are hurrying to Jerusalem for the tournament with death. All earlier images of journeying are gathered up into this tense narrative—Piers as a pilgrim to Truth, Christ as a way-farer, the dreamer as a 'seeker after ways'.[1] All paths converge here, upon Jerusalem, as indeed they should, for the battle with sin and death, imperfectly fought before this moment, with im-perfect weapons, will now be achieved perfectly, and will serve as model for all future conflicts in the life of the individual Christian. We cannot help but be reminded of Christ's words and actions, as he moves towards the goal of his earthly journey—Jerusalem:

And taking the twelve, he said to them, 'Behold, we are going up to Jerusalem, and everything that is written of the Son of Man by the prophets will be accomplished'. (Luke 18:31.)

The language is echoic: it harks back to earlier moments, in the Gospel of St. Luke:

He went on his way, through towns and villages, teaching and journeying towards Jerusalem. (Luke 13:22.)

Nevertheless, I must go on my way today and tomorrow and the day following, for it cannot be that a prophet should perish away from Jerusalem. (Luke 13:33.)

and it forecasts later moments, when Paul takes up that same journey, and hastens[2] to re-enact the sacrifice of Christ:

And now, behold, I am going to Jerusalem bound in the spirit, not knowing what shall befall me there. . . . (Acts 20:22.)[3]

---

[1] *Piers Plowman*, C. xv. 157.

[2] Acts 20:16, 'Festinabat enim. . . .'.

[3] All English quotations from *The Holy Bible and Apocrypha*, Revised Standard Version (London, 1965).

. . . I am ready . . . even to die at Jerusalem for the name of the Lord Jesus. (Acts 21:13.)

Much remains to be said and done if we are to explore thoroughly the significance of typological structure and the figural view of reality in *Piers Plowman*. The range of investigation is wide; it covers Langland's universally praised and often misunderstood 'realism': his sense of the past inseparable from, and active in, the present, the present active in the future;[1] his dealings with Christ's representatives in all ages—that perfect representative, Piers Plowman, that errant and stumbling representative, the dreamer, who is still learning how to 'fulfil' God's image in himself, at the very end of the poem:

'Consaileth me, Kynde,' quath ich . 'what crafte be best to leere?'
'Lerne to loue,' quath Kynde . 'and lef alle other thynges.'[2]

Thus, characteristically, Langland leaves for our wry comfort an admission that to see and understand God's act of redemption does not guarantee an easy process of transformation. Unlike Dante, the dreamer is not saved by the end of the poem, although he knows what to do to be saved: his conscience is alive, and stirring.

But it is in the creation of Piers the Plowman that Langland's debt to figural habits of thought is most satisfactorily—that is, most imaginatively—repaid. For not only do we see in him, as in the Good Samaritan, a 'type' of Christ, and an active illustration of how 'Christ has . . . by passing through them, sanctified every aspect of human existence'.[3] And not only do we see in him, as in Pearl and Beatrice, the crowned fulfilment of divine promise—the 'miracle whereby men are raised above other earthly creatures' and reveal divine truth. We see also part of the *process* of that miracle: the gradual conforming of a Christian life, which we meet first when it is instructed but inexperienced, to the pattern of Christ's life. And this conformation is so complete that Piers suffers the 'jousting at Jerusalem' with Christ. The echoing of Christ's words, sometimes their virtual

[1] Langland's time-concepts are essentially figural or typological: his treatment of the Good Samaritan and Piers Plowman as 'figures' of Christ should make this clear. Both are meant to be strikingly reminiscent of Christ, in doctrine and action, almost to the point of identification: but both are presented as existing before the Incarnation (see *Piers Plowman*, B. xvi, and B. xvii. 90 ff., C. xx. 81 ff.). In fact, Christ's existence is supra-temporal, and the 'figures' display this by refusing to conceive of time as an 'unbroken horizontal process' ('Figura', p. 59).

[2] *Piers Plowman*, C. xxiii. 207–8.

[3] Quoted from Irenaeus by Daniélou, op. cit., p. 38.

paraphrase, by the words of Piers,[1] the sharing, by Piers, in Christ's actions—

> . . . this Iesus of hus gentrise . shal Iouste in Peers armes,
> In hus helme and in hus haberion . *humana natura*. . .[2]

vividly recall the narrative of Christ's own life, and, at the same time, the lives of apostles and saints such as Paul and Stephen who strove to reflect as faithfully as possible—or in more technical language, to 'post-figure'—the pattern of that ideal life of sacrifice and love.[3]

So repetition is at the very heart of Langland's poem, as it is at the heart of his faith: form and meaning are, indeed, one, as lives, persons, journeys, questions and answers echo and prompt each other in unceasing creative flow.

As for fourfold allegory: a typological work, dealing as it must with man's past and future, his life, death, and salvation, is of itself most wealthy in significance. Although it does not require a multiple allegorical system to demonstrate this, it cannot be permanently injured by such treatment. By its very nature it is Christocentric, and moral and mystical truths are not inappropriately discovered in the presentation of the human search to know 'how I may save my soul'.

---

[1] Throughout the poem, but strikingly in C. xvi. 138 ff., Piers operates in this scene—the Feast of Clergye—very much as a 'figure' or 'type' of Christ, bringing, at l. 138, a fulfilment of the words of the Psalmist and a repetition of Christ's words on meekness and love.

[2] *Piers Plowman*, C. xxi. 21–2.

[3] Because I believe that *Piers Plowman* is concerned centrally with the transformation of the self in Christ's image, and only peripherally with an imminent, apocalyptic revelation of truth, I would prefer not to describe it as an 'apocalyptic work'. See M. Bloomfield, *Piers Plowman as a Fourteenth Century Apocalypse* (Rutgers University Press, 1963). Any medieval work which deals with the history of mankind is committed to medieval Christian eschatology. But the last words of the poem do not touch upon death and judgement: they touch upon regeneration and, in a truly figural way, call us back through Piers the Plowman to God's redemptive act in Christ.

THE NATURE OF ALLITERATIVE POETRY
IN LATE MEDIEVAL ENGLAND

By GEOFFREY SHEPHERD

Read 21 January 1970

I RECALL two problems which have troubled me in reading two alliterative poems written in the fourteenth century: familiar problems which have troubled other readers beside myself. The first is the so-called Pardon scene in *Piers Plowman* (in the second vision of the poem, as recounted in Passus VIII of the A-Text), where Truth has sent a pardon extending to all estates.[1] A priest asks to see the pardon which Piers holds. The dreamer looks on,

> And I bi-hynden hem bothe · bi-heold al the bulle.
>
> (A VIII, 93)

The priest reads the clauses of the Athanasian creed and pronounces that here is no pardon at all. In the A-Text, and in the B-Text, Piers in pure anger tears up the document. According to all three texts, a quarrel ensues between Piers and the priest, and the dreamer awakes and tells how he went on his way, wondering what the sight meant. He reminds himself that dreams are often not to be trusted, but also that some dreams in the Bible when properly understood conveyed truth:

> Al this maketh me · on metels to thenken
> Mony tyme at midniht · whon men schulde slepe,
> On Pers the plouh-mon · and whuch a pardoun he hedde,
> And hou the preost inpugnede hit · al bi pure resoun.
>
> (A VIII, 152–5)

Wise and ingenious men have written about this scene and given learned and ingenious interpretations. What remains surprising is that the scene should require so much ingenuity to give it meaning. All readers realize, with some dumb literary instinct perhaps, that they have reached a climax at this point

[1] *The Vision of William concerning Piers the Plowman*, ed. Walter W. Skeat (1886), vol. 1, A-Text, Passus VIII, pp. 226 ff.

of the poem. It is not satisfying to take the dreamer as a 'naïve narrator', or the tearing of the pardon as an arbitrary device to break the dream. The reader is surely right in feeling that the scene is relevant to the meaning of the poem. And yet the relevance is never made explicit. How could this poet, who is, as we come to know him, often powerful in utterance, and clear in exposition, sometimes resolutely tedious when he is determined to have his local meaning plain, offer in the A-Text, continue to offer in the B-Text, and still offer even in the C-Text —where he seems aware of some of the difficulties—a climax which remains scarcely intelligible? Did not the poet know the meaning of what he had himself composed? The answer given by the texts is surely, No.

The second problem is as familiar and much simpler. Most readers nowadays will agree that *Sir Gawain and the Green Knight* is a shapely and carefully constructed romance, lightly and deliberately moralized. The Lady's temptings of Gawain in the bedroom are seen to relate to the morality of the work. Each bedroom scene, we recall, is associated with a hunting piece. Yet to read the meaning of the poem into and through these hunting scenes has perplexed most interpreters. It is an excellent principle to insist that an impalpable allegory is no allegory at all. Many readers will have welcomed Professor Norman Davis's note on the first hunt: 'The noise, confusion and slaughter of this scene and the terror of the mass of hunted animals make unacceptable any suggestion of a symbolic parallel between it and the simultaneous quiet pursuit in the castle bedroom.'[1] What then are these hunting scenes doing in the poem? No doubt explanations can be sought and given in terms of a metonymic structure in the poem, or of social flattery of the audience. Part of the answer lies elsewhere.

In a society instructed by word of mouth, and by ear, any information or moralization is taken directly as it comes, in memorable and discrete parcels: the attention is directed simply to a succession of points; and if the points are sharp enough they will stick in the mind. Information is accepted within the frame of a story and extracted from it without discomfiture. The end of the first hunting scene in *Sir Gawain*, which deals with the breaking up of the carcass of the slain deer, may be taken as illustration. This is a full and detailed account in technical language of an elaborate ritual. We can assume a general

[1] *Sir Gawain and the Green Knight*, ed. J. R. R. Tolkien and E. V. Gordon, 2nd edition revised by Norman Davis (1967), p. 107, note on 1158 ff.

interest in hunting on the part of the audience: we cannot assume that more than a few members of the audience would have a detailed and expert knowledge of the advanced technique and its terminology. The direct and natural way for an audience to have taken this passage was in the first place as memorable instruction. While this part of the narrative was proceeding, they will have switched their attention from the story to the instruction.

There are other passages of *Sir Gawain* which could be considered as similarly, if less ostentatiously, mnemonic: the arming for instance, or the schematizing of the pentangle. We need not ignore simple if secondary intentions in writing poems, and simpler ways of responding to them. Metrical forms were in common use through the Middle Ages and beyond, for teaching and reinforcing moral, political, religious, sanitary, and behavioural commonplaces, and for fixing grammatical, logical, arithmetical, and legal formulas in the memory. Many passages in Middle English verse, at all levels of accomplishment, become more intelligible when they are admitted to be, if not primarily and detachedly mnemonic, at least vestigially mnemonic in form and content. Particularly is this true, in the later medieval period, of alliterative writing.

Alliteration as a formal device superimposed upon the verbalizations of a culture is itself a mnemotechnique. From the beginnings of the settlement of England by the Anglo-Saxons, alliterative composition had been a preservative of power, patrimony, and communal wisdom. The acquisition of a script, which also springs from a desire to make memorials, did not for centuries render alliteration superfluous; for alliterative usages had become as they have remained, part of the public language when it operates in a traditional and slightly formal register. In the curiously and deliberately archaising verse of the alliterative poets of the last medieval centuries, though these were now no spokesmen for an oral culture, the mnemonic use of verse is less submerged than it was in contemporary verse of a more bookish kind. Bookish verse tended to convert this inheritance into encyclopedism, as we see in Lydgate; but alliterative verse continued to appeal to the active memory more directly. Passages of *Piers Plowman* that may seem digressive—for example, the points of Patience (B XIV, 274–319), and much of the Samaritan's instruction (B XVII, 90–348)—may well be signs of the persistence of the mnemonic habit. Much more obvious is the long register of tradesmen in the *Gest Hystoriale of the Destruction of Troy*: or the list of Arthur's domains at the beginning of the alliterative *Morte Arthure* or the naming of the apostles in the *Siege of Jerusalem*; or the catalogue descriptions in *Susannah*, and in the *Parlement of the Thre Ages*, where the poet offers an account of the Nine Worthies:

> And I shall neuen you the names of nine of the beste

and having dealt with them one by one concludes:

> Now have I neuened you the names of nine of the best:

and similarly at the end of the *Wars of Alexander* with an attention mark added:

> Now sall I neuyn ȝow þe names · note ȝe þe wordis,

introducing a twenty-line catalogue of Alexander's conquests:

> þe pepill out of Panthi · is plant in first,
> Pruto, Picard, & Pers · & Pamphalie bathe,
> Portingale & Paiters · it paies me trouage,
> Arrabe & Artoyes · and Assie þe mare,
> Abbeon & Aufrike · & Acres anothire,
> Effosym & Ethiops · þire ebrues folke;
> All Ermony & Ewrope · enterely me serues,
> Ingland, Itaile, & Yndee · & Ireland costis,
> Meede & Mesopotayme · & Massedoyne eke.[1] *etc.*

Such lists even through print, manage to suggest that they were well-remembered by the poet and worth remembering by his audience.

The memorable catalogue could also be used as an unpretentious device in construction; for example in the assembly of banners in *Winner and Waster* or in the second part of *Mum and the Sothsegger* with its long list of libels.[2] And many familiar features of alliterative poetry seem to originate in the habit of composing detachable and memorable passages—what are

[1] *The Gest Hystoriale of the Destruction of Troy*, ed. G. A. Panton and D. Donaldson, EETS 39 and 56 (1869, 1874), ll. 1580–1600; *Morte Arthure*, re-ed. E. Brock, EETS 8 (1871), ll. 26–47; *The Siege of Jerusalem*, ed. E. Kölbing and Mabel Day, EETS 188 (1931), ll. 140–52; *Susannah*, ed. Alice Miskimin, New Haven and London (1969), ll. 66–117; *The Parlement of the Thre Ages*, ed. (Sir) Israel Gollancz, SEEP ii (1915), ll. 297, 580; *The Wars of Alexander*, ed. Walter W. Skeat, EETS, ES 47 (1886), (Ashmole 44) ll. 5655 ff.

[2] *Winner and Waster*, ed. Sir Israel Gollancz, SEEP iii (1920), ll. 143–92; *Mum and the Sothsegger*, ed. Mabel Day and R. Steele, EETS 199 (1936), ll. 1343–1751 (end).

called the set-pieces—descriptions of storm or weather, sea-voyages, battles, buildings, feasts, ordered pageantry. Such set-pieces are of course oral formulas writ long and large and had a special hold on memory as is shown by the subtle and pervasive correspondences in set-pieces in different alliterative poems. Many of these correspondences are not known to belong to an ancient traditional repertoire of phrase, but are apparently new transferable property among the later poets.

Most readers identify alliterative verse at sight; and certainly most alliterative poets left no doubt that they intended their compositions to be written down and read from the written page. Yet it is still true that their kind of poetry should be recognized by its sound, at least by its sound on the inner ear. It is the sound that distinguished alliterative verse from other verse of the late Middle English period. English prosody is notoriously obscure, so haunted by ancestral demons, that no sensible person would venture on this ground light-heartedly. It can be observed, however, that the alliterative poets themselves claimed to write in metre. Their metre is not to be called rhyme, in any of the historical senses of the word; plainly also it is not a syllabic or quantitative measure and it is not provided with regular feet. The audible basis of regular recurrence is the beat attached to the alliterating syllables (normally three) in a normally end-stopped line. The accentuation will be imposed upon and often distort the ordinary rhythm of utterance and the metre itself may well be more susceptible to analysis in terms of music, than of prosody.

The recognizable, memorable if unanalysed sound of alliterative verse is reinforced by the peculiar syntax, grammar, and diction, co-operating to give weight and distinction to this type of composition. The paratactic, itemizing constructions, some-times dependent for cohesion only upon the phonemic signal; the selection of words with a view to 'alliterative rank'; the use of variation and of epithets with a high level of predictability—such devices feed upon and strengthen the memorability of alliterative verse. From ancient times it had been understood that in devising mnemonics, what was to be committed to the memory should be made striking, and precise, simplified, slightly transfigured—that is made somewhat exaggerated or somewhat grotesque—and set within a homogeneous and familiar matrix. The alliterative style can be described in these terms. It simplifies as well as intensifies, it produces the effect of idealization under the appearance of realism, the sense of a high style hoisted up out of colloquialism. It also betrays its susceptibility to parody, its tendency to collapse into patterned noise, into rant.

The mnemonic cast of alliterative verse is for my purpose only an outward expression of a more intimate dependence of late medieval alliterative poetry upon memory. Much of this poetry commemorates the past as *testis temporum, memoria vitae, nuncia vetustatis*. The poet is often a memorialist. He tells the great *gestes* of antiquity. But the dependence on memory can be taken still further. The actual poetry-making is to be understood as a function of memory. Comprehensively, the poetics of alliterative poetry—in relation to form, matter and art—can be regarded as a poetics of memory.

The whole notion of the human memory is elusive and difficult to hold in mind. Of all the faculties there is none harder to account for or has perplexed the philosophers more. It would be advisable perhaps to follow Sir William Hamilton's advice and 'truncate a problem I cannot solve'. Fortunately, Dr. Frances Yates[1] has laid a delicate firm hand upon the Protean mystery and has fairly stabilized the role of memory in Western European thought, and demonstrated the continuity of the ancient arts of memory from classical to renaissance times. In all human affairs that depended upon transmitted learning these arts of memory were of supreme practical importance. Some acquaintance with them is usually implicit in the treatment given to memory under the fourth head of the art of rhetoric. No writer could escape their influence. Their drills often shape composition: thus the description of halls or pictorial panels in medieval allegory exploit the doctrine of places as taught in artificial memory.

Increasing literacy in the later middle ages, like the introduction of writing among the Egyptians of old, as Socrates said, was a recipe for forgetfulness; but it was only at the end of the middle ages, in the sixteenth century, that Englishmen emerged with astonishing acceleration from an intellectual world controlled by the spoken word, and began to dispense with their old props to intellect. Earlier the whole medieval system of education had depended upon memory. Just as scraps and terms of rhetorical theory turn up in all branches of medieval learning, so, as Miss Yates has shown, this associated art of memory was everywhere at work. It influenced the teaching of ethics and the practice of

[1] Frances A. Yates, *The Art of Memory* (1966).

the spiritual life. Thus, memory working within the imaginative faculty was treated as part of prudence: so *Imaginatif* in *Piers Plowman*, not unexpectedly, contributes to the understanding of the life of Dowel.

The psychology of memory remained Aristotelian—modified somewhat by the Arab commentators, and generally little disturbed by the schoolmen. But St. Augustine—particularly in *De Trinitate* and in the tenth book of the *Confessions*—had already inextricably entangled the theory with Christian experience of the inner life, and in the development of the new devotional movements from the eleventh century, Augustine's influence was strong. Thenceforward the *memoria Christi* is carefully promoted. *Agere memoriam* is the key to early Franciscan piety. In all the devotions of the Mind of the Passion there is conscious recall of the images of the crucifixion as a means of making real the presence of Christ. The memory stirs sentiment and motivates the will. Memory still has primacy in the *Spiritual Exercises* of Ignatius Loyola, and indeed in some of the English poetry of meditation of the seventeenth century which in this respect as in other aspects of thought and language prolonged a rich medieval inheritance.[1]

Memory, in poetry as in rhetoric, was not only concerned with guaranteeing delivery: it also had to do with invention. The poet's wit, in Dryden's phrase, 'like a nimble spaniel, beats over and ranges through the field of memory, till it springs the quarry it hunted after.' Traditionally, invention was defined as the excogitation of true or verisimilar material selected with a view to making a convincing argument. Late medieval handbooks on school-poetry or preaching or dictamen are much less concerned with invention than with arrangement and style; and the vernacular poets of medieval England were in similar case. Their material was usually at hand: their work most often translation or adaptation. Usually whatever remained of inventive activity was absorbed into the internal organization. In a debate, such as *The Owl and the Nightingale*, or in any composition according to a strict formal pattern, the choice of material was determined less by the need to promote a line of argument and more by its general convenience to the prescribed shape. The actual finding of arguments was restricted to amplification within a frame. Even Chaucer accepts this situation. Indeed in the *House of Fame* he encounters, debates, and politely turns down several

[1] See L. Martz, *The Paradise Within*, New Haven, Conn. (1964).

positive suggestions that might have enabled him to become a
poet of freer invention.

Alliterative poetry in general is different, not necessarily
superior of course, for there are many other things to poetry
beside invention. It is known that many alliterative pieces prove
difficult to classify: the difficulty always obtrudes in discussion of
Piers Plowman and its associated pieces: satire, complaint, preach-
ment, dream allegory, meditation, apocalypse, debate, moral
tract, epic—no label is adequate. There are other difficulties
with *Patience* and *Purity*. There has been debate enough about
Pearl. *St. Erkenwald* is not an ordinary Saint's life. There is difficulty even with *Auntyrs of Arthur*, *The Siege of Jerusalem*, and
Morte Arthure. None of these pieces is quite what a medieval English poem is expected to be like. They all transcend expectation
and strain the limits of genres. The difficulties may suggest that
we are dealing with compositions of individual invention.

At the same time, the alliterative poems present a remarkably
steady view of the poet and his activities. The poet of courtly
verse must show himself as the fresh young lover even if he allows
chronology to belie him: the voice of the narrator in the alliterative poems is always that of a man full of years. The author of
Winner and Waster has nothing but contempt for these modern
beardless boys who jangle as jays and tell their trashy tales
(24–6). The young can neither give nor take counsel. Truth is
declared in the *Parlement of the Thre Ages* by Elde whose 'berde
and browes were blanchede full whitte' (156): in *Mum and the
Sothsegger* by 'An olde auncyen man of a hunthrid wintre' (956).
In the same poem true Wit, taken as an image of the poet, and
surely close cousin to Long Will, is presented as

> Well homelich yhelid   in an holsum gyse,
> Not ouerelonge, but ordeyned   in þe olde schappe,
> With grette browis y-bente   and a berde eke,
> And y-wounde in his wedis   as þe wedir axith.
>   (III 212–15: cf. Introduction, p. xv)

Our alliterative poet is necessarily old in as much as wisdom is to
be acquired through long experience. He remains a practical
man, who knows about the world of affairs, who is eager to
present memorable instruction on public occasions about war
and peace, and on current topics of civil and religious debate.
He is clerkly but his concern is not primarily ecclesiastical. What
he has to say is grounded on a knowledge of common life. He
has an excellent memory for detail, and he is very ready to display it. He has read books, old good books, whose antiquity is

some guarantee of their value. Some of them are hard and misty, but none the less truthful for that. He himself may have to use the hard and obscure words, for what he has to say is often rather special. He is outspokenly contemptuous of mere entertainers, though, to the foolish, he himself may at times appear something of a fool. He is familiar with all sorts of people and yet he stands over against all society with understanding and detachment. He often withdraws; he walks alone to seek a retreat and focuses society through his glass of vision. And to the society he returns to tell the truth and to seek a reward.

We need not believe that many an alliterative poet deserves to be microcosmogrified thus. It gives him too antiquarian a gloss, anticipating even in detail that Minstrel of Sir Walter Scott's who sang the Last Lay. But a certain bookishness in an account of the alliterative poet would be significant. He no longer caters for an oral culture. In his conceit of himself as a sage and gifted littérateur, he is surprisingly like that ideal poet—aloof, high-souled, scornful of scurrility, a devoted amateur in theology, replete with counsel for princes—who was beginning to emerge from Boccaccio's Life of Dante and *De Genealogia Deorum*. All that the alliterative poet lacks is a good classical education. In his homely and wholesome English guise he remains on the side of the Trojans.

The alliterative poet protests that he is to be counted, above all else, a truth-teller. The prologue of the *Gest Hystoriale* treats the theme at length (5–98), lamenting first that many true stories have slipped from mind which could well bring comfort to men's hearts if they were faithfully rehearsed by poets who knew the facts and had studied what happened. This poet then devotes some seventy lines to a justification of his narrative and sources. Nor were such claims entirely specious. The poet of the *Siege of Jerusalem*, though recognizing that he is 'tied to the laws of poesy and not of history', organizes his learned sources with skill and ingenuity. There is a deliberate sobriety of tone and a matter-of-factness about this poem, about the *Gest Hystoriale*, and the Alexander poems which suggest that all of them could have been intended and received as morally authentic histories.

The poets display a similar confidence in their own veracity in *St. John, Joseph of Arimathie*, and in other treatments of faith and scripture. Even in *Sir Gawain* the poet sets his story in a recognized historical frame and vouches for its authenticity.

It would be superfluous to demonstrate the claim to truth-telling in *Piers Plowman*. Truth is the first of the abstractions named, and Conscience, still valiant for truth, accompanies the dreamer out of the poem at the end. With a narrower scope, an anxious search for doctrinal truth is pursued by the poet of *Piers Plowman's Creed* amid the conflicting testimony of human works:

> But all þat euer I haue seyd · soþ it me semeþ,
> And all that euer I haue writen · is soþ, as I trowe.
>
> (841-2)[1]

Mum and the Sothsegger may not be a shiningly eloquent composition but it fumbles to formulate the issue which was to dominate renaissance poetics: how to discern and communicate the realities of political action.[2] The poet confesses that he has looked through old books and consulted living authorities with little success, for they offer principles, and no guides to action. Now, in his sleep of despair he encounters the old Genius of the fruitful garden who gives him exemplary Senecan instruction, urges him to uphold the sacred cause of truth rejecting those 'who fikelly fable & fals ben within', and to look for truth where truth resides:

> Yn man-is herte his hovsing is, as hooly writte techet,
> And mynde is his mansion. . . .
>
> (1224-5)

It is God who breathed the spirit into man,

> For trouthe and þe trinite been two nygh frendes.
>
> (1248)

Langland also had announced this union of truth and the Trinity in the heart of man. In this claim, invention is liberated. Not for these alliterative poets the novelty of the Chaucerian invocation to the Muses for aid. They are much more ready to call upon God in Trinity:

> Maistur in mageste,   maker of Alle,
> Endles and on,   euer to last,
> Now God of þi grace,   graunt me þi helpe,
> And wysshe me with wyt   þis werke for to end.

And again,

> Now grette glorious Godd,   thurgh grace of hym selvene
> And the precyous prayere   of hys prys modyr,
> Schelde us ffro schamesdede   and synfulle werkes . . .

---

[1] *Pierce the Ploughmans Crede*, ed. Walter W. Skeat, EETS 30 (1867).
[2] See A. B. Ferguson, *The Articulate Citizen and the English Renaissance*, Durham, N.C. (1965), pp. 75-87.

And wysse me to werpe owte some worde at this tyme,
That nothyre voyde be ne vayne, bot wyrchip tille hyme selvyne;
Plesande and profitabille to the pople þat theme heres.[1]

A Biblical and an Horatian intention are here consciously brought together.

Frequently the emphasis in presentation reveals the high view of poetry. Some of the poets are interested in expounding the theology of the trinity: in *Piers Plowman* of course; more unexpectedly perhaps in the *Siege of Jerusalem* and in *Joseph of Arimathie*.[2] There is lengthy treatment of the worship of idols in the *Gest Hystoriale*, *Joseph*, the *Siege of Jerusalem*. *Patience* and *Purity* and *St. Erkenwald* take up the same theme.[3] Many of the poems that grow out of canonical or apocryphal scripture developed or emphasized prophetic episodes: the story of Jonah, Belshazzar's feast, the vision of the New Jerusalem, the special insights of the young Daniel in *Susannah*, the oracles delivered before the birth of Alexander, the predictive visions in *Morte Arthure*, *Auntyrs of Arthur*, *Joseph*, and *St. Erkenwald*. To tell of Tobit and truth was ever a proper theme.

The special knowledge spoken of is regarded as being locked up within a man and released by divine command. Speech is the 'spyre of grace' (PP1 B ix, 100). It is the gift possessed by the prophets of old, a Jonah, a Daniel

þat hatȝ þe gost of God þat gyes alle soþes.
His sawle is ful of syence, saȝes to schawe,
To open vch a hide þyng of aunteres vn-cowþe.[4]

Joseph is commanded by God to loose his lips and let the spirit work: and later receives direct instruction from Christ. Passages in *Piers Plowman*, *Winner and Waster*, *Mum and the Sothsegger*, and specifically the collections known as the *Scottish Prophecies* incorporate quasi-prophetic material of a kind first associated in England with Geoffrey of Monmouth's Merlin—allusive allegorical

---

[1] *Gest Hystoriale*, ll. 1–4, p. 1; *Morte Arthure*, ll. 1–3, 9–11; cf. *Death and Liffe*, ed. Sir Israel Gollancz, SEEP v (1930), ll. 17–19; *Chevelere Assigne*, ed. H. H. Gibbs, EETS, ES 6 (1868), ll. 1–4; *Pierce the Ploughmans Crede*, ll. 1–4.

[2] *Piers Plowman*, especially C-Text, XIX–XX; *Siege of Jerusalem*, ll. 97–120; *Joseph of Arimathie*, ed. Walter W. Skeat, EETS 44 (1871), ll. 121–211, 336–44.

[3] *Gest Hystoriale*, ll. 4264–461; *Joseph of Arimathie*, ll. 99–104; 371–402; *Siege of Jerusalem*, ll. 233–6; *Patience*, ed. (Sir) Israel Gollancz, SEEP i (1913), ll. 164–8; (*Purity*) *Cleanness*, ed. Sir Israel Gollancz, SEEP vii (1921), ll. 1341–48; 1719–20; *St. Erkenwald*, ed. Sir Israel Gollancz, SEEP iv (1922), ll. 15–32.

[4] *Cleanness*, ll. 1598–1600.

utterance which continued to exert a real and disturbing influence on politics, often at the fringes of literacy, well beyond
the Middle Ages. The alliterative line with its impressive
sonority and uncertain syntax was an apt medium for oracular
utterance.

The assumptions about poetry shared by the alliterative poets
are, as will be admitted, very ancient. These backward-gazing
poets were drawing upon the oldest traditions of European
poetry. Yet, unconsciously of course within the context of their
own times and with no perspective of what was to come, they
begin to anticipate renaissance poetics. The broad and recognizable channel by which the old ideas were being carried down
the stream to later times is Augustinianism, which even in the
flush of scholasticism had remained a strong secondary current
of thought. It was Augustine, who had provided the English after
the conversion with a theory of inspiration of the Scriptures; and
this theory, as modified by Gregory, had given them their guid-
ing principles of literary composition, that *Bibelpoetik* which has
been a recurrent feature in English poetry. And it was Augustine
above all other fathers of the church who, when studied afresh,
restored and then maintained a powerful Christian imprint on
the new poetics of Europe from Petrarch's time into the seventeenth century. A full evaluation of the literary implications of
the neo-Augustinianism of the late fourteenth century in its
relation to ultra-realist thought could well have important consequences for the understanding of the development of late
medieval poetry in England.

Augustine had sought and found the Trinity in the heart of
man. An understanding of memory overflows psychology and
invades metaphysic. In his great trinitarian analogy of the soul
Augustine had distinguished memory, intelligence, and will,
mutually related faculties, each enveloping the others. A man's
memory stores images abstracted by the intellect out of the flux
and buzz of experience and recalls them for the intellect's use
whenever he has made up his mind to think or speak. In a sense
then—but not in a Platonic sense, though using the Platonic
formulation—we remember, rather than start to learn, in all
acts of knowledge. In *De magistro* Augustine examined this process of thought from a consideration of what happens when we
read scripture or pray to God. We can have a knowledge of God
in doing these things because God is, already and always, there
in the memory. This presence of God within the mind is likened
to the presence of an inner teacher or master and it is this inner

master that illuminates the mind in acts of understanding. In reading to understand, or in prayer, the illumination operates on and activates a whole throng of familiar words in store. In telling the truth, that is in embodying the illumination in words, the reciprocally engaged and reciprocally modifying faculties of the mind working through words afford not only a human model of the Divine Trinity, but their activity is also directly linked with, and powered by, the Trinity in virtue of the illumination. The memory is thus 'a psychological focus through which conversion and reformation are gained out of time, multiplicity, and history'.[1]

None of the alliterative poets turns a steady inquisitive gaze upon his own composing. These poets recognize a gift of grace in themselves, they acknowledge it in scripture. As a group, whatever may have been their social status, they take themselves rather seriously. They also take the use of words seriously. They choose grave themes and believe utterance is powerful. But they have neither the occasion, the interest, nor the vocabulary to examine closely how they write. Their word for memory is still mind: the general agency and treasury of knowledge: *mens pro memoria accipitur*. And mind is much too comprehensive a term for them, or for us, to use in analysis of the mental processes involved in composition.

But the role of illumination in invention can be explored further. There were of course other vernacular writers who followed the workings of the mind and had a specialized interest in illumination, and within the context of their concern were careful and scrupulous in introspection. We are not interested here in the systematic psychology of the devotional and mystical writers such as is given in Chapters 63 and following in the *Cloud of Unknowing*, but with expressive accounts of what actually goes on within a mind engaged in discovering and shaping material which comes eventually to verbal formulation.

The Revelations of Juliana of Norwich describe the evolution of some mental processes which begin in perceptions and end in verbal dictation. On 8 May 1373 this woman, who is called simple and unlettered, experienced in sickness a series of 'shewings'. Some of these shewings seem to have been received as bodily sights, some she calls spiritual: sometimes she is not quite sure which. Some were associated at some stage with verbal

[1] G.-B. Ladner, 'St. Augustine's Conception of the Reformation of Man to the Image of God', in *Augustinus Magister* (Communications: Congrès international augustinien, Paris (1954)) ii, 875.

messages. At the moment of perception the shewings were not self-explanatory; but they were intensely memorable and Juliana considered them to be completely authentic. The Special Shewing, given in the longer version of the Revelations, suggests how understanding of an experience developed. She distinguished three stages: first there was a simple recognition of what the shewing is about; then a conceptual formulation developed; finally emerged a fuller understanding of a total meaning. Juliana regarded this further teaching as coming from Christ as the inner master. Each shewing was found to conceal mysteries which were made clear later by the exercise of the imagination, reminiscence, the association of ideas, and introspection. Even fresh detail was recalled in the original experience as a fuller cumulative meaning was acquired. Doctrine, allegory, scriptural exegesis were incorporated. She only knew what the initial shewing was, when she had fully learned what it meant. The whole process which extended over twenty years had a general educative effect and developed a compulsion to utterance.

The Revelations is the outcome: a precious and affecting document, written in a prose no doubt close to colloquial utterance, but cooled and superficially tidied by Juliana's amanuensis. But as a narration the book is disorderly and can scarcely be regarded as a model of the complete literary act, from conception to organized expression in a controlled medium. For a limited purpose, it serves admirably as an enlarged diagram of the originating phase of composition—a highly informative writing-up as of some laboratory experiments of the way in which invention worked with some medieval writers.

Complementary information about other aspects of the process can, with some difficulty it must be confessed, be extracted from Richard Rolle: in particular from Rolle's *Melos Amoris*, which is perhaps the most adventurous treatise on art by any medieval Englishman. Essentially it is an apologia for poetry, for Rolle's extraordinary gift of song. In this work, the form itself is part of the justification—so dominatingly that as a record of Rolle's experiences and of the stages of inventive activity it is heavily obfuscated by the manner of expression. *Melos Amoris* is organized as a linked series of expansions of scriptural texts and accumulates further verbal material from the scriptures, from service books, and from theological and devotional writings; and it is composed in a sustained alliterative Latin prose, rumbling and incantatory, dispersing meaning to the frontiers of unmeaning. Rolle with a vast, still unplumbed reservoir of phrases to draw upon, is very like an oral poet. He was extraordinarily assimilative, quick, and loquacious.

The process which results in composition begins with the activation of this material, assembled, assimilated, and revolving in the mind. Motion is induced on an act of will by concentrated reading, or by recitation, by psalm-singing, or simply by repeating verbal material. The old materials kindle, melt, and reform.

For page upon paragraph Rolle pursues, captures, and struggles to explain his new and wonderful *melos*. He rejoices in Jesu, in gests of joyful jubilation.[1] The *melos* is the musical vocalization of a truth discerned by the enlightened eye through the window made in the firmament itself where eternal truth is celebrated in angelic song. What Rolle brings thence and endeavours to reproduce in his book is the product of the *musica musa*: not only the unheard melody and jubilation, but a verbal and sonorous expression.

'The Eternal Light purges the mind, really, not imaginatively', Rolle writes in an Augustinian phrase.[2] In this condition when illumination shapes truth inside the mind, the old material in a new order acquires the flow and rhythm and structure of music. Thought has been turned into song.

Rolle's literary position is still very indistinct. Little is known about his sources or about direct influences at work within his intellectual milieu; or about his models in writing and his assumptions about composition. He is the first author within the Middle English period, practising in English as well as in Latin, in verse as well as in prose, to display a cultivated interest in form, style, and the complex art of literate composition. Plainly he attached importance to inherent rhythm and proportion in written composition, no longer completely dependent upon the speaking voice. Alliteration in his own prose and poetry, in Latin and in English, points these musical effects. Most of Rolle's so-called lyrics and other verse pieces are embedded in his didactic prose and then, as if the rising heart has suddenly quickened to the unheard *melos*, utterance becomes metrical. There can be little doubt that he is consciously exploiting an effective device.

What is paradoxical at first sight is that Rolle's English poems appear rough and irregular, so that Miss Hope Emily Allen could write that Rolle had 'no more sense of poetic form than

---

[1] The *'Melos Amoris'* of *Richard Rolle of Hampole*, ed. E. J. F. Arnould, Oxford (1957), p. 42, l. 13.

[2] Ibid., p. 6, ll. 17–18.

a child'.[1] But in discourse designed with a real as distinct from a metaphorical likeness to music, roughness and irregularity are the dynamics of vibrant utterance.[2] Such prosodic accidents of speech will inhere almost automatically in the composition of the oral poet. In literate poetry, these musical features have to be contrived by the poet and introduced by design. We must not repeat simply what Horstman said flatly about Rolle: *He revived the alliterative verse.*[3] The least that can be said, however, is that at the time when a new metrical form of vernacular poetry is developing in England, Rolle had realized the importance of the inner tune in written composition, believed he had caught the tune of a new song, and that his own composition is marked by a number of formal devices, chief among which is alliterative accentuation.

In their different ways Rolle and Juliana contribute to an understanding of the poetic and the practice of poetry that are developed in England and were most characteristically but not exclusively appropriated by the alliterative poets. These poets were making *melos* out of memory. They were transforming the recitative of oral poetry into a literate equivalent where the musical element subsumed in speech was reproduced as a formal feature of written style.

Alliterative poetry is not all of a piece. There is a variety in the composition of alliterative verse, so is there a range of treatment and theme. Nevertheless, as it is more than mere convenience that permits us to speak of alliterative writing in all its variations as one style, so alliterative poems in theme and treatment of theme stand in a continuum: the terms in this continuum are moral insight and historical truth.

On one side of this continuum will stand *Piers Plowman*, in our assessment dominating the whole alliterative achievement. It is this poem above all others that demonstrates how the active memory works in late medieval English poetry.

Modern editors have made the poem increasingly accessible, but we must believe that behind the necessary distinctions of the three texts, there was a sustained attempt by the poet to write one poem. Both the medium, still dependent upon the fluidity of

---

[1] Hope Emily Allen, *Writings ascribed to Richard Rolle* (Modern Language Association of America Monograph Series iii), New York and London (1927), p. 288.

[2] Cf. Northrop Frye, *Anatomy of Criticism*, Princeton (1957), pp. 255–8.

[3] C. Horstman, *Yorkshire Writers: Richard Rolle of Hampole and his followers*, London and New York (1896), ii, *Introduction*, p. xviii.

oral composition, and the method of invention—the elicitation of memory—work to keep the composition continuously exploratory and its language experimental. If we look at Langland's language and his modifications in composition in the light of Juliana's account of her experience and both in relation to the workings of memory, Langland's so-called realism may be regarded as an index of his method. For example, the description of the Tree of Charity—in a passage highly characteristic of the method—is presented with extraordinarily vivid and such extraordinarily inconsistent detail that it cannot be visualized. Such presentations are very much of a kind with the *picturae* which Dr. Beryl Smalley has examined in her accounts of Robert Holcot and John Ridevall.[1] As presented, *picturae* are not description or impressions of things seen, but verbal schemes for conceptualization. In Langland the detail is chosen, rejected, and replaced not with a view to its striking force on the sensuous imagination, but, according to its estimated usefulness, that, when fixed in the memory, it can generate concepts in the mind. The detail is not a penetrating point, but the barb which holds the *imago agens* in position. Invention operates to make abstraction memorable.

But originally, and fundamentally, Juliana's narrative depends upon a series of shewings, physical, imaginary, or conceptual. If we exercise our judgement upon the whole structure of *Piers Plowman* it is possible to detect behind the narrative also a series of illuminations, arbitrary in their initial occurrence, inexplicable in their succession, but accepted by the poet as compelling and authoritative. There is the scene of the field crowded with people, full of noise where a marriage is being arranged; a sight of the crowded court at Westminster; the sight of a man with a cross preaching in a field; a sudden meeting of a queer-looking palmer with a plowman who puts forth his head. There is of course the pardon scene: all these in the *Visio*. Later we may think to identify the dinner at high-table; the sight of a man in a dirty coat selling wafers; of a propped-up tree in an orchard; a scene of tournament and a sight of a man covered with blood; perhaps some ugly civil disturbance in the Antichrist passus. Some of these critical illuminations may have sprung from Langland's private experience, some from meditative reading. Langland's use of scriptural quotation may indicate that he regarded some as locutions. Identification of some

[1] Beryl Smalley, *English Friars and Antiquity in the early Fourteenth Century*, Oxford (1960), pp. 118, 165–83.

of these critical sights and scenes is surely debatable. There will
be others. There can be no doubt that some scenes of this kind
or the fragmentation of such scenes lie underneath the movement and development of the poem and give to the poem its
vertebrate structure. Around these vertebrateś are the accre-
tions of associative memory, the tissue and embodiment of long
experience and further thought and reading. In the A-Text the
sharp signs are still apprehensible by the reader, but even there
they exist behind the exposition and not as presentations of the
original sight.

For Langland it can be assumed that they were important,
but not in such a way that they had to be retained in their original clarity. They were *ferlies*, marvels, for which he had to
work to find the meaning. Indeed as shiny and elusive warrants
of truth, their significance becomes much plainer when their
immediacy and sensationalism is sloughed off and they can be
apprehended as approximations to a universal. This slow and
uneven abstraction from sense image to species to universal
marks the change that, usually with disfavour, critics have observed in the progress from the A- to the C-Text.

From our first reading of the poem we knew that the tearing
of the pardon was a climax. It ends the *Visio*. It can be accepted
now with less puzzlement, that when Langland had finished his
early draft of the poem, he could not explain what the scene
meant. He had to submit it to thought and to the other inner
faculties of the mind to find out. He tried to give some sort of
interpretation in the last four passus of the A-Text. He knew it
had something to do with the life of Dowel. But exactly what,
he has not been able to set out to his satisfaction in the last four
passus of the A-text. In the later revisions he struggles to make
it plainer. The additions in the B- and C-Texts over a period of
many years are, as has often been observed, elaborations of these
concluding passus in A. There is also a short version and a long
version of Juliana's Revelations. She had turned her illuminations over and over in her mind for twenty years; and much of
her final exposition can scarcely be linked directly with any
particular feature of a shewing as she recorded it. All sorts of
things are drawn in. But she never transcends her purpose of
recording her initial experiences. Langland of course goes much
further; and draws out of the experiences the true and verisimilar material from which he makes convincing his argument,
exploring and recommending the life of perfection. This is rare
and fresh invention as medieval writers understood it.

The poetics of the illuminated memory have never been clearly delineated in late medieval England, but they belong to a European tradition of thought which within an Augustinian context and with developed emphases is represented within the work of Dante, Bonaventure, the Franciscan poets, the poets of Chartres, the Latin poets of Anglo-Saxon England and of the Carolingian court.[1] It is a tradition that revives in the sixteenth century, in Puritan poetics, and in some writers of the Counter-Reformation. It is important in the development of European conceptism. It is most familiar to English readers in the works of Vaughan, Traherne, and Milton.

The spangle of illustrious names across centuries serves to emphasize that the English alliterative poets are not the waifs of time, thinly lining the route of English poesy with no standing in its triumph. Late medieval poetry even in England speaks with more than one voice. It should not all be deverbalized into allegorics of charity and into iconography. It is well to remember Eugenio Garin's observation that there were two opposed understandings of poetry among medieval Latin poets: one as pure rhetorical adornment and the other as a moment of supreme insight, vision, an intuition of an idea.[2]

In the English vernacular the alliterative poets offer a characteristic adaptation of this second understanding: none so impressively as Langland. But once the poetics are recognized they can be seen as informing and controlling many other pieces: *Winner and Waster*, *Mum and the Sothsegger*, *St. Erkenwald*, *Death and Life*, *The Three Living and the Three Dead*. They illuminate others; they are peculiarly applicable to *Pearl* with its two great moments of vision.

But the poetics of memory could also be studied in the historical pieces. In them a narrower horizontal window is opened up on the known history of man. For not only do the poets repeat and elaborate their memorial lists of the Nine Worthies. They see unfolded, and assess the common inheritance of fourteenth-century Englishmen: the legacy of Israel; Alexander and the wonders of the East; Troy and the origins of Britain; Arthur and his empire. They trace and join the lines of destiny into sombre patterns of glory and ambition. They offer a fourteenth-century English version of Augustine's vision in the *City of God*, wherein retrospective memory and a prospective intention must

[1] References can be found from Rosario Assunto, *La critica d'arte nel pensiero medioevale*, Genoa–Milan (1961), Index, *s. pittura*.

[2] Eugenio Garin, *Medioevo e Rinascimento*, Bari (1954), p. 52.

of force go together. The apocalyptic mood of the time which Professor Bloomfield has stressed[1] certainly looked towards the coming of the Kingdom of God, but it also anticipated the coming of the Kingdom of God's Englishman.

Time overtook our poets. Even in the fourteenth century they affected an antique fashion. By the late sixteenth century they were superannuated. English people had different ambitions, they were firmly committed to print and heard new tunes of speech in their ears. Most of those who knew anything about the old poetry remarked its provincialism in time and place and speech. The old gests had become dull matter for jesting. Yet something remained and some things were remembered. Let another teacher from the provinces speak. Holofernes in *Love's Labour's Lost* had a revealingly old-fashioned taste. He too composed a poem about hunting wherein he affects the letter. He also celebrated the Nine Worthies, the deeds of the sweet warmen of old. He was in no doubt that he himself had a gift and what he says about it can be applied directly and descriptively to these earlier poets of memory. They, in their time, exhibited 'a foolish extravagant spirit, full of forms, figures, shapes, objects, ideas, apprehensions, motions, revolutions: these are begot in the ventricle of memory, nourished in the womb of *pia mater* and delivered upon the mellowing of occasion'. Let me make Holofernes' complacent conclusion my own: '. . . the gift is good in those in whom it is acute, and I am thankful for it.'

[1] M. W. Bloomfield, *Piers Plowman as a Fourteenth Century Apocalypse*, New Brunswick (1963).

TOWARDS A CHAUCERIAN POETIC

By DEREK BREWER

Read 1 May 1974

IN 'The Prologue' to *The Legend of Good Women* (F. 97–100; G. 81–8)[1] Chaucer makes his most extended comments on literature, and emphasizes three main points: the importance of traditional stories; the problem of belief in them; and his presentation of the 'naked text'. Another point is implicit, his own presence in the poem, even though he refuses responsibility. From here we may make a start towards establishing the nature of his poetic.

We are directed first towards stories, narrative, an aspect of literature which has often been curiously despised by literary critics. A recent treatment of narrative by a philosopher[2] uncorrupted by literary prejudice, Professor W. B. Gallie, effectively demonstrates, using the analogy of games-playing, how a reader of a story must know, or learn by playing, the 'rules of the game'; he must get 'some sense of its point and

---

[1] All quotations are taken from *The Works of Geoffrey Chaucer*, ed. F. N. Robinson, London, Oxford University Press, 2nd edn., 1957.

[2] W. B. Gallie, *Philosophy and the Historical Understanding*, Chatto and Windus, London, 1964, pp. 22–50. E. M. Forster, *Aspects of the Novel*, Edward Arnold, London, 1927, represents the explicit contempt for story-telling as such. P. Zumthor, *Essai de poétique médiévale*, Editions du Seuil, Paris, 1972, maintains that narrative has nothing directly to do with Poetic (p. 177); Dante seems to have regarded *cantio* as the supreme essence of poetry, Zumthor, ibid., p. 189. For helpful analyses of literary narrative, see O. Pächt, *The Rise of Pictorial Narrative in 12th Century England*, Clarendon Press, Oxford, 1962; K. H. Jackson, *Welsh Tradition and the International Popular Tale*, University of Wales Press, Cardiff, 1961; R. Scholes and R. Kellogg, *The Nature of Narrative*, Oxford University Press, Inc., New York, 1966; A. B. Lord, *The Singer of Tales*, Harvard Studies in Comparative Literature, Cambridge, Mass., 1960; D. Mehl, *The Middle English Romances of the Thirteenth and Fourteenth centuries*, Routledge and Kegan Paul, London, 1968; W. W. Ryding, *Structure in Medieval Narrative*, Mouton, The Hague and Paris, 1971; E. Vinaver, *The Rise of Romance*, Clarendon Press, Oxford, 1971. Cf. also *Aristotle on the Art of Poetry*, trans. I. Bywater, Clarendon Press, Oxford, 1920, pp. 36–7: 'The most important (element in tragedy) is the combination of the incidents of the story. Tragedy is essentially an imitation not of persons but of action and life, of happiness and misery.'

purpose', and a range of concepts that will recognize those contingencies that may arise within the rules, and those that should not. We learn about the rules and point of stories from the story itself, and others like it. The quality of understanding involved, says Gallie, is more like *anticipation* than *imitation* of life.

The long and subtle discussion I have so briefly summarized has no literary axe to grind, but it falls in well with certain modern concepts, deriving from quite other arguments about the nature of signs, that a story, a poem, indeed all arts and sciences, are self-enclosed systems, whose essential subject-matter is themselves, not something other, and which may be said in consequence to have a centre of reference within themselves.[1]

This is a very partial truth, both generally and for Chaucer, but it establishes what was neglected in the eighteenth and nineteenth centuries, that poems, and even language itself, have their own ontological status: their validity does not consist only, or primarily, in a *direct* relationship to what is tendentiously opposed to them either as 'real' life or personal expression. They are not only reportage or exhortation, mirror or lamp.[2] We may support the concept of the autonomy of art and language by reference to another philosopher, J. L. Austin, who argues for what lovers of literature feel in their bones, that in some areas of language the very speaking of the word is the doing of the act.[3] There are verbal deeds. Austin refers to this as the performative element in language. He has to struggle hard to release himself from a doctrine of verbal meaning which sees words as essentially labels; a product of a doctrine of 'naïve realism' which seems to have arisen in England in the seventeenth century and is not held consciously by any thinking person, but which still underlies much of our common-sense empiricism and philistinism.[4] The performative element in words which may be seen in such verbal deeds as certain promises and bets, should certainly be extended to include prayers and works of literature, to indicate that the word *is* the deed, and has a certain self-sufficient, self-referring quality. It may be put in

[1] Zumthor, op. cit., e.g. pp. 143, 155, 311; cf. *The Times Higher Education Supplement*, 22 March 1974, p. 15, on F. Jacob, *The Logic of Living Systems*, trans. B. E. Spillman, Allen Lane, London, 1974.

[2] Cf. M. H. Abrams, *The Mirror and the Lamp*, Oxford University Press, Inc., New York, 1953.

[3] J. L. Austin, *How to do Things with Words*, ed. J. O. Urmson, Clarendon Press, Oxford, 1962.

[4] Cf. D. Emmett, *The Nature of Metaphysical Thinking*, 1945, corrected reprint of 1966, Macmillan, London, 1966.

Saussurean and semiotic terms by saying that literature is both *signifiant* and *signifié*, both the sign and what it signifies. I believe this to be generally true, but it is particularly true of literature written before the late seventeenth century. The advantage of recognizing this qualified ontological reality of language and literature is that it frees us from the concept of language as derivative, vicarious, secondhand; and therefore of literature as essentially either escapist or propagandist. When language and literature are recognized as autonomous systems we begin to see the true need for and function of rhetoric. We rediscover the justification, which ordinary language has never needed, of self-referring literary and linguistic devices like pun, proverb, and hyperbole, all banished from educated literature from the late seventeenth century till the early twentieth. The autonomy of language and literature, and the sense that they are their own self-referring self-centred systems, release us from now old-fashioned concepts that narrative is intrinsically un-poetic, that literature necessarily imitates 'life' or expresses the poet's own feelings; that it depends for its validity on referring to 'life' or feeling as a centre outside itself, and that 'realism' is the supreme literary virtue, consisting in careful so-called imitation of that non-verbal universe of appearance which is dignified by the term 'reality'.

When language, literature, and that part of literature which consists in narrative, are thus granted their own autonomy, free even from the creator of the poem, we are justified in seek-ing within each system its patterns, and further inner systems, which exercise controlling power. In the case of narrative, and any particular system of narrative, such as is offered by any given story, we are perfectly well accustomed to seek this inner system, and it is usual to refer to it, as Gallie does, as 'getting the point'. Getting the point of a story is not merely following the narrative sequence, so to speak, linearly and horizontally to find out how it ends, important as that is. As we read a narrative, the operations of memory, anticipation, and dis-covery construct from the sequential experience a hierarchy of impressions, from the most detailed to the most general, which has elaborate interconnections. The art of the correct connection of detail to generality within a narrative may be said to be the true art of reading. A performative verbal structure is thus created in the mind, which in the case of great literature is of the utmost complexity, but which is not in-considerable in any story of merit. Indeed, it is precisely that degree of ability of a story, and a work of literature, to create a complex inter-related structure in the imagination which constitutes its degree of essential value. In the end, literary merit will be found not to consist in its morality, nor its immorality, nor its plausibility, nor insight into human feelings, nor depth of thought, nor revelations of beauty or ugliness, for these are not particularly literary qualities. Any or all of these qualities and others, in that they constitute the referential base of much language, and arouse the sympathies of the imagination, necessarily constitute the subject-matter out of which literature is made; they may determine for an individual reader the attractiveness or otherwise of a work of literature; but the prime *literary* qualities must reside in imaginative verbal structures, and the rhythms with which the act of narration deploys them in order to make them comprehensible.

The multiplicity of connections and significances in a story, which constitute its 'point' or 'points', have been recognized from the earliest commentators on Homer and on the Hebrew Bible. No one knew better than their medieval successors working on classical texts and on the Bible that there are layers of significance in narrative, to be deduced by certain rules. The principles of allegorical exegesis are now well known,[1] and the first question for a purely Chaucerian poetic which considers narrative is whether allegorical meaning is intentionally built into Chaucerian stories. The general answer must be no. First, Chaucer himself, in the passage referred to in 'The Prologue' to *The Legend of Good Women*, emphasizes his interest in the 'naked text' of 'approved stories', which you may believe or not as you like. Since allegory is essentially didactic, and emphatically goes beyond the 'naked text', allegory is denied here. Chaucer's own references to 'glosing', by which allegory is deduced, are normally scornful. Next, Chaucer in his 'Retracciouns' condemns all his secular works as worldly vanities which do not give good doctrine, and these include all his major poems. Finally, internal evidence of the 'naked text' reveals

---

[1] On the exegesis of classical texts see, e.g., Sir J. E. Sandys, *A History of Classical Scholarship*, 3 vols., Cambridge University Press, 1903-8; and J. Seznec, *La Survivance des Dieux Antiques*, Warburg Institute Studies, 11, London, 1940, trans. B. F. Sessions, Bollingen Series xxxviii, New York, Pantheon, 1953; E. R. Curtius, *European Literature and the Latin Middle Ages*, trans. W. R. Trask, Routledge & Kegan Paul, 1953, pp. 203 ff. For medieval biblical commentary, cf. H. de Lubac, 'Exégèse Médiévale', *Théologie*, 41, 42 (1959); 59 (1964); Aubier, Editions Montaigne.

some traces of allegorization, as at the end of 'The Clerk's Tale' (*CT.* IV, 1142–55) and in 'The Tale of Malibeus', but not elsewhere. These particular tales were probably classed among 'the books of legendes of seintes, and omelies, and moralite and devocioun', for which Chaucer in his 'Retracciouns' gives thanks. Chaucer thus gives us a rule which divides secular from devotional narrative. The secular narratives are not allegorical. The devotional narratives have clear traces of allegory, which suggest that were more intended more would be explicit. Another rule is suggested here. Unless there is explicit, internal evidence to the contrary, the face value of a 'naked text' should be accepted, whether secular or devotional.

This does not deny value to recent work, notably by Professor D. W. Robertson,[1] which has argued for the presence of ecclesiastical allegory. The reason lies in the very nature of story. Modern work by Biblical scholars, folklorists, literary historians, and anthropologists[2] has amply demonstrated that stories have significance beyond their face value, without contradicting or invalidating the face value. A story is a system which has its own inner pattern, centre, or point. The better the story the more significant, or complex, its inner sense. Robertson's attempt to reach this inner sense, and to establish a poetic for Chaucer, has been a true response; yet in detail it must be questioned because it places Chaucer in the learned exegetical Latin tradition of the official culture; whereas it seems that the bulk of Chaucer's work must be placed in a different, secular and unofficial tradition, which was in certain respects opposed to the official. One of the reasons for Chaucer's fundamental inconsistency is that he could not in the end, as the 'Retracciouns' show, reconcile the secular with the devotional, the unofficial with the official, as Dante seems to have done.[3]

[1] D. W. Robertson, *A Preface to Chaucer*, Princeton University Press, Princeton, N.J., 1962.

[2] Biblical work is summarized in *Peake's Commentary on the Bible*, ed. M. Black and H. H. Rowley, Nelson, London, 1962; cf. works by C. Lévi-Strauss, e.g. *Structural Anthropology*, Basic Books Inc., New York, 1963 (Penguin Books, Harmondsworth, 1963, original French edition, 1958); *Mythology*, ed. P. Maranda, Penguin Books, Harmondsworth, 1972.

[3] Cf. D. S. Brewer, 'Gothic Chaucer', in *Writers and their Backgrounds: Geoffrey Chaucer*, ed. D. S. Brewer, G. Bell and Sons, London, 1974 (henceforward cited as *WBC*); and D. S. Brewer, 'Notes towards a theory of medieval Comedy', *Medieval Comic Tales*, translated by P. Rickard and others, D. S. Brewer Ltd., Cambridge, 1973. For Dante, cf. M. L. Colish, *The Mirror of Language*, Yale Historical Publications Miscellany 88, Yale University Press, New Haven and London, 1968.

So far what has been said of narrative applies to all, even novels. But the narratives Chaucer uses, whether secular or devotional, have the further specific quality of being traditional, not invented by him, therefore not in any way autobiographical or expressive. Thus he aligns himself with ancient and general human tradition. He seems moreover to have done so progressively, as part of his poetic development. In his earliest poetry, not purely translation, he already reveals his strongly narrative bent, which he uses particularly to embody problems. In *The Book of the Duchess*, *The House of Fame*, *The Parliament of Fowls*, which are modelled on French love-visions of the thirteenth and fourteenth centuries,[1] he shows himself in line with a general development of French poetry from lyric to narrative. Yet they are not purely narrative; nor are they full stories, for these love-visions may well be regarded as narratively expanded first-person lyrics, with the special expressivity that lyrics imply. The forms of Dream and Meeting were especially important in the thirteenth and fourteenth centuries. Chaucer approached even these narrative love-visions from the point of view of provincial English romances which, though he later mocked them, seem to have provided his earliest literary pleasure and to have conditioned his poetic diction.[2] His developing preference for impersonal narrative is further illustrated in *Troilus and Criseyde*. The direct source, Boccaccio's *Il Filostrato*, is, so its author claims, and it seems reasonable to believe, a first-person lament of rejected love displaced into a third-person narrative of romanticized history, or historical romance. Chaucer further removed the first-person element already displaced by Boccaccio, though he retained and even enhanced certain elements of lyric commentary, and did indeed also add the different drama of his own personal engagement with the story. Here he realized, perhaps for the first time following the narrative débâcle of *The House of Fame*, the advantage of using a given story. Boccaccio's *Il Filostrato* was, however, something of a newly invented story, even if a not very original one, and Chaucer made it in a sense less original by making it more

---

[1] J. I. Wimsatt, *Chaucer and the French Love-Poets*, University of North Carolina Studies in Comparative Literature No. 43, Chapel Hill, N.C., 1968, and 'Chaucer and French Poetry', *WBC*, pp. 109–36; Zumthor, op. cit., pp. 306 ff., 376; C. B. Hieatt, *The Realism of Dream Visions*, De Proprietatibus Litterarum, Series Practica 2, Mouton, The Hague and Paris, 1967.

[2] D. S. Brewer, 'The relationship of Chaucer to the English and European traditions', *Chaucer and Chaucerians*, ed. D. S. Brewer, Nelson, London, 1966.

traditional. From *Troilus and Criseyde* onwards Chaucer turned in his poems increasingly towards given, traditional stories, if we except 'The Squire's Tale', which itself collapses as completely as *The House of Fame*.[1] Just after *Troilus and Criseyde* he wrote 'The Prologue' to *The Legend of Good Women* in its earlier form, which mentions the large number of 'old approved stories' to which I have referred. In *The Legend* he retells stories from Ovid on his favourite theme of betrayed women, but when he came to *The Canterbury Tales* the range of sources is much wider. This Gothic manuscript miscellany evades comprehensive generalizations since it includes non-fiction and the 'Retracciouns'. Of itself it challenges the notion of a completely comprehensive poetic. Compared with Chaucer's literary beginnings it contains a high proportion of internationally popular tales, some at least of which were probably current orally. They are placed even more strikingly in a popular setting, not a courtly, let alone an ecclesiastical context. They are an imitation of an episode of popular tale-telling, going on for days, as sometimes happens even in modern times with the Irish *ceilidhe*. A framing device for a series of stories was not uncommon; but this relatively low social level is as unparalleled as the dynamic interplay of character.

Popular may include learned and devotional as well as secular, but the more popular a story is, the nearer it seems to fantasy. The apparently realistic *fabliaux* have plots more fantastic than the romances, and far more so than *Troilus and Criseyde*. Chaucer's poetic progress is from treatment of events of reality and personal experience, such as lay just beneath the surface of *The Book of the Duchess*, to the pure fantasy of 'The Miller's Tale', if pure is the word. We must pause a moment to

---

[1] C. S. Lewis remarked on Chaucer's 'medievalizing' *Il Filostrato* in 'What Chaucer réally did to *Il Filostrato*', *Essays and Studies of the English Association, 1931*, Clarendon Press, Oxford, 1932, pp. 56–75. Probably 'The Squire's Tale' should be dated before the main *Canterbury Tales* period. In it the teller characterizes himself as a 'dul man' (*CT.* v, 279), in accordance with Chaucer's generally self-mocking presentation, but very dissimilar to the Squire who is supposed to be telling the tale. But unlike Chaucer's principal early poems and 'Palamon and Arcite' which became 'The Knight's Tale', the 'Squire's Tale' is not mentioned in 'The Prologue' to *The Legend of Good Women* (cf. *Pro.* F. 420). 'The Squire's Tale' may be in a very special category if it is in part built on a framework of astronomical allusion—a remarkable inner point—as maintained by J. D. North, with much plausibility; 'Kalenderes Enlumyned Ben They: Part II', *Review of English Studies*, N.S., vol. xx (1969), pp. 155–262.

distinguish, within fantasy, the marvellous from the impossibly ingenious, which explains this apparent paradox. In secular tales, specifically romance, Chaucer tends to exclude the marvellous, as far as he can, and even appears to despise it. He always mocks Arthurian romance, that hodge-podge of marvels,[1] and all fairy-tale romance, as in 'The Tale of Sir Thopas'. The romance of *Troilus and Criseyde*, except for the ending, is entirely free of the marvellous. 'The Knight's Tale' has the bare minimum, accepted from the source, *Teseida*. But Chaucer accepts the marvellous in religious tales. This is another general rule. Marvels occur only in religion. When Chaucer brings religious and secular, official and unofficial, cultures together there is always a clash, which is often the source of humour, certainly of ambiguity, perhaps of inconsistency and incompatibility. The outstanding examples are the ending of *Troilus and Criseyde*, where the religious element follows a secular story and accompanies the posthumous marvel of Troilus's apotheosis;[2] and the ending of 'The Clerk's Tale' of Patient Griselda, where jesting secular comment follows the serious marvel, presented with religious overtones, of Griselda's patient obedience. There is a characteristic Chaucerian duality here.

Nevertheless, it is a duality within the general class of fantasy, which occurs in the structure of the stories he uses. His stories, taken from so many diverse sources, though he emphasizes their origin in books, have a natural affinity with folktale and fairytale.[3] This may be partly what causes his reserve. Believe them if you like. They arouse an ambivalent fascination in him, which raises the ultimate problem of truth. But for the moment we notice the structural element. The vast majority of narratives available to medieval men shared this affinity, even if they were not actually folktales themselves, and I include here the Biblical narratives. The marvellous is only one aspect of the general appeal of folktale. There are others. Both Chaucer and Boccaccio seem quite consciously to have dipped into the general folkloric tradition, enjoying especially the popular farcical tales, just as Chrétien in the twelfth century seems to have

[1] There is no doubt of the mockery, though there is also some ambivalence: cf. D. S. Brewer, 'Chaucer and Chrétien and Arthurian Romance', in *Chaucer and Middle English Studies in Honour of R. H. Robbins*, ed. B. Rowland, Allen and Unwin, London, 1974.

[2] J. M. Steadman, *Disembodied Laughter*, University of California Press, Berkeley, Los Angeles and London, 1972.

[3] Zumthor, op. cit., p. 399; F. L. Utley, 'Some Implications of Chaucer's Folktales', *Laographia* iv, Athens, 1965, pp. 588–99.

sought Arthurian folklore, perhaps with different purpose, but in each case seeking a secular, not an ecclesiastical interest. They were the more able to do this because the difference between medieval literary narrative and folklore narrative was one only of degree, with many qualities shared. Oral delivery was still an influence on Chaucer's highly intellectual poetry, just as it still is in that folklore narrative observed by scholars in modern times, in Ireland, Yugoslavia, and Russia. These narratives reflect the ancient general European and Judaic tradition which extends far back behind the written records.[1] Yet this tradition was largely broken in the seventeenth century and it is now extraordinarily difficult to recreate except by natural sympathy, which is in certain respects beyond argument. In the case of Shakespeare, for example, if a person cannot naturally see that the leaden casket, not the gold, should be chosen, and that the man who chooses the leaden casket is *for that reason* the hero, and a good man, there is not much that argument can do, except recommend a course of reading Grimm's *Fairy Tales* and hope that something will click. The situation is even more complex with Chaucer, who is more rationalistic than Shakespeare. If a person does not see that Dorigen and Griselda are good women, Troilus a good man, the duck in the *Parliament* a coarse fool, then, like the terslet, 'I cannot see that arguments avail'. But short of battle, perhaps a consideration of folktale and a reminder of historical perspective may demonstrate that what I hold as certain may at least be possible. The situation with Chaucer is complex because of his own self-contradictoriness. He gives us a popular tale like that of Griselda, and himself expresses pain and incredulity of a quite modern kind; or relates a romantic tragedy apparently of a modern kind like that of Troilus, and himself expresses at the end a detached derision for earthly suffering. Consideration of the traditional tale may help to show how Chaucer was able to utilize its structure for such contradictory effects.

If traditional tales, including modern folktale, Grimm's fairy tales, popular tales of all kinds, classical legends, some Biblical narratives, are borne in mind, we may abstract some general characteristics. Like all stories, they have a 'point'; but the

[1] R. Crosby, 'Chaucer and the custom of oral delivery', *Speculum* 13 (1938), pp. 413–32; A. B. Lord, *The Singer of Tales*, 1960; J. H. Delargy, 'The Gaelic story-teller', *Proceedings of the British Academy*, xxxi (1945), pp. 177–222; M. Lüthi, 'Parallele Themen in der Volkserzählung und in der Hochliteratur', *Laographia* iv (1965), pp. 248–61.

point is not an imitation of what life is 'like', though in the nature of things it will concern a topic of human interest, not necessarily profoundly. Nor is the point necessarily a developing theme which is followed through. The story imitates not 'life' but an earlier version of itself. This is what it is to be traditional. The story is about 'itself', an impression which the fondness of the traditional tale for repeating incidents, and even phrases, much emphasizes. Its basic structure is a series of events to which characters are secondary, and variable, as Aristotle points out, as does the Russian folklorist, V. Propp.[1] The tale may violate naturalistic standards of possibility and behaviour, but it is self-regulating according to its own 'point' or inner centre. Details of narration may refer either to the surface narrative or to the inner centre, or of course to both. The very concept of a traditional, that is, a repeated, tale is a social concept, which enfolds the actual story in a larger entity. Though not a group-product, it is nevertheless a product formed and sometimes modified by the successive minds that have held it, and of the social and literary conventions dominant in the minds of those who tell and those who receive it. And, incidentally, one version of a story may retain features at first devised to fit special circumstances in an earlier version which have themselves altered or disappeared.

The social element is to be seen most clearly in the oral folktale or folk-epic as reported by scholars. A sympathetic audience is required, who knows the conventions. The highly sympathetic Irish scholar Delargy himself comments on how tedious, that is to him and to the modern reader, are certain long interpolations in the oral tale, which are much relished by the traditional audience. The singer or sayer shares with the audience a common stock of conventional, that is 'self-centred', not naturalistic, motifs and themes, and larger segments of story, down through episodes, stock descriptions of all kinds, to formulaic verbal phrases. The singer or sayer usually has a better command of the traditional repertoire than his audience, or he would not be performing his function, but the traditional repertoire does not originate with him, however creative a bearer of the tradition he may be. Even learned poets in the Middle Ages,

---

[1] *Aristotle on the Art of Poetry*, trans. I. Bywater, Clarendon Press, Oxford, 1920, p. 38. V. Propp, 'Morphology of the Folktale', edited with an introduction by S. Pirkova-Jakobson, trans. L. Scott, Indiana Research Centre in Anthropology, Folklore and Linguistics Publication 10, 1958. Cf. Geoffrey of Vinsauf, *Poetria Nova*, ll. 60–2.

trained in rhetoric, were in a similar position. Rhetoric notoriously does not discuss original invention in our sense, but teaches the conventional rehandling of familiar material.

Both folk-singer and rhetorical poet may vary their material and method, but variations themselves follow rules and use familiar materials. Alternatives are usually available from the traditional stock, whether of formula, proverb, or larger section. What is allowable as a variant depends mainly on the specific tradition of the community and language concerned. In Ireland the modern and ancient traditional tale exists as an outline or summary, governed by its inner point, but it has no fixed form. Its specific realization depends on the skill of the individual teller and the circumstances of that particular telling.[1] Learned poets like Chrétien and Chaucer appear to be in a similar relationship to given material, though unlike the oral singer, they practise a *conscious* choice of change within clear limits. They accept the basic story structure, but reinterpret it in various ways.[2] In Chrétien's phrase, they accept the *matiere*, or matter, but provide the *sen*, which is the way the matter is specifically rendered.[3] The method adopted was frequently the insertion of long digressions, that is, by the technical rhetorical device of amplification, which could be used for explanatory monologue as well as various kinds of descriptions and adornments.[4] This is little different structurally from the way in which modern but traditional Irish or Yugoslav singers or sayers of tales, with the general shape of the story in mind, may insert or omit, as circumstance may suggest or require, the formal description of a journey, a battle, a person, or a decorative alliterative run, a king's boastful speech, or a section of dialogue where direct and indirect speech merge into each other.

[1] Delargy, loc. cit., p. 209.

[2] Aristotle, *Poetics*, ed. cit., p. 53. 'The traditional stories, accordingly must be kept as they are. . . . At the same time even with these there is something left to the poet himself.'

[3] Chrétien, *Le Chevalier de la Charrette*, ed. M. Roques, Les Classiques Français du Moyen Age, 86, Champion, Paris, 1958, ll. 1-29. On the topic generally, and in particular on the development by French courtly poets of an explanatory type of narrative in the light of *grammatica* and *rhetorica*, see *The Works of Sir Thomas Malory*, ed. E. Vinaver, Clarendon Press, Oxford, 1967, vol. i, Introduction, pp. lxxiii-xciii. Malory, like Chaucer, appears to be much less thoroughgoing in the establishment of a theme than it is claimed French writers were.

[4] Geoffrey of Vinsauf, *Poetria Nova*, ll. 206 ff., ed. E. Faral, *Les Arts Poétiques du XIIᵉ et du XIIIᵉ Siècle*, Champion, Paris, 1924; trans. M. F. Nims, Pontifical Institute of Medieval Studies, Toronto, 1967.

The language used may be briefly stated here to be as traditional as the matter. The nearer to oral delivery, the more formulaic it is, but both popular and learned poets make full use, as popular language still does, of hyperbole, proverb, sententious apophthegm, mixed metaphor, puns, and wordplay of all kinds, not necessarily comic. This is the performative, creative element in language, where language itself, like the story, has its own autonomy, its own life, and reference to the non-verbal world is not its only validation. But a major distinguishing mark of a good singer or sayer will of course be the skill of his individual verbal realization of his material.

The traditional tale may thus be described in terms of descending generality, from its most general 'point', to its general shape, down to the detail of a possible specific realization. This is how the rhetorician, Geoffrey of Vinsauf, recommends composition at the beginning of the *Poetria Nova*. The tale may be said metaphorically to have two centres of reference or of validating originality, closely similar in nature; one within itself, and one within the tradition. Such a structure has implications far different from those ideas about the nature of language and literature which, though with their roots in the Middle Ages, first began to become dominant in the seventeenth century and still exert an implicit hold on much of our thought about literature. A brief survey of these later notions may remove some difficulties.

The notions were first introduced into English literary culture by Sidney's *Apology for Poetry* (1595), and it is convenient to call them Neoclassical, for the Romantic and Symbolist movements issued from them and altered their balance rather than their quality. A very rough summary of Neoclassical, Romantic, and Symbolist concepts of literature is that the literary text originates in what the writer feels about the world. There are thus two centres of reference for the text: one the poet's subjective feeling, the other, some aspect of 'life'. The text is judged by its personal expressivity, and the accuracy or penetration with which 'life' is described. These notions are still current. The concept of two centres is beautifully illustrated by the modest remark attributed to T. S. Eliot in the facsimile edition of *The Waste Land*.

Various critics have done me the honour to interpret the poem in terms of criticism of the contemporary world, have considered it, indeed, as an important bit of social criticism. To me it was only the relief of a personal and wholly insignificant grouse against life; it is just a piece of rhythmical grumbling. (T. S. Eliot, *The Waste Land: A Facsimile and Transcript*, edited by Valerie Eliot, Faber and Faber, London, 1971, p. 1.)

Expressivity and description in a text not only vary in proportion; they may be dissociated, as Eliot here suggests. Various devices have been used, from Sidney's concept of a second, golden Nature onwards, to unite expression and description. Moral judgement is a favourite one, easily merging into moral propaganda about the state of the world. There is a passionate desire for 'moral realism' with which literary virtue is equated. A Neoclassical reformulation of ancient notions about the superiority of poets to ordinary mortals in moral, realistic, and intellectual terms is equally firmly expressed by Sidney, Milton, Samuel Johnson, Shelley, and, to cut a long story short, D. H. Lawrence.[1]

The development of such concepts of literature and reality, about the subjective and objective worlds, went parallel with, and were perhaps connected to, the new developments in empirical science, which were also connected with new notions about language. Not only scientists and philosophers, but literary critics, deeply influenced by Bacon, Hobbes, and Locke, wanted language to be primarily an instrument of accurate description of ideas and material reality. To put it briefly, words ought to be labels of things. This is effectively to deny all the creative, performative, systematic, and self-referring elements in language, leaving only the descriptive. The seventeenth and succeeding centuries saw the beginning of an attack on rhetoric, on metaphorical language itself, let alone mixed metaphors, on hyperbole, puns, proverbs, all the characteristics of traditional literary language and its sententious or witty aspects, which continued until the middle of the twentieth century, and is still implicit in much criticism.[2] The doctrine

[1] Sidney in the *Apology*; for Milton, cf. I. Langdon, *Milton's Theory of Poetry and Fine Art*, Cornell Studies in English 17, New Haven, 1924; Johnson, *Rasselas*, chapter x; Shelley, *A Defence of Poetry*; D. H. Lawrence, *Selected Literary Criticism*, ed. A. Beal, William Heinemann, London, 1955, pp. 102–18.

[2] For the seventeenth century the main picture is drawn by R. F. Jones, *The Seventeenth Century*, Stanford, 1951, who quotes, e.g., Hobbes's *Leviathan* (1651), and Thomas Sprat, *The History of the Royal Society* (1667); further evidence can be found in Locke, *An Essay concerning Humane Understanding* (1690), Pope, *Peri Bathos* (1727), and in the eighteenth-century editions of Shakespeare. Cf. T. S. Eliot on Hamlet's puns, etc., his condemnation of 'the strained and mixed figures of speech in which Shakespeare indulged himself', and condemnation of the rhetorical style, *The Sacred Wood* (1920), pp. 79, 102, 143–4.

was limited until the twentieth century by moral and social inhibitions, including that of class, but is still strong now that it has lost these inhibitions.

The literary forms which naturally express the basic Neoclassical feeling about literature and language are the expressive autobiographical lyric, and the descriptive novel, which is often much more autobiographical than it seems. A brief glance at almost any modern collection of poems will illustrate the dominant first person, the 'personal grouse', even if no longer rhythmical. The novel's claim to be descriptive may be focused in the frequently reiterated claim that the characters are thought of first, and that the story follows on from their interaction as it would in ordinary life, but coherently, within a stable framework and perspective.[1] Both novel and lyric are private experiences, designed for the solitary reader of print in a quiet room. Imitating life they seek originality, avoid repetition, though they are often paradoxically didactic as well. There are nowadays many signs of change from this essentially Neoclassical position: language and literature, like linguistic thought, are rapidly breaking away. But it is still firm enough to influence ideas about, and often to misconceive, the nature of traditional, pre-Neoclassical literature.

The novel and the lyric are in almost every respect the contrary of the traditional tale, whose general rules we may briefly formulate thus: the story is familiar in general shape, and not personally expressive; the series of events is primary, the

---

[1] L. C. Knights, *How Many Children had Lady Macbeth?*, Gordon Fraser, The Minority Press, Cambridge, 1933, collects statements to this effect from contemporary novelists, and from critics of Shakespeare, pp. 2–5. The doctrine of lyric expressiveness and the primacy of 'life' in combination is illustrated by Ezra Pound's quotation of a late nineteenth-century French critic's condemnation of the Georgian poets because they mastered writing without having 'lived', and sought feelings to fit their vocabulary, rather than words to express their personal passions and ideas: cf. T. S. Eliot, *The Waste Land: a Facsimile and Transcript*, ed. Valerie Eliot, Faber and Faber, London, 1971, pp. 11 and 126. The combination of 'realism' (i.e. a plausible verbal report of commonplace appearances), with autobiography, real or assumed, to create the novel, and oust the prose romance, seems first to begin in Europe under Humanist (i.e. Neoclassical) auspices in Spain in the second half of the sixteenth century. 'The literary ideal of Valdés [a Spanish Renaissance Humanist], in particular, was coherence within a framework of events and characters that could happen and exist in reality; in short, an ideal of realism that was not then, in the 1530's, being exemplified in fiction.' A. A. Parker, *Literature and the Delinquent*, The University Press, Edinburgh, 1967, pp. 5–6, 20.

characters secondary; traditional topics and adornments may be inserted by association, the principle of metonymy, either with the course of events or with reference to the inner point, but they may be omitted. Repetition is optional but agreeable. There is no rule of plausibility. Formal interests determine local subject-matter. Language is often formulaic, self-referring. Wordplay and the sententiousness of conventional wisdom are often present, though instructiveness being the reiteration of commonplaces, it does not confer upon the tale any special status of moral significance or insight, exemplary as the tale may be. The subject-matter is not personal expression. The concept of organic unified development from beginning to end is inapplicable. Rather the form is controlled by a general idea and specific realizations vary according to teller and social circumstance. Hence the multiplicity of narrative, and the wide range of tone, the fluidity of form, which are so surprising, baffling, and indeed offensive to Neoclassical principles of organic unity, decorum, and single-ness of tone.

The natural point of entry into a traditional tale seems to be by following the sequence of events which creates the recogniz-able pattern of the story and which is the ultimate control. Events are the specific realizations of what Propp calls the abstract concept of an event. Two events need not be identical in fact, to be identical in function, as folklorists know, and as practical reading experience shows. The story by the thirteenth-century German, der Stricker, which is called in translation 'The Judge and the Devil', has hardly one detail of narration, except an old woman, in common with Chaucer's 'Friar's Tale', yet they are very obviously in one sense the same story.[1] So we generalize from events to functions and thus to at least part of the general point of the story; or we proceed from events towards greater particularity of story, to the characters associ-ated with events, or to various other attachments to the story which make it more and more specific to that particular telling or version.

The notion that a story has an inner point implies the possibility of symbolic transposition, which is not the same thing as allegory. This possibility will vary according to the story and,

[1] *Sources and Analogues of Chaucer's Canterbury Tales*, ed. W. F. Bryan and G. Dempster, University of Chicago Press, Chicago, 1941, pp. 269–74; *Medieval Comic Tales*, trans. P. Rickard, D. Blamires, and others, D. S. Brewer Ltd., Cambridge, 1973, pp. 72–3.

no doubt, to the ingenuity of the receiver.[1] Obvious traditional examples of great symbolic power and great naturalistic implausibility are the story of the Fall in Genesis, and of Oedipus. Popular tales are frequently popular because they symbolize certain states or situations, or generate pregnant, if familiar, propositions. This is part of the richness of story as literature, and part of the value of an improbable, or impossible, series of events, which create such powerful impressions. Symbolizations of this kind can hardly be said to be themes in the ordinary sense of a recurring yet developing statement which the whole tale is designed to illustrate. They generate rather such obvious sententious comments on life's little ironies as, in 'The Reeve's Tale', 'the biter bit'; or in 'The Merchant's Tale', both the incompatibility of youth with crabbed age and also, that 'a woman is never at a loss for an answer'.[2] They can be more profound: 'The Man of Law's Tale' of Constance embodies the obvious message about constancy and shows it in combination with a flow of natural motherly feeling; but it also embodies concepts of the divisiveness of religion, the loneliness of integrity, the benevolent neutrality of nature. 'The Clerk's Tale' of Patient Griselda, apparently so similar, is very different because it shows the obvious lesson about patient suffering as a good through its *conflict* with the flow of natural motherly feeling.[3] Both tales use the device of repetition of event with only slight variation, but 'The Clerk's Tale' in particular needs to be accepted in traditional terms, as established by the structure of events and the happy ending. Griselda is shown to be good through the series of events that repeatedly test her, and which are the centre of the story. Any naturalistic reading, concerned merely with probability of event, or of motive in her husband Walter, or with his and Griselda's own character and motives as primary and generative of the action, like a novel, turns the story upside down, and not only makes Walter

[1] e.g. C. Lévi-Strauss, op. cit.; E. Herzog, *Psyche and Death*, trans. D. Cox and E. Rolfe, Hodder and Stoughton, London, 1966; H. Zimmer, *The King and the Corpse*, ed. J. Campbell, Bollingen Series xi, Pantheon Books Inc., New York, 1948; and generally, G. C. Jung and Kerenyi, *Introduction to a Science of Mythology*, trans. R. F. C. Hull, Routledge & Kegan Paul; A. H. Krappe, *The Science of Folklore*, Methuen, London, 1930, repr. 1962.

[2] See further, D. S. Brewer, *Chaucer*, 3rd (supplemented) edn., Longmans, London, 1973, pp. 172–82.

[3] D. S. Brewer, 'Some metonymic relationships in Chaucer's poetry', *Poetica*, Tokyo, i (1974), pp. 1–20. The notion of incompatible good values is unfamiliar in modern thought; less so in earlier poetry.

an incredibly monstrous mixture, but Griselda herself a con-
temptible coward who will not protect her poor innocent
children. Such judgements would be only a beginning of the
absurdities and affronts to our sense and sensibilities that any
novelistic reading of the tale offers. Here, if ever, is a tale self-
centred and tradition-centred, arising from a complex amalgam
of traditional stories of testing, traditional concepts of loyalty,
promise-keeping, endurance, masculine and feminine roles, and
so on, which lie deep in the human consciousness and relate to
myth, although Boccaccio's version in the *Decameron* is the first
complete one we know. Since then, a hundred later written
versions and over fifty oral versions have been traced, almost
all derived from Boccaccio, and the tale has been set in the
context of numerous analogues.[1] There can be little doubt that
until our own day the popularity of this tale far surpassed that
of any of those libertine tales for which the *Decameron* is now
renowned. Such widespread appeal of a story which violates all
the canons of a novel is an index of the power of those other
qualities of the traditional tale which I have tried to suggest,
and I cannot believe that such great popularity is totally independent of literary merit, any more than it can be totally
identified with merit.

The question arises: how legitimate is such interpretation?
The nature of the traditional tale frees us from any bondage to
simple intentionalism on the part of the teller, because he did
not invent the tale, and he is in the same relationship to the inner
point as the audience. But he may tell the tale well or ill; or he
may attempt to change it; or as in Chaucer's case with the
Tale of Griselda, he may by a realistic telling call into question
the inner point. Each case must be treated on its merits. What
Chaucer does in this case is to build up a painful tension between
the non-naturalistic 'point' and the naturalistic telling; but the
presence of the tension proves the presence of the traditional
point and meaning.

Troilus and Criseyde offers another case. Here the story structure is relatively thin in contrast with the wealth of naturalistic
detail. Nevertheless an interpretation of the story as such is
necessary if we are to grasp the whole and establish a true hierarchy of connections. The poem is subject to almost as many
interpretations as *Hamlet*, and this in itself offers a clue. Any

---

[1] W. E. Betteridge and F. L. Utley, 'New light on the origin of the Griselda
story', *Texas Studies in Language and Literature*, XIII (1972), pp. 153–208.

general interpretation that does not place a question at the centre of the poem is likely to be too dogmatic. Chaucer tends in his earlier poems to embody a problem in narrative, with his own self as questioning and questing within the poem. That a narrative conveys a problem is a likely rule in Chaucer's poetic. In *Troilus and Criseyde* the named poet is absent from the poem, though many critics put him in as the Narrator, in response to the highly personalized telling, and the quite unusually large number of references to the 'author' or source. The general problem in the earlier poems concerns the deprivation, or even the nature, of love. It comes to a grand climax in *Troilus and Criseyde*, and fades out in *The Legend of Good Women*. More specifically and variously the underlying problem, in *Troilus and Criseyde*, is perhaps how to reconcile the goodness of love with its transience; and beneath it all, there lies that deep sense of loss and betrayal to which Chaucer so often returns in the list of betrayed heroines, which he found in Ovid. Another way of putting the problem at the heart of *Troilus and Criseyde* is that some values are essentially in conflict, as already noted in 'The Clerk's Tale', but occurring in other forms elsewhere; for example in 'The Knight's Tale', and, especially, in 'The Franklin's Tale' where it is found in the clash between *trouthe* and honour.[1] Boethius reflects such problems in the clash between this world and the transcendent world, Fortune and Providence, transience and permanence, and no doubt thus provided Chaucer with the incentive to study and translate the *Consolatio Philosophiae*. It is notable that Chaucer chooses secular, not theological means, to embody this recognition of a common human experience, that sense of fracture between what we know of the world and what we think it ought to be, or indeed was; as Chaucer writes explicitly in a lyric,

> The world hath mad a permutacioun
> Fro right to wrong, fro trouthe to fikelnesse.
> (Lak of Stedfastnesse.)

It is the subject of The Fall of Man, but the Bible as a sacred text was not available to Chaucer for rehandling as secular literature was.

Such generalizations arise out of contemplation of the series of events. A poet may even, in the light of his perception, then remodel in part his original source, and set up a process of

---

[1] D. S. Brewer, 'Honour in Chaucer', *Essays and Studies 1973*, John Murray, London, 1973, pp. 1–19.

interactions, which may or may not be complete in the specific verbal realization of the events, and in the rhythm in which they are deployed. It seems likely that a practising traditional writer will devote most of his conscious attention to the practical art of verbal realization. Chaucer reflects on the need to get to what he calls the 'knot' of the story in 'The Squire's Tale' (*CT.* v. 401). In *Troilus and Criseyde* he comments on the impracticality of a full-blown realism, conscious, as always, of a potentially impatient audience or reader (*TC.* III, 491–504). In *The House of Fame* the Eagle prides himself on making reasons to an ignorant man so 'palpable' that he may shake them by the beaks without any subtlety of speech, scientific terms, figures of poetry, colours of rhetoric (*HF.* 855–69). The series of events was probably visually imagined before being verbally realized. Much medieval French poetry was introduced by the words *je vois.*[1] In 'The Knight's Tale' as in *The Parliament of Fowls* stories are painted on walls.[2] But in particular *The House of Fame*'s account of the Aeneid, with its non-naturalistic, but quite natural synæsthetic blend of reading and seeing, hearing and remembering, suggests how a story was held in mind. Elsewhere, Chaucer varies casually between 'write' and 'say'. The *Gawain*-poet does not only tell, he will *schawe*.[3] Such pictures may be held with varying degrees of fluidity and precision. To judge from Chaucer's verbal realizations, his mental pictures were animated, highly selective, without perspective or over-all view, but with vivid local detail. Chaucer's narratives tend to proceed in scenes, marked by passages of dialogue, monologue, description, or comment, linked by brief passages of transition. On a larger scale that is the structure of *The Canterbury Tales* itself: the Tales being the 'scenes', the links being the transitions. The links, on large or small scale, are more literal, carry less weight of implication, than the scenes.

The structure of events, with their underlying point and potential realization in scenes, constitute the context in which the details operate.

The importance of context is obvious: a small detail of a

---

[1] Zumthor, op. cit., p. 207.

[2] V. A. Kolve, 'Chaucer and the visual arts', *WBC*, pp. 290–319.

[3] A. C. Spearing, 'Patience and the *Gawain*-poet', *Anglia* 84 (1966), pp. 305–29 (repr. *The Gawain-Poet*, Cambridge, 1972), comments on visualization in medieval poetry. Aristotle recommends that the poet should keep the actual scenes of his story as far as possible before his eyes while composing (ed. cit., pp. 60–1). He should first simplify and reduce his story to a universal form before proceeding to lengthen it out by the insertion of episodes (p. 61).

painting is infinitely ambiguous if isolated.[1] The same is true
for words and the larger verbal units of formulae, set-pieces,
topoi. Within fairytales, according to Propp,[2] a function can
only be correctly understood when its place in the sequence is
established. Even stories themselves may require some sense of
context, as in the case of the tale of Patient Griselda, which is
why they may be regarded as centred in tradition, and why
literary texts and language itself can never be completely self-
enclosed, completely self-referring and 'circular'. The context
controls the intention of the story, and is important because it
limits the potential ambiguity of detail. Unlimited free association, especially after six hundred years, which disregards the
poet's intention as revealed by context,[3] is likely to put the
critic in the same position as the Summoner in 'The Friar's
Tale', which is a story to illustrate the supreme importance of
intention in speech. Not understanding this, the Summoner
was carried off to hell.

Traditional story may be said to establish two kinds of context in narrative. One is horizontal, referring to the sequence
of events. The other, which is multiple, may be described as
vertical, cutting across the sequential horizontal line in many
ways and referring variously to traditional topoi, to the
audience, to the general point of the whole sequence. It is a
crude metaphor but may be useful.[4] The horizontal context
proceeds in sections delimited by the non-naturalistic course of
many stories, the shortness of memory, the tendency to move
sharply from one scene to another in narrative. It may also be
interrupted by the vertical context. Hence inconsistencies in
some time schemes, or between widely spaced passages, such as
descriptions in 'The General Prologue' and the same character's
presentation as a storyteller. The Monk is a good example.
There is no more point in trying to reconcile such inconsistencies in a naturalistic way over a long space of the horizontal

[1] See E. H. Gombrich, Art and Illusion, Bollingen Series xxxv 5, Pantheon
Books Inc., New York, 1960, passim, both for the varieties of ambiguity and
the need for establishing a controlling context by empathy with the artist's
or speaker's intention, e.g. pp. 232, 313. Cf. also E. H. Gombrich, Symbolic
Images, Phaidon, London, 1972, p. 4. Without context one thing may
signify various, even contradicting things, says St. Thomas Aquinas, quoted
ibid., p. 14.

[2] Op. cit., p. 19.

[3] Cf. D. S. Brewer in Modern Language Review 68 (1973), pp. 630–4.

[4] Cf. E. Auerbach, Mimesis, trans. W. Trask, Doubleday Anchor Books,
New York, 1957, pp. 14–17.

context than in trying to reconcile the two accounts of Creation in Genesis 1 and 2. We have to dive beneath the surface to discover some more general set of concepts or intentions. The principle of limitation of meaning by intention is often a principle of limitation of applicable context. Verbal phrases may be quite strictly limited. In *The Parliament of Fowls* mythological Venus is described with implications of disapproval (260–73), but when the formel four hundred lines later says that she will not, as yet, 'serve Venus ne Cupide' (652) we are in a different scene and there is no reason why we should not accept the normal face-value meaning of 'Venus ne Cupide' as a synonym for love. Equally, the description of Venus in different poems will have different implications according to how the context establishes her good or bad mythological or planetary qualities.

Formal elements may establish a vertical context, corresponding to the reference to the general tradition. The formal description of a person is an example. Estates literature provided a number of frameworks, on which details might be embroidered.[1] These could be set in a series with a weak horizontal connection and context, such as culminates in the *danse macabre*. In 'The General Prologue' Chaucer establishes a somewhat stronger horizontal context, and a stronger one still in the Links between the tales, and it is interesting to note that the stronger horizontal context in the Links, becoming more and more naturalistic, results in a weaker vertical context.

Occasionally the juxtaposition of contexts results in naturalistic confusion. An example of a horizontal context is the cursive confession, which following Jean de Meung's *Faux Semblant* is three times used by Chaucer as a satirical device, for the Wife of Bath, the Pardoner, and the Canon's Yeoman. It may be considered as partly a grammatical device. Instead of saying 'He or she did, or was, such and such a bad thing' the poet substitutes the first person. The words are still to be taken literally within the fiction. But a vertical context has been introduced by the non-naturalistic formal device and psychological probability, though not satirical and comic effect, is upset.

The Book of the Duchess offers another example, which does not trouble the hearer but only the literalistic scholar. The poet represents himself, in the poem, as overhearing the Black Knight's sorrowful song that his lady is dead (475–86), but yet he appears not to realize what the Knight plainly says.

[1] J. Mann, *Chaucer and Medieval Estates Satire*, Cambridge University Press, Cambridge, 1973; Zumthor, op. cit., p. 135.

There have been many attempts to remove the inconsistency by creating a consistency of the poet's assumed stupidity. In truth the inconsistency is real, but not important, because the poem does not ask for a 'suspension of disbelief' and is not about the dreamer or his character; we look through his eyes at the Black Knight. We forget that the dreamer has overheard the solution to the question he is asking because we are not interested in him, but we identify ourselves with him and accept that he is ignorant if he says so a good many lines later. The reason we can thus interrupt the horizontal context is partly sheer spacing, but also because we accept the strong vertical context, related to the general point of the poem, the death of Blanche the Duchess, which must be unequivocally established early on. The duality of vertical context against horizontal repeats the contrast between death and the progress towards recognition of death, which is part of the greatness of the poem. But a novel-istic creation of the consistently behaving distractingly stupid character of the dreamer is not part of that greatness.

Another example of the two contexts in *The Book of the Duchess* is the formal, traditional description of Blanche. This is 'vertical' because it refers to the tradition. The description is the same for all medieval heroines. It is worth noting that there is no attempt to describe an individual woman. The traditional literary formula absorbs life, not imitates it, and may be truly said to be self-referring.

The notion of horizontal and vertical contexts is meta-phorical and must not be schematically applied. It is a way of describing the multiplicity of reference beyond naturalism, and the importance yet limitation of context, of elaborate traditional literature, especially in Chaucer. *Troilus and Criseyde* offers many examples, some of which may be briefly noted. Troilus's songs and his Boethian meditation do not show that he was a highly educated young man. Nor are Criseyde's sententiously Boethian remarks about transience evidence that she is philosophically inclined. They are lyrical or sententious adornments relating to non-naturalistic vertical contexts. The wonderful scene of Pandarus's interview with Criseyde at the beginning of Book II is on the other hand naturalistic enough within its own limits. Yet it is equally an adornment, not developing the action but enlivening and commenting on it. The characterization of the agents in *Troilus and Criseyde* is clearly secondary to the action, as we know from their difference from Boccaccio's version. In this sense they too share vertical contexts. The character of

Troilus partakes of the idealized and idealizing lover, independent of his actual seduction of Criseyde. His feebleness from
grief in Book v is rapidly succeeded by slaying his thousands.
The hyperboles of weakness and valour are markers of the nature
of his grief and bravery, acceptable as the ordinary hyperboles
of everyday animated language, part of traditional understanding, not plausible descriptions of a character acting in a coherent
framework of events that could happen naturally.

Many passages in *Troilus and Criseyde* must have been slotted
in just as they occurred to Chaucer while he translated with
Boccaccio's text in front of him. Such a process, operating by
association, or metonymy, evoking different contexts, with
local inconsistencies, is a characteristic of the Yugoslav oral
folk-epic singer, *mutatis mutandis*, as it is of the amplification of
the rhetorically trained writer, but of course it violates the Neoclassical naturalistic unities. If the reference to Troilus's loss of
love and life at the beginning of Book iv (l. 27) means what it
seems to mean, Chaucer planned ahead in only the roughest
way, very much like a folk-singer, with just the general shape
of the story in mind. Hence a number of gaps when the story is
considered as a naturalistic structure. Where, it has been asked,
did Pandarus sleep when Troilus and Criseyde spent their first
night together? The narrative is telescoped. Pandarus laid
himself to rest. Are we to imagine he slept on the floor in the
same room? We are not told yes or no. There is no mention of
the palliasse which is quite prominent on a somewhat similar
occasion when Troilus sleeps at Deiphebus's house. Nor is
anything made of the possible fact that Pandarus was sleeping
without pillow or bedding in the same room in which Troilus
and Criseyde were talking and making love in a curtained bed.
The following morning we get a strong impression that he
comes in from outside, which is marginal to the central concern.
Similar gaps exist in *The Book of the Duchess* when the poet
apparently represents himself as taking horse direct from his
bedchamber, and in the uncertainty whether the Wife of
Bath's fifth husband is still alive. The narrative method skips
such gaps because they are unimportant to its purposes.[1]

---

[1] Gombrich, op. cit., emphasizes how few clues we work on in imagining
character and action. Cf. R. Champigny: 'In fiction as opposed to "real life"
we cannot make the implicit explicit by applying causal laws. ... The implicit
meaning of tenses changes when we turn from history to fiction. In both
cases (causality and temporality) a gain in esthetic resonance can correspond
to a loss in cognitive resonance.' *PMLA* 85 (1970), pp. 988–91.

The process of insertion may be seen operating everywhere in
The Canterbury Tales. A literary instance is Dorigen's formal
'complaint' in the often misunderstood 'Franklin's Tale'. It is
an adornment attached to a received story, its formal character
clearly marked by its introduction and diction. The length of
such a passage is no index of its emphasis in the story. It has
some slight horizontal naturalistic context, in that Dorigen
expresses distress. Its formality and content establish a vertical
context, connected with Chaucer's favourite topic of betrayed
women.[1] The passage is not naturalistically expressive nor
symbolic; it is a rhetorical marker to elaborate upon Dorigen's
situation, generalize it within a long tradition, and also to
isolate it. It should be taken at face-value; which is not to say
that it is entirely successful. The analogy that springs to mind here
is that of grand opera, which also has strong popular associations,
and seems often to be regarded by critics as absurdly non-
realistic and unintellectual. Dorigen's complaint is an aria and
fulfils similar functions. The aria breaks the horizontal narrative
context but the vertical context as usual expresses a direct
relationship between text and audience governed by a traditional convention. Within the narrative context of opera
characters are conversing with each other, while actually they
are singing, not talking, and facing the audience, not each
other. The singing is the medium which comments on what is
supposed to be naturalistically felt but only indirectly evoked.
Much the same may be said of Shakespeare's plays. The formal
singing corresponds to the rhetoric in Chaucer and Shakespeare;
it is part of the medium and the tradition, not part of the fiction,
and so must be taken at face value, like Dorigen's complaint, or
the Franklin's own self-description, or the rhetorical art of his
tale, although in naturalistic terms it is inconsistent with what
is supposed to be happening.

Chaucer's rhetoric has been well studied in recent years, and
needs no detailed discussion here.[2] I shall merely point to one
fundamental aspect, alien to much modern thought about
poetry. Rhetoric rests on the ancient concept that there is a
clear distinction in words between inner meaning and outer
realization, which corresponds to the relationship between the

[1] D. S. Brewer, 'Love and marriage in Chaucer's poetry', *Modern Language
Review* 49 (1954), pp. 461–4.
[2] R. O. Payne, *The Key of Remembrance: A Study of Chaucer's Poetics*, New
Haven, 1963; and in *Companion to Chaucer Studies*, ed. B. Rowland, Oxford
University Press, Inc., Toronto, 1969, pp. 38–58.

inner point of a story and its possible specific realization. The inner meaning is what Chaucer calls the *sentence*. He explains this in 'The Prologue' to 'The Tale of Melibee', commenting on the different versions of Christ's Passion given in the four Gospels:

But douteles hir sentence is al oon.
(*CT*. vii, 952.)

Popular feeling and learned medieval doctrine again coincide here, and there is no sense of 'the heresy of paraphrase'. John of Salisbury maintains that the same truth may be conveyed by different words.[1] The *inner* meaning is in control. Words themselves were conceived of as sharing an inner and outer nature, mind and face, in modern terms perhaps *signifié* and *signifiant*. As Gower says, 'The word is tokne of that withinne'. In literature the rhetoricians made use of the same concepts in their remorseless emphasis on variation of language. This is what justifies the fullness, the sententiousness, of rhetorical poetry. Explicitly in 'The Prologue' to 'Melibee' just referred to, and implicitly elsewhere, Chaucer practises the sententious adornment which this non-mimetic use of language encourages. Both popular and learned traditions encouraged proverbs and the sententious style. They survive in ordinary speech even today, like the puns and hyperboles associated with them, though the literalism of Neoclassical principles banished them from polite literature.[2]

[1] John of Salisbury, *Metalogicon*, Libri IIII, ed. C. C. I. Webb, Clarendon Press, Oxford, 1929, IV, cap. 32; trans. D. D. McGarry, University of California Press, Berkeley and Los Angeles, 1962, p. 253. John Gower, *Confessio Amantis*, E.E.T.S., 2 vols. e.s. lxxxi–lxxxii, 1900, vii, l. 1737; cf. v, ll. 1825 ff. For Dante, signs are never identical with their objects, Colish, op. cit., p. 344. The notions that thoughts come first, and that words have an inner mind and an outer face, are remarked by J. Richardson, *Blameth Nat Me*, Mouton, The Hague and Paris, 1970, pp. 29, 35. Once again, T. S. Eliot identifies the contrast with Neoclassical principle. 'A disadvantage of the rhetorical style appears to be, that a dislocation takes place, through the hypertrophy of the auditory imagination at the expense of the visual and tactile, so that the inner meaning is separated from the surface. . . .' (He claims that there is no such dislocation in Shakespeare and Dante.) 'Milton I (1936)', *On Poetry and Poets*, Faber and Faber, London, 1957, p. 143.

[2] Cf. Elizabeth Gaskell, *Wives and Daughters* (1866), ch. 28, 'All proverbs are vulgar'. For classical and medieval Latin background, cf. F. di Capua, *Sentenze e Proverbi*, Libreria Scientifice Editrice Napoli, 1946; Curtius, op. cit., pp. 57 ff. Cf. D. McDonald, 'Proverbs, *Sententiæ*, and *Exempla* in Chaucer's comic tales', *Speculum* 41 (1966), pp. 453–65, for one of the rather rare discussions of this important aspect of Chaucer's style. Pandarus's use of proverbs is a mark of both his common touch and his notable amount of literary expertise.

Chaucer's puns have now been rediscovered. Now we need beware of excess, lest we be misled by the tendency of Neo-classical literalism to disregard intention and context, combined with the modern appetite for sexual obscenity. If we isolate a word or a phrase from its controlling context it is inevitably ambiguous. Traditional poets, like Chaucer and Shakespeare, who use puns and make jesting sexual references are peculiarly vulnerable, if context and intention are disregarded, to perverse modern interpretations. Shakespeare himself identifies and mocks this identical error when he shows Leontes in *The Winter's Tale* taking up Camillo's innocent word *Satisfy* and giving it a totally unwarranted obscene sexual implication. The habit of such misinterpretation should be called 'The Leontes Complex'.

Chaucer's sententiousness, however, still needs rescue. His rhetorical adornment is sometimes taken to be bad poetry, or, to save it, is attributed to that Narrator who is always taken to be a bad poet. The relationship of this Narrator to the poet is sometimes hard to find. Sometimes again the bad poetry is assumed to be ironical. In *Troilus and Criseyde*, Book v, when Criseyde goes to bed in the Greek camp, a beautiful stanza describes the state of the heavens. This has been seen by Pro-fessor Donaldson, the most acute of Chaucer's modern critics, as an ironic cosmic fuss to get a sorry little woman to bed in a tent (v, 1016–22).[1] But a similar passage is applied to Troilus a little later (v, 1107–13) which cannot attract a similar comment. Later still in the poem the poet comments elegiacally that such is this world:

> In each estat is litel hertes reste,
> God leve us for to take it for the beste.
> (*TC.* v, 1749–50.)

This comment fits both horizontal and vertical contexts: it is traditional;[2] it is true; it should be taken at face-value. The anti-rhetorical pressure of Neoclassical literalism, and the Neoclassical desire for originality and rejection of popular social linguistic registers all tempt us to regard such conventional wisdom as banal, therefore at its face value unworthy of a great poet; therefore ironical. But there can be no irony here, because there can be no double meaning: that is, nobody can argue

[1] E. T. Donaldson, *Speaking of Chaucer*, The Athlone Press, London, 1970, p. 78.

[2] Cf. 'Thomas de Hales' Love Ron', *English Lyrics of the Thirteenth Century*, ed. C. Brown, Clarendon Press, Oxford, 1932, no. 43, l. 31.

that the world is really a most enchanting and continuously delightful place, where we are all thoroughly at home. Nor can the banality be regarded as deliberately bad and pompous poetry, because the line does not contain within itself the model of what is being parodied, as the lines of 'Sir Thopas' self-evidently do. The line is not absurd. Parody is important in Chaucer, but its signals are always plain. If this line is bad, then it is accidentally and unintentionally bad. We are meant to take it at face-value. If we fail to recognize the controlling limiting contexts and intentions of the poems, anything and everything may be ambiguous; may be attributed to the Narrator, which means discounting and devaluing it; and chaos is come again.

But there is a contradictory element in Chaucer's poetry which justifies much modernistic criticism, and it is now important to identify its sources. It may be summarized as the establishment by Chaucer of two other centres of validating originality or reference which do indeed correspond to those emphasized by Neoclassical criticism: 'life', and the poet's own self-expression. These have their origin in the Middle Ages too, in our culture, and Chaucer produces a characteristically complex, even inconsistent, combination.

In the twelfth and thirteenth centuries in France new impulses towards making stories intelligible have been detected in both romance and history.[1] Chrétien demonstrates the difference between *sen* and *matiere*, and one way of understanding the *sen* is as an invention of motivation to account for the series of events, which is the *matiere*. A 'varnish' of realism is given to the incomprehensible yet fascinating detritus of Celtic mythology. Succeeding authors of Arthurian romance continue the process, by accepting the ending and main structure of a story, but inventing a beginning to account for it. Boccaccio expands the story of Troilus in the same way. Chaucer continued the process in *Troilus and Criseyde*. 'The end is every tales strengthe' as Pandarus and the rhetoricians say, but the poet has to lead up to the end.[2] In this process we may see part of the root of the novel's imitation of life, though the process is not in itself anti-traditional. It shows the learned secular poet taking more responsibility for his story. In this respect the influence of learned clerical poets, and of the whole Latin tradition, may

[1] Vinaver, *The Works of Sir Thomas Malory*, Clarendon Press, Oxford, 1967, vol. i, pp. lxxiv–lxxxv; Zumthor, op. cit., pp. 361–5.
[2] *TC*. II, 260.

be felt. An elaborate theory of the value and the instructiveness of poetry, deriving both from the ancients and from Christian theology, was elaborated in the Middle Ages in association with Latin, and may be found for instance in the work of Alanus de Insulis, known to Chaucer. Variations of this theory flourish in Dante, Petrarch, Boccaccio, and others.[1]

There is also in French poetry from early on a steady assertion of a truth claim.[2] It has been said that even in the twentieth century the older tellers of Irish folklore believe the marvel tales. Yet such belief is usually specialized, not part of everyday assumptions, and the Irish fairytales often end with a formula which disclaims responsibility—'if there be a lie in it, be it so! It is not I who made or invented it!'[3]

The English tale-rhyme romances frequently assert their truth, and Chaucer tells the parody 'Sir Thopas' *verrayment*—a word he does not use elsewhere—and follows 'Sir Thopas' with the discussion of the relation of variable words to *sooth* in 'The Prologue' to 'Melibee' already mentioned.

The desire for intelligibility and coherence, the greater sense of responsibility of the learned poet, the ambivalent truth claim, all accompany or cause a greater self-awareness in the poet. Much early narrative is introduced by the first-person pronoun. The history of the first-person poem or similar work can be traced back to the third millennium B.C. It occurs amongst the earliest records of our own culture in Genesis 37, perhaps written down in the fifth century B.C. It is significantly associated with dream and vision, which are incontestably events in our lives, yet incontestably subjective, and always the subject of speculation. Medieval poets personalized the dream-vision and made it an extraordinarily useful vehicle, from the twelfth century onwards, for the new feeling about love, also intensely significant and subjective. One of the fundamental activities of all literature is to externalize our inner life, thereby to test it, and share it, and so give it a validity beyond the merely individual. Fourteenth-century dream poems began to develop in a special way what I have called the fourth centre of validating originality, that of the poet's own personal feelings. Machaut, particularly in his last poem, *Le Voir Dit*, appears to approach genuine autobiography, thus reuniting with narrative some of the inner expressivity of the lyric, and yet also reaching

[1] Cf. Brewer, 'Gothic Chaucer', *WBC*, p. 7; Curtius, op. cit., pp. 214 ff.
[2] Zumthor, op. cit., pp. 115–16.
[3] Delargy, art. cit., p. 194.

out directly into the actual world. Professor Kane[1] has established beyond question some degree of actual, if unmeasurable, degree of autobiographical content in the references by Chaucer and Langland to themselves in their poems, which are in ambiguous relationship with their fictional self-representation.

Chaucer uses traditional forms to enable him to respond with unusual fullness to such developments. He positively seeks both the traditional and the new. He imitates the popular storyteller by refusing to take responsibility for the tale, not only in 'The Prologue' to *The Legend of Good Women* but even in 'The Prologue' to 'The Miller's Tale' (*CT.* I, 3167–86) where he clearly has a reader in mind. The older he grows the less he suggests even those hints of personal expressivity found in earlier poems written under the influence of Machaut, and the more he poses as an old-fashioned traditional storyteller, the climax being his own telling of that drasty rhyme 'Sir Thopas', where he represents the traditional gestour, disour, or minstrel whom he must have heard in youth declaiming the English romances. From this point of view Chaucer is the last of the English minstrels who walked wide over the land, whose tone he had early caught, and whose modesty and deference to his audience he adopts, in such contrast to the vatic aura of the traditional primitive court-poet, as in Ireland,[2] or the official didacticism of some medieval Latin poets, or Dante's authority, or Petrarch's avid desire for personal fame as a sage, or Neoclassical claims of the poet's moral and intellectual supremacy. The personal modesty is also to be taken at face value, provided it is not confused with the lack of self-confidence.

Yet the use of traditional tales and forms paradoxically allowed Chaucer to insert into his tales that extraordinary amount of scientific, historical, philosophical, and rhetorical comment which reflects the new desire for intelligibility and comparison with the non-verbal world of actual experience. He also inserted, in various ways, the description of himself which is essentially the product of the new literary and intellectual forces, and which connects the poems with the world of actual experience.

[1] G. Kane, *The Autobiographical Fallacy in Chaucer and Langland Studies*, Chambers Memorial Lecture, University College of London, H. K. Lewis & Co. Ltd., London, 1965, p. 17: 'it is almost certain that the dreamers and narrators of Chaucer and Langland are not fictions in any total sense; that they do mirror to some extent the actual men who created them'.

[2] J. E. Caerwyn Williams, 'The court poet in medieval Ireland', *Proceedings of the British Academy*, lvii, 1971.

There is some variation in his practice. At first, in *The Book of the Duchess*, *The House of Fame*, *The Parliament of Fowls*, he follows Machaut and others and specifically includes himself within the action, thus establishing a real, though equivocal, relationship with the world outside the poem, which thus, through the poet, exerts a pull of validating originality. He slightly characterizes himself as a dull man within the poem, which is obviously absurd. He thus both does and does not extend the autobiographical and expressive interest that was developing among his immediate French predecessors.

In *Troilus and Criseyde* the situation is different. The poet is not within the fiction, nor does he describe himself. Nevertheless, he dramatizes himself as a teller of the story. The effect is to project with greater vigour the varying and to some extent mutually inconsistent successive limited contexts of the narration. The notion of the Narrator, developed by many critics after Professor Donaldson,[1] has helped to reveal the dramatized telling and the multiplicity of points of view in *Troilus and Criseyde*. But the notion that the Narrator represents actually and deliberately bad, or paradoxically bad, poetry in the poem, as a technical device, is unconvincing, because there are no signals beyond the often disputable suggestion that the poetry is bad. There are undoubtedly flaccid or awkward passages in *Troilus and Criseyde*, but there is no evidence that they are intentionally bad, which would be absurd, or parodic. Nor are they directly the subject of a theory of poetic, since good or bad poetry may be produced by the same poetic, as by the same poet. *Troilus and Criseyde* exists first on a literal narrative level of the poet telling a story in terms of direct address to an acknowledged audience, whom we join and who must take at face value at least the beginning and the ending of the poem, though recognizing the rapid changes of tone. Chaucer then takes advantage of the pre-existence of the story, and of the varieties of narrative element provided by traditional forms, to treat the story partly as an independent entity, as a popular storyteller might. But he also represents himself as intensely engaged with, and moved by, the story, in several different ways. Popular tellers are also moved by the stories they tell, but Chaucer's involvement is personal, historical, to some extent responsible, partly contradictory, and ultimately ambiguous. The basic unity of the poem resides in the sequence of events,

[1] E. T. Donaldson, op. cit., pp. 1–12, 65–101.

not in the multiplicity of comment and reaction that it gives
rise to, first in the poet, then in his readers. But much of the
richness of the poem lies in this poetic representation of the
poet's own dramatic attitudes to the story, which make a
sequence of vertical contexts. If the poem is about the poet's
responses to the variety of events that constitute the story,
there is no need to seek a unity within the variety of his presented feelings, attitudes, or judgements. Their variety is allowed
by the limitations of the contexts of traditional narrative, and
held together metonymically by the chain of events, which
carry us through a living process of response where change is
natural. Process is as important as product. From this variety
may be ultimately sifted out a general view, but it will be
complex, and must contain elements whose incompatibility is
hard to resolve.

In 'The Prologue' to *The Legend of Good Women* and in *The
Canterbury Tales* Chaucer once more introduces himself. His
comments, made within the poem, about himself outside the
poem, must sometimes be taken at face value, for example
when he gives lists of his works. He thus increases that uncertainty of perspective and of the limits of the containing
frame, increases the mixing and fluidity of forms, the combination of learned and popular; in a word, he increases that
ambiguity of relationship between art and 'life', which characterizes so much Gothic art, and entitles us to call Chaucer a
Gothic poet.

When the poet describes himself as a 'dull man', as he does
in 'The Squire's Tale', or says that 'The Tale of Sir Thopas'
is the best rhyme he knows, these seem to be examples of the
only kind of self-description in Chaucer's poetry that we cannot
take at face value. Yet they have a special status since they
refer to a character who is not in fact entirely fictitious. There
is thus a tension, or interplay, between the fictional and non-
fictional centres of validating originality. This tension exists,
though not so strongly for us, in some of the other character
descriptions of 'The General Prologue'. Manly's work of
historical identification is somewhat out of fashion nowadays,
but there can be no doubt that some of the characters described
in 'The General Prologue' refer, however problematically, to
real people, and the purely self-contained, self-referring nature
of the poem cannot be maintained.[1] What is peculiar is that

[1] J. M. Manly, *New Light on Chaucer*, Henry Holt Company, 1926, repr.
Peter Smith, Gloucester, Mass., 1959.

the reference outside the poem may be false, as with Chaucer's dullness. The reason for this is that references outside the poem are apparently always satirical, even if only self-satirical. In satire, the ideal is asserted, at the cost of the real person or object in the world. So that in satire Chaucer still in a sense maintains the dominance of the internal reference over the external.

One example will show how equivocal this dominance is; the portrait of the beautiful lady, who is always the same; this topòs absorbs the reality of the Duchess Blanche. The same formula is applied to Alisoun, the wanton village carpenter's wife.[1] The joke is against her. To take one detail: to praise a girl because she is clean, and thus as shiny as a new coin, is evidently comic. It is the more comic in the vertical context of the traditional topos, which is the main context, since the description contributes almost nothing to the horizontal context. There would be little joke without the vertical context, the traditional self-referring topos. Nevertheless, Alisoun is not, like Blanche, entirely absorbed within the topos. That is the whole point. She does not fit. Hence the joke. But in order to make the joke, a competing centre of originating reality has been set up, that of ordinary life, and it pulls against the internal centre. The parody allows the tradition to continue to function with new subject-matter, and so to triumph still. But it is a Pyrrhic victory.

We find ourselves again in an area that might have been designated by our great Neoclassical empiricist, Samuel Johnson, as that where there is always an appeal open from literature to ordinary experience, and, as always, there is a tension between the two.

Chaucer appears to be peculiarly conscious of such tension, and to exploit it, especially in *The Canterbury Tales*. 'The Clerk's Tale of Griselda' is an outstanding example where the realism of his telling of an implausible traditional tale creates an almost intolerable tension. This itself is high virtuosity and it is released by the extraordinary technical virtuosity of the Envoy, totally ambiguous as to fictional status and speaker, breaking every Neoclassical rule of decorum, unity, and frame one can think of.

He exploits the same tension in the variably dramatic propriety of the tales as spoken by their tellers. The

[1] D. S. Brewer, 'The ideal of feminine beauty', *The Modern Language Review* 50 (1955), pp. 257–69.

elegant, patronizing, rhetorically rich 'Miller's Tale' is put in the mouth of a coarse uneducated man. The limited range of context allows Chaucer to put a long speech on true *gentilesse*, undoubtedly to be taken at face value, in the middle of the 'Tale' by the Wife of Bath whose character and expressed opinions are far different. There is no need to reconcile the inconsistency by elaborate naturalistic theories. The confessions of the Wife of Bath, Pardoner, and Canon's Yeoman similarly move between life and literature, defying any purely naturalistic interpretation, and not calling for any elaborate over-all reconciliation, though in limited local contexts they are sufficiently naturalistic to justify many critical insights based on naturalistic premisses.

The tension between literature and life need not be represented as a struggle, though it often leads to paradox. In certain respects it can be represented as the continual effort of literature to absorb life, to hold and fix it, merely moving from traditional methods to newer ones. The parodic use of ancient topoi pours new wine into old bottles. Sometimes the bottles break, but the wine is not lost. The reaching out of Chaucer's poetry into new areas is also demonstrated by the great number of new words in his vocabulary.[1] This does not mean that he introduced such words into English in the sense that he personally invented or naturalized them; but that they are first recorded in his works is significant of his literary absorption of the developing vocabulary.

In Chaucer's use of words, as in some other respects, an intense *literariness* of a rather modern kind is the cause, or effect, of his new realism, as of his new responsibility and intelligibility, all different from the traditional qualities he chose to imitate, or, sometimes, to pretend to imitate. Although he remarks on the possibilities of variation in 'The Prologue' to 'Melibee', Chaucer insists on the preservation of the detailed precision of his words and metrical forms in a way very unlike that of the truly oral poet, and here again we must take his meaning at face value. His success is marked by the fact that hardly any of his scribes 'participated' in the composition of his poems, apart from a few tiny scraps, as they certainly did with other English Gothic poetry,[2] adding, subtracting, or

---

[1] N. Davis, 'Chaucer and fourteenth-century English', *WBC*, pp. 58–84.

[2] Cf. *Piers Plowman, The A Version*, ed. G. Kane, The Athlone Press, University of London, 1960, pp. 126 ff., and J. Mills, *Six English Romances*, Dent, Everyman's Library, London, 1973, Introd., pp. xxvii ff.

changing the order of words and stanzas, taking part in the process of tradition. Even the revisions of *Troilus and Criseyde* that Chaucer pretty certainly made do not much affect the relative stability of the text, for all the carelessness of scribes, and for all Chaucer's own carelessness about certain kinds of naturalistic detail. Even when Chaucer uses 'oral-formulaic formulas' they are normally carefully placed; an imitation of oral delivery quite as much as an example of actual practice. In *The Canterbury Tales* particularly, but also in many aspects of *Troilus and Criseyde*, a reader is clearly envisaged who is likely to be concerned with the accuracy of the text. The accuracy of his text deeply concerned Chaucer;[1] and the implication of this seems to be that the face of the word must accord with its mind; the text must be true to itself. In this respect the development of Chaucer's literariness has moved far towards the precisions of Neoclassical principle and print culture, and away from the formulas of traditional culture.

It may well be that this sharper sense of literary precision, paradoxically balanced against the traditional and popular modes that he partly inherited and partly imitated, contributed to a final dismaying sense in Chaucer that secular fictions were not only incompatible with devotional writing, but that such sustained ambiguity was no longer tolerable. The 'Retracciouns' at the end of *The Canterbury Tales* must also be taken at face value. They are not ambiguous. They represent the non-fictional elements that had already appeared in the earlier fictions: they represent that new desire for intelligibility, responsibility, in the written word; they also represent most strongly the pull of what Chaucer thought of as the real world, and they represent the poet's own sincere, expressive, auto-biographical view. They thus represent those third and fourth centres, as I have called them, which brought so much new life into traditional secular literature that eventually they over-whelmed the popular tradition, as happened in later centuries; and as Chaucer paradoxically forecasts when he denounces his own secular works in favour of a greater moral realism, which destroy literature in the name of that very unsatisfactory substitute, 'life'.

[1] Cf. *TC.* v, ll. 270, 1793–9, and the poem 'Adam Scriveyn'; *CT.* I, ll. 3176–7.

LANGLAND AND THE IDEOLOGY OF DISSENT

By PAMELA GRADON

Read 16 October 1980

PERHAPS one of the most curious conjectures as to the authorship of *Piers Plowman* is the note on the Harleian manuscript of the C-text by the catalogue's compiler: 'Now among the several persons to whom the poems of Piers Plowman have been ascribed,' the author writes, 'I remember not any William; so that if Geffrey Chaucer was the man, he disguised his name for feare of the clergy, who are bitterly inveighed against in these poems.'[1] Scholarship has now established William Langland as the author of the poem, but its nature is still a matter of debate. The anticlerical stance of William Langland gave the poet status as a reformer and Piers Plowman, taken to be the author,[2] blended with Chaucer's Ploughman to become the hero of many a fifteenth- and sixteenth-century poem of social complaint as well as a hero of the Protestant reformation.[3] Bale regarded the poet as *ex primis Iohannis Vuicleui discipulis*;[4] later editors and critics continued to debate the poet's

---

[1] *Catalogue of the Harleian Manuscripts* (London, 1808), ii. 673.

[2] Cf. Thomas Warton, *History of English Poetry*, ed. W. C. Hazlitt (London, 1871), ii. 244.

[3] As well as the well-known fifteenth-century examples *The Ploughman's Tale* and *Pierce the Ploughman's Crede* we may note *The Praier and Complaynte of the Ploweman unto Christe* (*Harleian Miscellany*, vi (1745), 84–106: *STC* 20036); *A proper Dyaloge betwene a Gentillman and a Husbandman* (ed. E. Arber, *English Reprints*, (1871), 129–69: cf. *STC* 6813); *How the Ploughman Learned his Paternoster* (*Reliquiae Antiquae*, ed. T. Wright and J. O. Halliwell (London, 1841), pp. 43–7: *STC* 20034); *A goodly Dyalogue betwene Pyers Plowman and a popysh Pryest* (*STC* 19903); *I playne Piers which can not flatter* (*STC* 19903a); a curious example in this kind is *Pyers Plowman: Man's Exhortation unto the Knights and Burgoyses of the Parlyament House* (*STC* 19905) which is less a complaint of clerical corruption than a pamphlet on enclosures. Cf. M. Aston, 'Lollardy and the Reformation', *History*, xlix (1964), 149–70; A. N. Wawn, 'Chaucer, *The Plowman's Tale* and Reformation Propaganda: The Testimonies of Thomas Godfray and *I playne Piers*', *BJRL* lvi (1973), 174–92.

[4] *Scriptorum illustrium maioris Brytannie . . . Catalogus* (Basel, 1557–9), ii. 673.

indebtedness to Wyclif.[1] In the first part of the twentieth century, however, interest in the historical background receded and R. W. Chambers represented a generation and more of critics when he wrote in 1939: 'The light thrown upon contemporary history ... was only incidental; the poem as a whole tells the story of the struggle of the human soul.'[2] Yet, some forty years on, a recent editor sees Langland again as 'in a way ... in close relation to the Lollards,'[3] and a recent study sees the poem as both an exposition of the Christian ethic and a critique of this, a poem whose poetry grows from the fissures within the clerical ideology of the age.[4] It would thus seem worth looking again at the possible connections between Langland and Wyclif and to consider the implications of the historical material in the light of these investigations.

Any study of the relationship between Langland and Wyclif invites three questions: firstly, is what we know of the chronology and dissemination of Wyclif's work compatible with such a relationship? Secondly, does the text of *Piers Plowman* supply any evidence of such a relationship? Thirdly, how important is such a study to our understanding of the poem as a whole? In reply to the first question, it must be said straightaway that if we accept a date in the late sixties for the A-text, the influence of Wyclif can hardly be in question. For at this period Wyclif, according to modern dating, was writing his logical and philosophical works.[5] The earliest reference to his views on dominion is probably one to be found in a sermon by William Rymyngton delivered in 1373.[6] Whether the author of the A-text could have been acquainted with the preaching of John Ball, whose activities had attracted the unfavourable notice of the authorities as early as 1366, is another

---

[1] Cf. W. W. Skeat, *The Vision of William Concerning Piers the Plowman* (Oxford, 1886), II. xxxviii-liii.

[2] *Man's Unconquerable Mind* (London, 1939), p. 102.

[3] D. Pearsall, *Piers Plowman: An Edition of the C-text* (London, 1978), p. 15.

[4] David Aers, *Chaucer, Langland and the Creative Imagination* (London, 1980).

[5] It is likely that Wyclif's works on logic, physics, metaphysics, and theology were written before 1373. See S. Harrison Thomson, 'The Order of Writing of Wyclif's Philosophical Works', *Českou Minulósti: Essays Presented to V. Novotny* (Prague, 1929), pp. 146-66; id. 'Unnoticed MSS. and Works of Wyclif', *JTS* xxxviii (1937), 24-36, 139-48; J. A. Robson, *Wyclif and the Oxford Schools* (Cambridge, 1961), pp. 115-16. For the suggestion that Wyclif was blacklisted in Oxford as early as 1366 see M. J. Wilks, 'The Early Oxford Wyclif: Papalist or Nominalist', *SCH* v (1969), 98. If such blacklisting existed it was presumably a purely academic affair.

[6] R. O'Brien, 'Two Sermons at York Synod of William Rymyngton', *Citeaux*, xix (1968), 59 and n. 79. I owe this reference as well as many helpful suggestions to Dr Anne Hudson.

question.[1] But what of the B-text? Here we enter a much more difficult area. For to the later seventies, when most critics would suppose the B-text to have been written, belong Wyclif's most important polemical works on doctrine and politics[2] which were to usher in 'a new age in which the tyrant priests would be deprived of their wealth and political power by the lay rulers, and redeemed as new men into a primitive purity.'[3] The impact of this programme can be measured by the schedule of heresies and errors which Wyclif was called upon to answer in 1377.

Moreover, it may be demonstrated that, even if Wyclif's works were unknown to Langland, if the B-text was written in London as its familiarity with the events of 1376 would seem to suggest, he would not have lacked opportunity to imbibe radical ideas; nor do we need to rely for evidence of Wyclif's preaching in the vernacular on his somewhat puzzling reference to his *sermones . . . ad populum*.[4] Indeed he boasts in the *De Veritate* that he has spread

[1] David Wilkins, *Concilia* (London, 1737), iii. 64–5, cf. 152–3.

[2] Gwynn's view that Passus xiii–xx were written not later than 1370–2 has not been generally accepted. See 'The Date of the B-text of *Piers Plowman*', *RES* xix (1943), 1–24. The dating of most of Wyclif's works is a matter of debate. The *Postilla* and the *Principium* are probably from c.1371–5 (cf. B. Smalley, 'John Wyclif's *Postilla super totam Bibliam*', *Bod. Lib. Rec.* iv (1953), 203; id. 'Wyclif's *Postilla* on the Old Testament and his *Principium*', *Oxford Studies Presented to Daniel Callus O.P.* (Oxford, 1964), p. 256; G. A. Benrath, *Wyclifs Bibelkommentar* (Berlin, 1966), p. 8); for other works the dating of the Wyclif Society editors is still in some cases useful, but some later opinions may be noted. The *De Benedicta Incarnatione* is probably 1371–2 or possibly as early as 1370 (cf. M. Hurley, '*Scriptura Sola*: Wyclif and his Critics', *Traditio*, xvi (1960), 280); the *Sermones Quadraginta* are from c.1375–9 (cf. W. Mallard, 'Dating the *Sermones Quadraginta* of John Wyclif', *Medievalia et Humanistica*, xvii (1966); Benrath, pp. 378–86); probably written between 1373 and 1378 are *De Dominio Divino, De Mandatis, De Statu Innocentiae, De Civili Dominio, De Veritate Sanctae Scripturae, De Officio Regis, De Potestate Papae, De Ecclesia, Dialogus, De Eucharistia*, and some of the short treatises such as *De Paupertate* and the *Determination against Binham*. For discussion see H. B. Workman, *John Wyclif: A Study of the English Medieval Church* (Oxford, 1926); A. B. Emden, *A Bibliographical Register of the University of Oxford to A.D. 1500* (Oxford, 1957); for further discussion of *De Civ. Dom.* cf. T. J. Hanrahan, 'John Wyclif's Political Activity', *Med. Stud.* xx (1958), 154–66; E. C. Tatnall, 'John Wyclif and *Ecclesia Anglicana*', *JEH* xx (1969), 19–24; George Holmes, *The Good Parliament* (Oxford, 1975), pp. 167–78; for the *Determination against Binham* cf. J. Dahmus, *The Prosecution of John Wyclyf* (New Haven, 1952), pp. 22–3; for the relative order of *De Civ. Dom.* and the *Determination against Binham* see J. I. Catto, 'William Woodford, O.F.M. (c.1330–c.1397)', p. 175 (unpublished Oxford B.Litt. thesis, 1969).

[3] Michael Wilks, '*Reformatio Regni*: Wyclif and Hus as Leaders of Religious Protest Movements', *SCH* ix (1972), 118.

[4] Iohannis Wyclif, *Sermones*, i, Praefatio, l. 11. References to Wyclif's works are to the editions of the Wyclif Society where these are available.

his doctrines *per magnam partem Angliae*.[1] The Chronicles also testify to Wyclif's preaching activities. Walsingham describes how in 1377 Wyclif preached in the city of London and how, elated by the support of the nobility, he ran from church to church proclaiming his errors to the citizens.[2] In the *Historia Anglicana* he also describes how Wyclif preached his heresies *nude et aperte* to the people of London, who received them gladly.[3] We may perhaps surmise that these sermons were not unlike a famous sermon preached in 1382 by Nicholas Hereford in the churchyard of St. Frideswide's, Oxford, a summary of which is extant in MS Bodley 240. The theme was the abuse of mendicancy and the corruption of the clergy and he calls upon the king to confiscate their possessions.[4] That a similar attack on clerical wealth was made in London in the seventies we know also from a sermon preached at Paul's Cross by Bishop Brinton in 1374 or 1375 in which he denounced those who attacked the temporalities of the church.[5] And while Walsingham's testimony may be suspected of hindsight,[6] that Wyclif was indeed spreading heretical ideas in the seventies seems demonstrated by the charge against him in 1377 that he advocated the confiscation of temporalities. The impact of Wyclif's teaching in London may also be inferred perhaps from Walsingham's story of the intervention on his behalf during the indictment of 1378.[7] Moreover, some evidence from a later date and other areas may also indicate the impact and dissemination of Wyclif's teaching in the late seventies. For example, the statute of 1382 against illegal preaching no doubt reflects, not only increasing ecclesiastical anxiety about the spread of heresy, but also general anxiety about public disorder and sedition in the light of the Peasant's Revolt of 1381. Nevertheless, it seems reasonable to suppose that those men who in the words of the statute 'under pretext of great sanctity' preached without licence 'not only in churches and cemeteries but also in markets, fairs and other public

---

[1] *De Veritate*, i. 349/21-2.

[2] *Chronicon Angliae*, ed. E. Maunde Thompson (RS 1874), pp. 116-17.

[3] *Historia Anglicana (HA)*, ed. H. T. Riley (RS 1863), i. 363; *Chronicon Angliae*, p. 115. For the date cf. Dahmus, *Prosecution*, p. 21.

[4] *vnde si rex et regnum vellet eis auferre possessiones 7 thesauros eorum superfluos ut deberet tunc non oporteret regem spoliare pauperem communitatem regni per talagia sicut solet* (MS Bodley 240, p. 850).

[5] *The Sermons of Thomas Brinton*, ed. M. A. Devlin (CS, Third Series, lxxxv, 1954), p. 48.

[6] For Thomas Walsingham cf. V. H. Galbraith, 'Thomas Walsingham and the St. Albans Chronicle', *EHR* xlvii (1932), 12-30.

[7] *HA* i. 356.

places . . . heresies and notorious errors' did not spring up overnight.[1] Indeed the events of 1381 would tend to support such a contention. The same inference may be made from the instruments against the preaching of Lollard doctrines by the followers of Wyclif in Wykeham's Register[2] and from the letter written by Courtenay to Peter Stokys on 28 May 1382 in which he speaks of 'certain sons of perdition' preaching in his diocese both 'in churches and squares and other public places'.[3] It may also be that Walsingham's denunciation of Wyclif under the year 1382 may have wider chronological implications: *suas damnabiles opiniones, modo per se*, he writes, *modo per sequaces suos, modo scriptis, modo praedicationibus, per totum tempus illud dilatare contendit.*[4] I think we may therefore suppose, in the light of the evidence I have presented, that Langland could well have imbibed the ideas of Wyclif in the late seventies when he was writing the B-text.[5]

It will not have escaped attention that I have made no mention of the vernacular sermons and tracts preserved in the collections of Arnold and Matthew.[6] There is in fact no solid evidence for attributing them to Wyclif let alone to Aston, Repingdon,

[1] *RP* iii. 124-5, item 17. Cf. Dahmus, *Prosecution*, 98-101. For the association of Lollardy and sedition see M. Aston, 'Lollardy and Sedition, 1381-1431', *Past and Present*, xvii (1960), 1-44.

[2] *William of Wykeham's Register*, ii. 337-8, Hants Record Society, 1899.

[3] *Fasciculi Zizaniorum (FZ)*, ed. W. W. Shirley (RS 1858), pp. 275-6.

[4] *HA* ii. 51; cf. *Continuatio Eulogii*, ed. F. S. Haydon (RS 1863), iii. 354-5.

[5] It must always be remembered that heretical ideas may have come from other than Wycliffite sources. There are numerous parallels between the ideas of the Lollards and the Brethren of the Free Spirit, the Waldensians and other continental groups. It has long been thought that there was no heresy in England before the Lollards (cf. M. D. Lambert, *Medieval Heresy* (London, 1977), p. 217). But Eric Colledge has drawn attention to some contrary evidence (see *The Chastising of God's Children*, ed. Joyce Bazire and Eric Colledge (Oxford, 1957), pp. 49-54). We may also note that, in speaking of the flagellants in England, he speaks of 'the indulgent neglect which until the days of the Lollards was the lot of religious enthusiasts in England' ('A Penitential Pilgrimage', *The Month*, xx (1), (1958), 8). It is difficult to believe that there were no beghards or Brethren of the Free Spirit among the Flemings of London, and it is perhaps worth noting that cloth workers were a prominent class in the Lollard movement (K. B. McFarlane, *John Wycliffe and the Beginnings of English Nonconformity* (London, 1952), p. 180). Certainly the ideas of the beghards were known in England. Wycliff speaks of *ratio beghardorum* (Benrath, p. 212 n. 516). This information he may indeed have picked up in Bruges but the heresy was also known to Bradwardine (see H. A. Oberman, *Archbishop Thomas Bradwardine: A Fourteenth-century Augustinian* (Utrecht, 1957), p. 151 and n. 2). Cf. also *De Civ. Dom.* i 177/4-7 and n. 4.

[6] Thomas Arnold, *Select English Works of John Wyclif* (Oxford, 1869-71); F. D. Matthew, *The English Works of Wyclif Hitherto Unprinted*, EETS os 74, 1880.

or Purvey,[1] although some may derive from works by Wyclif. This erroneous attribution dates back to the Catalogue of Shirley[2] and is based on the slightest evidence. It must be remembered that reforming zeal and hostility to the friars were once regarded as evidence of Lollardy. We now know that this is not the case. But there is an even more important reason for questioning the relevance of these texts to the B-text of *Piers Plowman*; there is little solid evidence for their dating. It is not, in my opinion, demonstrable that any of them dates from the seventies; some are datable to the middle or late eighties.[3] Most of them cannot be safely dated at all. It would seem likely, however, that many of them were written after 1382, a period of rapid dissemination of the Lollard movement.[4] I shall not totally ignore the evidence of these documents, but in our present state of knowledge it can only be regarded as suggestive and confirmatory. Students of Langland will realize that such a self-denying ordinance deprives the student of much traditional evidence.[5] It may perhaps be added that it is not even clear that all the tracts are Wycliffite; some express merely anticlerical or antifraternal commonplaces.

We turn now to our second question; does the text of *Piers Plowman* afford any evidence of Wycliffite thought? I shall deal first with passages common to all texts, or common to B and C where A is not extant. Passages peculiar to C (quite few in number) I shall deal with later. The speech of Anima (or Liberum Arbitrium) in B. xv may first engage our attention. Much of the criticism of the clergy with which the speech is concerned is probably not significant. In an age when, as Owst showed, denunciations of clerical corruption poured from the pulpit;[6] in an

---

[1] See Workman, i. 329–32.

[2] W. W. Shirley, *A Catalogue of the Original Works of John Wyclif* (Oxford, 1865), pp. 31–49, has a section entitled *Extant English Works*. This section was omitted in Loserth's revision of 1924.

[3] For discussion of the dating of the vernacular texts cf. E. W. Talbert, 'The Date of the Composition of the English Wyclifite Collection of Sermons', *Speculum*, xii (1937), 464–74; M. W. Ransom, 'The Chronology of Wyclif's English Sermons', *Research Studies of the State College of Washington*, xvi (2), (1948), 67–114; for the tracts see the introductory material in Arnold and Matthew.

[4] For the dating of the Lollard Movement from 1382 see K. B. McFarlane, *Lancastrian Kings and Lollard Knights* (Oxford, 1972), p. 140.

[5] Margaret Deanesly questions the attribution of the sermons to Wyclif in 1920 but her doubts seem to have remained unnoticed by literary critics. See *The Lollard Bible* (Cambridge, 1920), p. 317.

[6] G. R. Owst, *Preaching in Medieval England* (Cambridge, 1926), especially pp. 1–47. It should be noted, however, that Owst does not always sufficiently

age when Parliament records complaints against the concubines of the clergy, against simony and absenteeism, and especially alien incumbents, an age when Parliament further claims that Holy Church is more harmed by such bad Christians than by all the Jews or Saracens of the world;[1] in an age when anticlerical invective even by the laity already had a long history and antifraternal literature was commonplace,[2] it is hardly necessary to invoke the name of Wyclif to explain denunciations of clerical corruption.[3] Nevertheless, there are points of interest in Anima's speech. Some may be mentioned briefly as suggestive merely. Thus the tantalizing reference to tithes which clerics have *wiþouten trauaille . . . þat trewe men biswynken*;[4] or the attack on titular bishops;[5] nor perhaps need we discuss Paull's view that the material on Mahomet shows the influence of Wyclif;[6] his case seems unproven. The reference to the Donation of Constantine might appear more interesting, for Langland here shares with both Wyclif and the vernacular works a reference to the legend of the voice proclaiming the poisoning of the church:[7]

> *Dos ecclesie* þis day haþ ydronke venym
> And þo þat han Petres power arn apoisoned alle.[8]

But, in fact, the legend goes back at least to the thirteenth century and became a commonplace of anticlerical satire.[9] These

distinguish between anticlerical material delivered to the clergy and the same material delivered to the laity.

[1] *RP* ii. 313-14, items 41 and 42; 338, items 97-9.

[2] Cf. P. R. Szittya, 'The Antifraternal Tradition in Middle English Literature', *Speculum*, lii (1977), 287-313.

[3] Cf. John A. Yunck, *The Lineage of Lady Meed* (Notre Dame, 1963). Gower's *Vox Clamantis* gives a notable example of lay criticism of the church by an anti-Lollard writer.

[4] B xv, 488. On tithes see Anne Hudson, *Selections from English Wycliffite Writings* (Cambridge, 1978), note to Text 2, lines 81-7. For the collocation *trewe men* see Anne Hudson, 'A Lollard Sect Vocabulary', *So Meny People Longages and Tonges: Philological Essays Presented to Angus McIntosh*, ed. M. Benskin and M. L. Samuels (Edinburgh, 1981), pp. 15-30.

[5] B xv, 509-10; C xvii, 187-90, 259-61. The references are to the editions of Kane-Donaldson for the B-text and to Pearsall for the C-text.

[6] M. R. Paull, 'Mahomet and the Conversion of the Heathen in *Piers Plowman*,' *ELN* x (i), (1972), 1-8.

[7] See Matthew, 122/33-123/1, 374/22-4, 379/30-380/4, 399/31-3; Wyclif, *Polemical Works*, ii. 575/16-17; *Supplementum Trialogi* (*Joannis Wiclif Trialogus*, ed. G. Lechler (Oxford, 1869), 408/31-409/2); *De Pot. Pap.* 168/32-169/1.

[8] B xv, 560-1; C xvii, 223-4.

[9] Beryl Smalley, *English Friars and Antiquity in the Early Fourteenth Century* (Oxford, 1960), pp. 195-6. For the Donation more generally cf. D. Maffei, *La*

ambiguous passages, however, perhaps assume more importance
when we turn to Anima's climactic apostrophe demanding that
the clergy should live, in Langland's phrase, *per primicias et
decimas*,[1] or in the words of the vernacular tracts *on dimes and
offerings*:[2]

> Takeþ hire landes, ye lordes, and leteþ hem lyue by dymes.
> If possession be poison and inparfite hem make
> (Charite) were to deschargen hem for holy chirches sake,
> And purgen hem of poison er moore peril falle.[3]

A number of writers have suggested that we have here Wyclif's
teaching on dominion.[4] Wyclif's attack on the temporalities of the
church can be traced back at least to 1373 but it is perhaps
sufficient here merely to refer to the charge in the schedule of 1377
that Wyclif taught that *domini temporales possunt legitime ac meritorie
auferre bona fortunae ab ecclesia delinquente*.[5] Yet, while at first sight we
seem to have caught Anima propagating Wycliffite ideas, the
charge is not easy to sustain; for the idea was neither new or novel
when Wyclif advanced it. It had been taught by Marsilius of
Padua and John of Jandun, *damnatae memoriae*;[6] even some of the
Austin Friars, as Gwynn has pointed out, advanced a doctrine of
dominion similar to that which led to Wyclif's heretical stance;[7] its
egalitarian tendencies came to light in the doctrines of John Ball;[8]
it was part of the prophetic programme of John of Rupescissa
whose seventh intention was to devise 'a way of depriving the

---

Donazione di Costantino nei Guiristi Medievali (Milan, 1964). Criticism of the
Donation is common in Wyclif's work but by no means confined to him. Cf. *De
Civ. Dom.* ii. 195/30–196/28; iii. 215/12–218/9; *De Ecclesia*, Bk. xvi; *Dialogus*, 66/
10–17; *Polemical Works*, ii. 670/1–9, 701/7–14, and so on. There may be a veiled
reference to the Donation in B x, 317–20. The Abingdon Chronicle tells of a
traditional association between Abingdon and Constantine (*Abingdon Chronicle*,
ed. J. Stevenson (RS 1858), i, 7–8). A. Gwynn, however, sees a reference to the
Austin friars (*The English Austin Friars in the Time of Wyclif* (Oxford, 1940),
pp. 221–3).

[1] B xv, 556–556a; C xvii, 219–219a.
[2] Cf. Arnold, i. 199/26–8, 282/28–30; iii. 150/18–19; *De Off. Reg.* 52/9–11; *De
Ecclesia*, 308/22–7.
[3] B xv, 564–7; C xvii, 227–32.
[4] Workman, i. 278; Gwynn (1940), p. 223; M. McKisack, *The Fourteenth
Century, 1307–1399* (Oxford, 1959), p. 291; cf. Pearsall, p. 106 (n. to lines 168–71)
for a different view.
[5] *HA* i. 324; cf. *FZ*, pp. 248–9.
[6] *FZ*, p. 243.   [7] Gwynn (1940), pp. 59–73.
[8] R. B. Dobson, *The Peasants' Revolt of 1361* (London, 1970), pp. 370–1, 374;
R. Hilton, *Bondmen made Free: Medieval Peasant Movements and the English Rising of
1381* (London, 1973), p. 227.

universal church of all temporal things'.[1] Nor was the removal of
temporalities from the clergy entirely a novelty. Wyclif claims that
Edward III removed the *temporalia* of the Bishops of Norwich,
Exeter, and Ely *pro contemptu* and held them for twelve years.[2]
Certainly there is evidence of the seizure of Courtenay's temporalities and of those of William of Wykeham,[3] although none of these
cases implies the permanent confiscation of temporalities from the
whole church. A curious example of the blending of practical
politics and reforming zeal which seems to have informed the
argument about temporalities is to be found in the articles which
Bankyn and another Austin friar laid before Parliament in 1371,
arguing the disendowment of the monastic orders in order to
finance the war effort. This was in a sense a special plea designed
to meet a special situation, but nevertheless the articles go to the
heart of a controversy 'that was exciting angry passions' in the
1370s.[4] And it should be noted that the articles conclude with a
citation from Augustine on clerical poverty which Bankyn
adduces in support of his concluding contention that 'a powerful
man who, for their unnatural behaviour, would take from the
monks their possessions and their liberty would be blessed of
God'.[5] In an era when public finance was strained by the war with
France and by the exactions of the papacy,[6] it was perhaps
inevitable that men should look enviously at the church's wealth;
equally, it was perhaps inevitable in an age of anticlericalism that
such a progamme should be supported by moral arguments about
clerical poverty. Therefore, while it must be conceded that our
text echoes both the article against Wyclif of 1377 and the
requirement of clerical poverty commonly voiced in Wyclif, and
while it may perhaps be surmised that the Dreamer has the same
idea in mind when he speaks of Dowel and Dobet as *dominus and*

---

[1] *Vade Mecum in Tribulatione*, ed. E. Brown, *Fasciculus Rerum Expetendarum et
Fugiendarum* (London, 1690), ii. 500.

[2] *De Ecclesia*, 332/4–10; cf. Tatnall, p. 33.

[3] See J. Dahmus, *William Courtenay: Archbishop of Canterbury, 1381–1396*
(Penna. State Univ. Press and London, 1966), pp. 12, 24; McKisack, p. 291.

[4] See Gwynn (1940), p. 216.

[5] *Adonques dit il qe un home puissant estoit beneit de deu qe lour voudreit tolir de lour
avoir et libertes pour lour desnaturesse ensi apperceu*; V. H. Galbraith, 'Articles Laid
before the Parliament of 1371', *EHR* xxxiv (1919), 579–82. For discussion of
this Parliament see Dahmus, *Prosecution*, pp. 8–9.

[6] That anti-papal claims were not confined to the laity is shown by the
curious pamphlet of 1374 in the *Eulogium Historiarum* (cf. Gwynn (1940),
pp. 219–21, and J. I. Catto, 'An Alleged Great Council of 1374', *EHR* lxxxii
(1967), 764–71).

kny3thode,[1] yet Anima perhaps stands out as much as an English patriot as a Wycliffite. Indeed, Anima would have been a credible participant in the famous scene depicted by Walsingham as taking place in 1385, when Parliament responded to Courtenay's refusal to accept lay taxation of the clergy *cum summa furia*, and demanded that the clergy should be deprived of their temporalities as a remedy for their overweening pride.[2]

I shall deal next with a number of passages dealing with the life of the clergy. Wyclif envisaged the dispossessed clergy living in evangelical poverty and innocency of life.[3] Accordingly, passages in Langland advocating clerical poverty have been thought to be Wycliffite. Such a claim has been made by Pearsall for Loyalty's contention that:

> If preestes weren (wise) þei wolde no siluer take . . .
> *Spera in Deo* spekeþ of preestes þat haue no spendyng siluer,
> That if þei trauaille truweliche, and truste in god almy3ty
> Hem sholde lakke no lyflode.[4]

Such a claim, however, is difficult to sustain; still more Skeat's claim that it refers to the 'poor priests'.[5] Wyclif was by no means the first to invoke a clerical age of innocence. Leff has pointed out that a primitive past was invoked in different ways by writers as diverse as Marsilius of Padua, Dante, Ockham, and Dietrich von Niem.[6] While it is difficult to determine the paternity of many of these ideas, they must surely be seen in the wider context of that attempt to return to first principles and to primitive virtues which has always given impetus to Christian reform. The picture in Acts of a primitive church with all things in common has always haunted the minds of Christian writers. When Wyclif writes *omnia*

---

[1] B x, 336.

[2] *Milites Comitatuum, cum quibusdam ex proceribus regni, cum summa furia deprecarentur auferre temporalia ab ecclesiasticis, dicentes clerum ad tantam excrevisse superbiam, quod opus esset pietatis et eleemosynae per ablationem temporalium quae ecclesiasticos extollebant eos compellere ad humilius sapiendum*; cf. *HA* ii. 139–40.

[3] *Clerum . . . deberet esse pauper, similis statui innocencie*: *Dialogus*, 3/17–20.

[4] B xi, 283–9; C xiii, 99–102; Erzgräber thought that the passage in C on the good shepherd (C xvii, 292–3) showed the influence of Wyclif: W. Erzgräber, *William Langlands 'Piers Plowman': Eine Interpretation des C-Textes* (Heidelberg, 1957), p. 223. It could equally well show the influence of Grosseteste (cf. E. Brown, ed. *Fasciculus Rerum Expetendarum*, etc. ii. 260–3); but the image is commonplace. The same may be said of the passage in B xiv, 271–3 (C xvi, 111–13) in which Pearsall sees possible Wycliffite influence.

[5] Skeat, ii. 175.

[6] Gordon Leff, 'John Wyclif: The Path to Dissent', *PBA* lii (1966), 153; cf. Leff, 'The Apostolic Ideal in Later Medieval Ecclesiology', *JTS* xviii (1967).

bona cleri sunt bona pauperum[1] he is giving voice to the concept of a clergy living in humble poverty such as Langland voices in the passages under discussion. But it was a view expressed by many Christian writers, and the phrase itself was commonplace. For example, that writer much read in the Middle Ages, Julianus Pomerius, adjures the clergy that the property of the church is *patrimonia pauperum*,[2] and again that those who live *de evangelio* wish to have nothing of their own but possess all things in common.[3] And within the context of the theme of poverty, all pervasive in the later Middle Ages, it is difficult to suppose that the words from Augustine cited by Bankyn to Parliament in 1371 would not find an echo in the hearts of many in England: *bona omnium pauperum non pauperibus dare sacrilegium est*.[4] And it is to be noted that that reforming patriot Anima uses virtually the same words for the same purpose as Bankyn:

> Ac Religiouse þat riche ben sholde raþer feeste beggeris
> Than burgeises þat riche ben as þe book techeþ,
> *Quia sacrilegium est res pauperum non pauperibus dare.*[5]

The concept of a return to a primitive simplicity of life by an evangelical clergy is to be seen in two other matters which preoccupy both Wyclif and Langland; the matter of the participation of the clergy in the royal administration and in war. The participation of the clergy in the royal administration is criticized by Langland in the Prologue to *Piers Plowman*:

> Bisshopes and Bachelers, boþe maistres and doctours,
> That han cure vnder crist, and crownynge in tokene
> And signe þat þei sholden shryuen hire parisshens,
> Prechen and praye for hem, and þe pouere fede,
> Liggen at Londoun in Lenten and ellis.[6]

It is indeed the case that Wyclif and the Lollards denounced the Caesarean clergy. Thus in the *De Ecclesia* Wyclif claims that strife will never cease in the church until the usurpation of secular office by the clergy ceases,[7] and this consistently held view appeared in

---

[1] *De Veritate*, iii. 41/21-2. Cf. *Sermones*, iv. 274/19-20.
[2] *De Vita Contemplativa*, ii. ix (*PL* lix. 454).
[3] Ibid. ii. xiv (*PL* lix. 458).
[4] Galbraith (1919), p. 582.
[5] B xv, 342-3. For the source of the Latin see Skeat, ii. 226.
[6] B Prol. 87-91; C Prol. 85-9; cf. A Prol. 90-5 (ed. Kane, London, 1960).
[7] *De Ecclesia*, 292/3-7; cf. *De Civ. Dom.* iii. 173/14-176/7; *Opera Minora*, 21, 48/10-49/26; *De Off. Reg.* 27/3-29/10, 52/4-24.

the vernacular writings with equal vehemence.[1] Moreover, in
1376 Wyclif took part in the attack on William of Wykeham by
preaching against him in London.[2] Yet while Wyclif's views
derived from his theories of dominion and were, in a sense,
academic, they corresponded to a political mood in the country
which was hostile to the predominance of the clergy in secular
affairs. Thus in 1371 a group of lay lords petitioned for the
removal of the Bishop of Winchester from the Chancery and the
Bishop of Exeter from the Exchequer.[3] The motives indeed were
secular but they well illustrate an aspect of the late fourteenth-
century attack on the clergy which led Professor McKisack to
characterize the period as one of notable anticlericalism.[4] Langland in this matter, as in others, was as much in tune with his age
as with Wycliffite views.

Denunciations of fighting clerics are common in the Lollard
vernacular.[5] It is not surprising therefore that critics have seen in
the lewed vicory's condemnation of warring popes a reflection of
Lollard thought.[6] It is likely that the wars which broke out
between Urban VI and Clement VII in 1379[7] were the immediate
inspiration of these passages, although a similar protest in the C-
text against warring clerics who *with moneye maynteyneth men to werre
vppon cristene*[8] could have been inspired by the Despenser Crusade
of 1383, another favourite target of Wycliffite and Lollard
invective. The theoretical background is not so easy to determine.
The question of clerical participation in warfare was the subject of
Gratian's attention[9] in the twelfth century and continued to be
debated throughout the Middle Ages.[10] As there were those who
maintained the right of clerics to hold property so there were those

---

[1] Cf. Arnold, i. 270/6-7; Matthew, 168/16-26. Cf. also *The Twelve Conclusions*
of 1395 (see Hudson, 26/62-71).

[2] G. Leff (1966), p. 144.   [3] Cf. *RP* ii. 304, item 15.

[4] McKisack, p. 289.

[5] Cf. Arnold, i. 116/13-16, 123/3-8, 167/9-12; iii. 141/11-29; *The Twelve
Conclusions*, ed. Hudson, 28/135-153.

[6] B xix, 428-9, 442-6; C xxi, 428-9, 442-6. Cf. O. Mensendieck, *Charakterent-
wicklung u. ethisch-theologische Anschauungen des Verfassers von 'Piers Plowman'*
(Leipzig, 1900), p. 83.

[7] See J. A. W. Bennett, 'The Date of the B-text of *Piers Plowman*', *Med. Aev.* xii
(1943), 63. But cf. B. F. Huppé, 'The Date of the B-Text of Piers Plowman',
SP xxxviii (1941), 40-4; Gwynn (1943), 13-14.

[8] C xvii, 234.

[9] *Decretum*, C xxiii, q. viii: A. Friedberg, *Corpus Iuris Canonici* (Leipzig, 1879),
i. 953-65; cf. S. Chodorow, *Christian Political Theory and Church Politics in the Mid-
twelfth Century* (Berkeley, 1972), esp. pp. 223-46.

[10] See F. H. Russell, *The Just War in the Middle Ages* (Cambridge, 1975).

who maintained the right of clerics to take part in war, though not to fight. Wyclif's views on this matter were plain; appealing behind, as it were, the decretals to the earlier authority of Gratian,[1] he denounces the participation of the clergy in bloodshed. Clerical fighting is clearly associated with clerical worldliness. In the *Dialogus* he claims that the endowment of the clergy compels them to take up arms,[2] and in the *De Officio Regis* he devotes chapter xii to the discussion of the just war, and the inevitable connection between a Caesarean clergy and clerical bloodshed. Nor is his posture purely academic; for in the *De Paupertate* he must surely be speaking *ad hominem* when he says: *Peccatum mortale foret ecclesiam Anglicanam . . . ministrare domino papae bona ecclesiae ad expugnandum Cristicolas.*[3] The lewed vicory's indictment of that worldly prudence which involves the popes in warfare is indeed in keeping with the thought of Wyclif but was not without parallels elsewhere in medieval thought.

We have so far considered a number of passages in which Langland might well be thought to express widely held popular views rather than purely the views of Wyclif himself. We may now consider some points of doctrine which might appear to be more fundamental than matters of political import. We may first deal briefly with the topic of penance. There is no question that repentance is an important theme in the poem; nor that Langland condemns the prostitution of the sacrament for financial gain. The confession of Mede and the form of the final Passus of the poem make this clear. What is in question is Langland's understanding of the nature of the sacrament of penance. His views have been seen as contradictory.[4] Thus the Dreamer in Passus xi of the B-text (80-2) appears to argue, in a passage perhaps significantly omitted in the C-text, that *sola contricio delet peccatum.* Such a claim would seemingly match the heresy, known on the Continent,[5] and attributed to Wyclif in the schedule of 1382: *Item quod si homo fuerit debite contritus omnis confessio exterior est sibi superflua, vel inutilis.*[6] Imaginatyf seems to be making a similar claim when he says:

---

[1] Just as he cites Grosseteste in support of an attack on the Caesarean clergy. See Tatnall, p. 41.

[2] *Dialogus*, 8/7-8; cf. also *De Civ. Dom.* ii. 233/24-275/19, iv. 447/35-451/12; *De Pot. Pap.* 388/13-30.

[3] *Opera Minora*, 25/17-19.

[4] For discussion cf. Mensendieck, op. cit., p. 82; Greta Hort, *Piers Plowman and Contemporary Religious Thought* (London, 1938), pp. 130-55; Erzgräber, pp. 227-9.

[5] See R. E. Lerner, *The Heresy of the Free Spirit in the Later Middle Ages* (Berkeley, 1972), p. 90.   [6] *FZ*, p. 278.

For if þe clerk be konnynge he knoweþ what is synne,
And how contricion wiþoute confession conforteth þe soule,
As þow seest in þe Sauter in Salmes oon or tweyne
How contricion is comended for it cacheþ awey synne;
Beati quorum remisse sunt iniquitates, et quorum tecta sunt etc.[1]

On the other hand, we find passages seemingly commending auricular confession. At B xiii, 410-11,[2] Sloth is defined as failure to perform the penance imposed by the priest; at B xiv, 16-21, Conscience recommends contrition, confession, and satisfaction; in the same Passus[3] Patience claims that *shrift of mouþ sleeth synne be it neuer so dedly*. In the final Passus of the poem we find emphasis on true penitence. Thus the horses of Piers' cart are Contrition and Confession[4] and through Contrition and Confession the Dreamer comes to Unity.[5] In B xx,[6] we find confession to parish priests commended and the Battle with Antichrist ends with the theme of penance.

Two points may, I believe, be made about this seeming confusion. In the first place, Wyclif's attitude to the sacrament of penance is not as clear-cut as that of the vernacular writers whose works have influenced comment on this passage. In the *Postilla*[7] and the *Sermones Quadraginta*[8] Wyclif seems to support the orthodox view of the sacrament as including auricular confession. But even in a comparatively late work, such as the *De Blasphemia*, he seems to sanction auricular confession while claiming that when invalidated by the unworthiness of the priest it can still be efficacious if the sinner is contrite.[9] In *De Potestate Papae* he envisages auricular confession as legitimate and meritorious but *preternecessarium quoad salvacionem*.[10] This permissive attitude, while not strictly orthodox, except in its emphasis on the importance of contrition, is far from the angry denunciations of *rowning in the ear* found in the vernacular texts.[11] Secondly, Gratian opens *De Poenitentia* with the following question: *Utrum sola cordis contritione ...*

[1] B xii, 174-7; C xiv, 114-17.
[2] C vii, 71-2.
[3] B xiv, 91.
[4] B xix, 331; C xxi, 332.
[5] B xx, 212-13; C xxii, 212-13.
[6] B xx, 281-4; C xxii, 280-3.
[7] Benrath, p. 147.
[8] *Sermones*, iv. 299/31-3.
[9] 134/9-27.
[10] 310/26-311/2.
[11] Cf. Arnold, i. 196/3-7, 351/4-6; ii. 87/25-8, etc., and Hudson, 20/69-21/80 and note.

absque oris confessione quisque possit Deo satisfacere.[1] That Langland is here indeed dependent on canon law or some derivative seems to be suggested by the line *And þouȝ a man myȝte noȝt speke contricion myȝte hym saue.*[2] For in Canon Law it is stated that *etiam ore tacente* may a man obtain pardon . . . *ut Dominus ostenderet, quod non sacerdotali iudicio sed largitate diuinae gratiae peccator emundatur.*[3] It is, I think, therefore, difficult to sustain the view that Langland's views on the sacrament of penance are Wycliffite; rather I would assume that he is making a debating point to which his protagonists provide a perfectly orthodox answer, although it may not be entirely chance that these orthodox formulations are, in a number of cases, omitted in the C-text.

In discussing a number of short passages from the B-text we have had occasion to note discrepancies between the B- and C-texts. It might therefore be appropriate here to notice two passages in C which might be thought to indicate a sympathy with contemporary dissent before passing on to discuss more widely diffused topics in the poem. The first passage appears in the C Prologue

> ydolatrie ȝe soffren in sondrye places manye
> And boxes ben yset forth y-bounde with yren
> To vndertake þe tol of vntrewe sacrefise.
> In menynge of miracles muche wex hangeth there.[4]

Pearsall comments that 'attacks on relic-mongering were a feature of Wycliffite writing'. To mock relic-mongering, attacked also in the B-text as well as by Chaucer, is not necessarily a sign of religious dissent. But the use of the word 'idolatry' as well as the accusation in line 119 that the clerics allow men to *worship maumettes*, seems to imply that Langland is not attacking merely the fraud implicit in the touting of false relics but also questioning relics and images as objects of veneration. It is certainly true that Wyclif attacks both relics and image-worship although these matters do not occupy the important place in his thought that

---

[1] *Decretum*, C xxxiii, q. iii, d. i (Friedberg, i. 1159). Cf. *Luce clarius constat cordis contritione, non oris confessione peccata dimitti*, ibid. c. xxx (Friedberg i. 1165). Langland's immediate source could have been some such writer as Raymond of Pennaforte. It is worth noting that this work may have been the inspiration of the banquet scene with the Doctor (cf. *Summa de Poenitentia et Matrimonio* (Rome, 1603), 442-5, §§ 8-9; cf. 447, § 13). If so, it would seem to indicate that the fundamental theme of the scene is not learning but penitence.

[2] B xiv, 85.

[3] C xxxiii, q. iii, d. i. c. xxxiv (Friedberg, i. 1166).

[4] 96-9.

they do in the vernacular works. For example, in the *Postilla*, in a commentary on Psalm 135, he compares *sculptilia moderna* to idols and comments tartly on images of Christ and the saints with golden locks and garments encrusted with gold, silver, and jewels.[1] In the *De Ecclesia* too he attacks the abuse of the relic cult and of pilgrimages, another target equally of Lollard polemic and Langland's satire.[2] For avarice, he claims, motivates the buying of relics so that they may become the lucrative objects of pilgrimage.[3] It is also likely, as Jeremy Catto has suggested, that the debate on images antedates the discussion in Wyclif himself.[4] It is worth noting that a story told by Henry Knighton under the year 1382 of a certain William Smith who used an image of St. Catherine as firewood,[5] is told also of a beghard of Cologne who stole images from a church and used them to kindle a fire to keep warm.[6] The passage in the C-text may thus represent an attack on images not necessarily Wycliffite. But it should be noted that even if we date the C-text before 1387 on the evidence of supposed borrowing in Usk, and even more if we accept a date in the nineties, the possibility of Lollard influence exists.[7] Joy Russell-Smith has pointed out that there is no reference to the veneration of images in the schedule of 1382, and she claims that it was only in the nineties

[1] Benrath, pp. 337-8.

[2] See AB Prol. 46-9; C Prol. 47-50; C iv, 122-4. John Burrow is no doubt correct in claiming that the pilgrimage to Truth is polemical ('The Action of Langland's Second Vision', *EIC* xv (1965), 252-3). On the other hand, the reference to pilgrimages at B xiv, 196-8 (C xvi, 39-41) implies that they are potentially good. For a general survey of Lollard views on images and pilgrimages see Hudson, pp. 179-81.

[3] *De Ecclesia.* 465/14-22; cf. *De Mandatis*, 155/26-160/13; *De Off. Reg.* 16/31-3.

[4] Catto (1969), pp. 150-5; cf. also Wyclif's early *De Benedicta Incarnacione*, 42/16-28.

[5] Knighton's *Chronicle*, ed. J. R. Lumby (*RS* 1895), ii. 182-4.

[6] Lerner, p. 118. For the Waldensian disapproval of images see Lambert (1977), p. 154.

[7] For a summary of opinions see E. Talbot Donaldson, *Piers Plowman: The C-Text and its Poet* (New Haven, 1949), pp. 18-19. But if the Ilchester manuscript (London University Library MS v. 88) is correctly dated as not much earlier than the 1390s, the earlier date is more probable (see A. I. Doyle and M. B. Parkes, 'The Production of Copies of the *Canterbury Tales* and the *Confessio Amantis* in the Early Fifteenth Century' in *Medieval Scribes, Manuscripts and Libraries: Essays presented to N. R. Ker*, ed. M. B. Parkes and Andrew G. Watson (London, 1978), 195 n.78). A date in the 80s may also be indicated by the C text of MS Bodley 851, a manuscript which belonged to John Wells who died in 1388. Cf. George Rigg, 'Medieval Latin Poetic Anthologies', *Med. Stud.* xl (1978), 387-407.

that the topic became violently polemical.[1] Thus we find Richard Wiche in 1395 saying that *In primis imponitur me praedicasse quod imagines non sunt adorandae, sed potius igni tradendae.*[2] In 1399 William Sautry, charged with heretical beliefs, asserts that he would rather adore an earthly king than the cross which, as far as he was concerned, was merely wood. Nor was he willing to venerate the bodies of saints.[3] Furthermore, the public concern which such matters were attracting in the 1390s is indicated by the following item in *The Twelve Conclusions* of 1395: *þe pilgrimage, preyeris and offringis made to blynde rodys and to deue ymages of tre and of ston, ben ner of kin to ydolatrie and fer fro almesse dede.*[4] But however we date the C-text, it is probably true to say that here again Langland may be reflecting contemporary controversy rather than academic debate.

But could we assume that Langland heard such matter discussed among the Lollers of Cornhill? I think this is unlikely. Discussion of the term *loller* is made more difficult by the conflicting manuscript evidence. In the relevant passages in Passus v, viii, and ix[5] there is occasional variation between the terms *lorel* and *loller* (especially in Cotton Vespasian B xvi) and sometimes *lollard*, a reading often found in Douce 104, but in one instance only shared with other manuscripts.[6] It should be noted, however, that at Passus ix, 215-18 all manuscripts agree in the readings *lolleth* and *lollen*:

> He þat lolleth is lame . . .
> Rihte so sothly such manere ermytes
> Lollen aȝen þe byleue and þe lawe of holy churche.

This agreement of all the manuscript witnesses would seem to substantiate Langland's assignment of the meaning 'to lean, to limp' and thus 'to be idle', a sense recorded in English dialects.[7] These *lollers* are often associated in Langland with *lewed hermits*,

[1] J. Russell-Smith, 'Walter Hilton and a Tract in Defence of the Veneration of Images', *Dominican Studies*, vii (1954), 180-214.

[2] *FZ*, p. 370.

[3] Ibid., pp. 408-9.

[4] Hudson, 27/93-6.

[5] v, 2, 4, 31; viii, 74, 287; ix, 101, 103, 107, 137, 140, 158, 159, 192, 194 (some MSS), 213, 240. For the affiliation of the manuscripts cf. Donaldson. 227-31. At ix, 137 Pearsall's reading *loreles* appears only in XMDYI. The reading should perhaps be *lolleres*.

[6] Namely at v, 4 where the reading also appears in BL MSS Add. 34779, Harley 2376 and Cambridge CUL Ff. 5. 35. *Lorel* for *loller* appears at v, 2 and 4; viii, 75; ix, 103, 107 also in Royal 18 B xvii; at viii, 75 also in Douce 104.

[7] See *EDD* LOLL *v*¹ and *sb*¹; LOLLARD *sb*.

hermits who live under no fixed rule and have no fixed abode. But it would seem from Passus ix, 246-56 that the *lollers* are not heretics, for they are pictured as occupying a position of dignity and, unless the odd change of number indicates an omission in the text, to be under the protection of the bishop.

> Ac aboute mydday at mele-tyme y mette with hem ofte,
> Come in his cope as he a clerk were;
> A bacheler or a bew-pere beste hym bysemede,
> And for þe cloth þat keuereth hym ykald he is a frere,
> Wascheth and wypeth and with the furste sitteth.
>
> .   .   .   .
>
> The cause of al this caytiftee cometh of many bischopes
> That soffreth such sottes and oþere synnes regne ...

It appears from Passus ix, 139 that these *lollers* bear *bagges* and *botels* under their cloaks and they are again compared to 'lewd hermits'. They are idlers who earn their living by begging presumably with the sanction, or at least with the connivance, of the bishop. Moreover, while the word *Lollard* as a term of abuse in England dates from 1382,[1] it does not appear to become widespread until the nineties when it is so used by Gower.[2] The word *Lollard* originally used to describe various kind of continental heretic[3] seems to have become blended in England both with the word *loller* 'idler', *gyrovagus*, and with *lolia* 'tares'; Lollards are thus those who *springen cokkel in our clene corn*.[4] In Langland the reference may be to *gyrovagi*, wandering religious who had left their houses and joined the numerous wayfarers who infested fourteenth-century England. As for the *lunatick lollers*,[5] it seems to me that they are most likely to be itinerant prophets as Donaldson suggested.[6] Whether such prophets were heretical it is difficult to say, but it may be worth noting that, while various heretical sects in the Middle Ages such as the Fraticelli, the Apostolic Brethren, and the Joachists concerned themselves with

---

[1] Cf. James Crompton, 'The Leicestershire Lollards', *The Leicestershire Archaeological and Historical Society* (17 April 1969), p. 11; *MED* s.v.

[2] *Confessio Amantis*, Prol. 349; V, 1810-11; cf. Chaucer, *Canterbury Tales*, B 1173, 1177.

[3] Cf. E. W. McDonnell, *The Beguines and Beghards in Medieval Culture* (NY, 1969), pp. 246, 266-7; Lerner, pp. 31, 40-1.

[4] *Canterbury Tales*, B, 1183.

[5] C ix, 107, 137. The reading *lollers* at 137 is supported by all the manuscripts except Huntington 143, Cotton Vesp. B. xvi, Douce 104, Digby 102, and the Sterling Library V 88 (Ilchester MS).

[6] Donaldson, op. cit., pp. 144-7.

prophecy,[1] prophecy was not an especial concern of the Lollards. Cola da Rienzo observed that had St. Francis returned to the world of his day he might well have been considered *fantasticus et bestialissimus idiota*,[2] and it may well be that Langland, in speaking of his *lunatic lollers*, had in mind some prophetic simpleton who so appeared to his worldly contemporaries. It may be noted that the nomenclature is quite different from that customarily thought to have been applied to the 'poor priests', who have been seen in Wyclif's writings behind the common epithets *sacerdotes simplices*, *sacerdotes fideles*, *viri apostolici*, or *viri evangelici*.[3] It seems to me therefore improbable that Langland's *lollers* are Lollards, and the fact that the word *lollers* is used already in the B-text (B xv, 213) would support this contention.

We have so far considered a number of points which are less part of the fabric of the poem than problematic moments, the product of textual interpolation maybe, or of a dialectical stance on the part of the poet or the dramatis personae. We should, therefore, now ask ourselves whether there are any more pervasive topics or dominant characters that might suggest sympathy with Wycliffite thought. There seem to be two main candidates for such a consideration; Piers Plowman and Langland's attitude to the church. Burdach suggested that the figure of Piers Plowman represented the same ideal as the poor priests of the Lollard movement.[4] Could Piers represent the *praedicator evangelicus* whose duty, according to Wyclif, is to take the yoke upon his shoulders and to plough the soil of sinners' hearts?[5] Does he demonstrate the natural affinity of manual labour with contemplation and with preaching which Wyclif speaks of in the *De Civili Dominio?*[6] Or does he perhaps represent the priesthood which Wyclif regards as a surrogate of Christ's humanity?[7] The priest is not merely a symbol

[1] Cf. M. Reeves, *The Influence of Prophecy in the Later Middle Ages* (Oxford, 1969), *passim*.

[2] See K. Burdach, *Der Dichter des Ackermann aus Böhmen u. seine Zeit*, Vom Mittelalter zur Reformation, III (2) (Berlin, 1926–33), p. 306n.

[3] See H. L. Cannon, 'The Poor Priests: A Study in the Rise of English Lollardry', *The Annual Report of the American Historical Association*, 1900 (1), 463.

[4] Burdach, p. 210; for the poor priests cf. Cannon, 451–82; Dahmus, *Prosecution*, p. 85; McFarlane (1952), p. 101; M. J. Wilks, 'Royal Priesthood: The Origins of Lollardy', in *The Church in a Changing Society* (Uppsala, 1978), pp. 63–70.

[5] *De Civ. Dom.* i. 329/1–7: The metaphor is, indeed, not new. Cf. S. A. Barney, 'The Ploughshare of the Tongue: The Progress of a Symbol from the Bible to *Piers Plowman*', *Med. Stud.* xxxv (1973), 261–93.

[6] *De Civ. Dom.* iv. 382/36–383/3.

[7] *Dialogus*, 2/14–16; cf. *De Off. Reg.* 13/10–12, 137/21–2. Cf. M. J. Wilks, *The Problem of Sovereignty in the Later Middle Ages* (Cambridge, 1964), pp. 376–7.

of Christ's humanity but by virtue of a shared quality, patient poverty, is truly his representative.[1] The semiotics of the figure of Piers can, I believe, be illuminated by reference to an observation of Wyclif in the *Trialogus*. *Non sequitur*, he writes, *Petrus secundum suum esse intelligibile est Deus, igitur Petrus est Deus*,[2] which we might paraphrase as 'a shared essence is not necessarily a shared individuality'. Thus when Wyclif claims that the priest is a surrogate of Christ's humanity he is not claiming identity with Christ nor that he is merely a symbol of Christ; rather he has the quality of humble service which characterized Christ's humanity and, by virtue of this, is his surrogate on earth. In an analogous fashion, each pope becomes a new Peter, the physical embodiment of the perpetual personality of the church. In demanding the separation of the papacy from the Bishopric of Rome, Wyclif was concerned to recreate the pope as *Petrus evangelicus*, 'qualified by his poverty and humility to superintend the rebirth of the church'.[3] Such a *Petrus Evangelicus* perhaps lies behind the Piers of the last passus of the poem. I would therefore suppose that Piers Plowman is in this sense both a ploughman and Christ,[4] the Son of Man;[5] hence the Dreamer's question:

> 'Is þis Iesus þe Iustere', quod I, 'þat Iewes dide to deþe?
> Or is it Piers þe Plowman? Who peynted hym so rede?[6]

But in essence he is patient poverty, a realization of the *vita apostolica*, a life which involved the imitation of the primitive church conceived of as poor, simple, and humble,[7] a fitting opponent of Hobbe the Robber, the symbol of avarice. This life was common to Christ and the true ploughman whose simple

---

[1] The virtue of humility in the view of Augustine lead to truth. He writes (*via ad obtinendam veritatem*) *est autem prima, humilitas, secunda, humilitas, tertia, humilitas*. Epistola 118, III. 22 (*PL* xxxiii. 442).

[2] *Trialogus*, p. 47.

[3] M. J. Wilks, 'The *Apostolicus* and the Bishop of Rome', *JTS* xiii (1962), 292. B xv, 212 (... Piers þe Plowman, *Petrus id est Christus*) may contain an ironical reference to the concept of the pope as Christ. The pope *should* be identified with Piers Plowman, the embodiment of charity.

[4] Cf David Mills, 'The Rôle of the Dreamer in *Piers Plowman*', in *Piers Plowman: Critical Approaches*, ed. S. S. Hussey (London, 1969), p. 211: 'To be Piers-like is to be Christ-like'.

[5] Burdach (pp. 322–3) calls attention to the reflection in Piers Plowman of the dual nature of the Son of Man; as an earthly ploughman and as a divine representative of God, the first and second Adam.

[6] B xix, 10–11; C xxi, 10–11.

[7] The purpose of this life was *zelus et salus animarum* and involved poverty and manual labour. Cf. McDonnell, p. 141.

prayer, said in charity, as Lollard writers claim, is better than a thousand masses said by a covetous priest; or that of any order that loves God less than he, *blabere þei neuere so meche wiþ lippis*.[1] That an essential component of the figure of Piers Plowman is his patient poverty seems to be suggested by a sermon *ad status* by Jacques de Vitry in which he draws a picture of three farmers who equally labour in the harvest; one may accept labour as a penance proper for sinful man, another labours to gain money, another to steal the corn. They all labour outwardly but the first gains eternal life, the second temporary gain, and the third the pains of hell. In the second place, Jacques de Vitry maintains that, at a spiritual level, we have *Christus agricola* who took the ploughshare of the cross upon his shoulders and who ploughs the human heart.[2] It is only a short step from this metaphor to the figure of *Christus agricola* of late medieval paintings in which Christ is accompanied by the rural instruments of his trade instead of the instruments of the passion,[3] his sufferings here identified with the *poenitentia* of labour illustrated by the good farmer of Jacque de Vitry's sermon. Here truly the husbandman and Christ are identified by the bond of patient poverty. Therefore I do not believe that we can identify Piers with the poor priests or indeed with the priesthood, although in emphasizing the qualities common to both Burdach, I believe, provided an essential clue to the figure of Piers.

We turn now to Langland's attitude to the church. Here it seems to me we find a sharp contrast between the Wycliffite and the Langlandian point of view. For nowhere in Langland, I believe, do we find that dualism, deriving from Wyclif's predestinarianism and ultimately from his realism, which lead him to distinguish between the *ecclesia malignantium* and 'the true reality of an Ecclesia of the just . . . the *respublica* of the rightous',[4] and to posit within the institutional church a true church consisting of the elect alone.[5] This was a recurring theme in Wyclif's works[6] and in

---

[1] Matthew, 274/7-10, 321/10-12.

[2] Ed. J. B. Pitra, *Analecta novissima Spicilegii Solesmensis* (ii, 1888), pp. 435, 437.

[3] M. Mollat and P. Wolff, *The Popular Revolutions of the late Middle Ages* (London, 1973), p. 291.

[4] M. J. Wilks (1972), 119. Already in the *De Mandatis* Wyclif contrasts the *ecclesia malignantium* with the *ecclesia praedestinatorum* 372/34-373/2.

[5] Cf. Gordon Leff, *Heresy in the Later Middle Ages* (Manchester, 1967), ii. 516-19; in Wyclif's words *Manifestum videtur quod nullus praescitus sit membrum illius ecclesie* (*De Ecclesia*, 83/21-2).

[6] For example, *De Ecclesia*, 71/29-74/31; cf. *De Veritate*, iii. 126/8-22; *Dialogus*, 5/5-11; *Sermones*, iv. 42/15-45/21; *Opera Minora*, 100/8-101/3, 179/26-30, *Opus Evangelicum*, i. 119/16-27; 120/20-38; *Supplementum Trialogi*,

the works of the vernacular writers.[1] Nowhere it seems to me does Langland indicate such a view of the church. On the contrary, in Passus I we find Holy Church in a pedagogic role which seems to suggest authority and which is consonant with the Dreamer's own views on wealth and the importance of love. Piers's will also implies a loyalty to the church which can hardly be regarded as cynical.[2] Nor can Liberum Arbitrium's definition of the church be regarded as in any way Wycliffite:

> 'What is holy churche, chere frende?' quod y
>   'Charite', he saide;
> Lief and loue and leutee in o byleue and lawe,
> A loue-knotte of leutee and of lele byleue,
> Alle kyne cristene cleuynge on o will,
> Withoute gyle and gabbyng gyue and sulle and lene . . .[3]

Holy Church is here represented as Unity of the Spirit in the Bond of Peace. Again at B xi, 96-100 Loyalty warns the Dreamer not to speak against prelates and priests, and at B x, 412 the church is described as the ark, it is *goddes hous to saue*. Above all, in the last passus, the Church is Unity. Nor I think is there any indication that Langland identified Antichrist with an Anti-church although he does seem to identify the pope with Antichrist.[4] Nor does the apparent association of the friars with Antichrist imply a belief in the two churches[5] although it is true that the anti-church in Wycliffite writings is often called the church of Antichrist. Nor does the form of the Battle with Antichrist at the end of *Piers Plowman* suggest a church of Antichrist, incapable from all eternity

415/1-416/2. The heresy of the two churches was also characteristic of Waldensians, the Fraticelli, the Apostolic Brethren, and the Brethren of the Free Spirit (cf. Reeves, pp. 203-7, 213, 407-8, 411; Lerner, pp. 179, 205; W. L. Wakefield and A. P. Evans, *Heresies of the High Middle Ages* (New York and London, 1969), p. 405). It may be noted that the *Lanterne of li3t* which distinguishes between the church of God and the church of the fiend attributes a similar dualism to Lyra. See Hudson, no. 22.

[1] Cf. Arnold, i. 50/27-31, 287/20-288/7; iii. 134/13-23, 339/19-25, 395/ 6-29; Matthew, 198/33-199/4.

[2] A vii, 83-7; B vi, 91-5; C viii, 100-4.

[3] C xvii, 125-9.

[4] C xxii, 126-8. For the association of Antichrist with the corruption of the church cf. Wyclif, *De Ecclesia*, 377/26-30; in the *De Off. Reg.* he associates Antichrist with the Schism (*De Off. Reg.* 225/34-226/10). For the vernacular works see, for example, Arnold, i. 97/21-4, 205/21-4; ii. 394/9-395/17; iii. 245/ 26-246/3. For the widespread belief in Antichrist see Norman Cohn, *The Pursuit of the Millennium* (London, 1957).

[5] Cf. Pearsall, p. 364, note to line 58.

of redemption; rather it is on the Psychomachia model of the French allegories.

It is true that the Dreamer raises the question of that favourite contemporary topic, predestination, and his question might be taken as implying the simple predestinarianism which lies behind the theory of the two churches:

> For Clergie saith þat he seyh in þe seynt euayngelie
> That y man ymaed was and my nam y-entred
> In þe legende of lyf longe ar y were.
> Predestinaet thei prechen, prechours þat this sheweth,
> Or prescient inparfit, ypult out of grace,
> Vnwriten for som wikkednesse, as holy writ sheweth,
> *Nemo ascendit ad celum nisi qui de celo descendit.*[1]

The Dreamer's words seem to suggest that the *prescient*, the reprobate are denied God's grace, *ypult out of grace*, and thus incapable of good works and committed to damnation. But I suspect that this passage is not only making a debating point but that it may have a dramatic function too, for in *The Chastizing of God's Children*, in a passage reminiscent of the *The Stimulus Amoris*,[2] fear of reprobation is presented as a temptation to be overcome. The account of the temptation in the *Chastizing* might well stand as a description of Will's state of mind or, in the case of the C-text, that of Recklessness: *þus it farith bi hem also þat wolen imagyne of predestinaciouns, and of the prescience or of þe foreknowynge of god; and suche men sum tyme bien dredeful for synnes don bifore . . . Wherefor sum bien in poynt to falle in dispeir.*[3] Such is the plight of the Dreamer when he hears the parable of the wedding feast:

> Al for tene of here tyxst tremblede myn herte
> And in a wer gan y wex and with mysulue to despute
> Where y were chose or not chose[4]

I think we may, therefore, presume that Langland does not envisage the divided church of Wycliffite thought.

But could it be claimed that Langland does argue for a de-institutionalization of the church such as Wyclif's views on predestination and dominion led him to adopt? For since his church consisted of the *corpus predestinatorum*, the function of the priesthood and the sacraments was diminished. Thus, for example,

---

[1] C xi, 205–10; B x, 379–82.
[2] Cap. III (Bibl. franc. med. aev., iv, 1949); *The Goad of Love*, tr. Clare Kirchberger (London, 1952), cap. 33. Cf. Bazire and Colledge, *Chastizing*, pp. 45–6.
[3] Bazire and Colledge, *Chastizing*, pp. 119–20.
[4] C xii, 48–50; B xi, 115–17.

Wyclif claims that the excommunication of the church cannot separate the elect from the body of Christ.[1] Even as early as 1377 the danger to the institutional church of Wyclif's views on dominion was realized; thus Gregory XI speaks of these views as 'Propositions which attempt to subvert and weaken the whole polity of the church and even the secular state'.[2] In some cases Langland seems to reject the Wycliffian point of view. For example, he declares that though the ignorant priest in celebrating mass

ouerhuppe . . . oure bileue suffiseþ.[3]

But perhaps something might be learnt about Langland's attitude to the institutional church from the Dreamer's encounters with churchmen. There are three figures that might repay consideration; the priest in the Pardon Scene, the two friars at the beginning of Dowel, and Need. Are we to assume, for example, that the Dreamer's musings on the topic of indulgences indicate a rejection of these documents?[4] Wyclif would seem to be on the side of the pardon from Truth. In the *Sermones Quadraginta* he emphasizes the instability of those who trust in indulgences *a pena et a culpa: Oportet enim omnem hominem proporcionaliter ad proprium meritum vel demeritum premiari.*[5] This view, which rejects the concept of the treasury of merit, the priest correctly challenges. Yet the ploughman, whose knowledge of the Bible is mocked by the priest,[6] as though he were indeed a Lollard, continues the debate; nor is the Dreamer convinced by the priest. A similar case may be seen in the scene with the two friars. The Dreamer proposes the text *Septies cadit iustus.* He is, in effect, asking a question related to the topic of penitence. Thus Canon Law reads in the *De Poenitentia: Septies cadit iustus et resurgit. Si cadit quomodo iustus? Si iustus, quomodo cadit?* And the gloss adds: *Dicitur hic quod iustus septies . . . cadit per venalia peccata*

---

[1] *De Ecclesia,* 111/21–6; cf. *De Off. Reg.* 166/8–10 and Leff (1966), pp. 165–7.

[2] *HA,* i. 346; *FZ,* p. 243. The charge is echoed by Courtenay in his letter of 1382 to Peter Stokys (*FZ,* pp. 275–6).

[3] B xv, 387; C xvii, 117–19. The idea that a priest in mortal sin is unable to exercise his priestly function can be found in the heretical sects of the Continent. In *c.* 1252 Wm. Cornelius of Antwerp was accused of an heretical opinion that a priest in mortal sin is unable to consecrate, absolve, or impose penance (cf. McDonnell, p. 489) and a similar opinion is recorded for 1292 (McDonnell, p. 513).

[4] B vii, 173–86; C ix, 319–33. The passage is, no doubt, ironical (cf. *The Vision of Piers Plowman,* ed. A. V. C. Schmidt (London, 1978), note to lines 174–9 (p. 326)), and to that extent is questioning the value of papal indulgences. For indulgences cf. *De Ecclesia,* cap. xxiii, and Hudson, note to text 2, ll. 105–18. For rejection by the Waldensians cf. Wakefield and Evans, pp. 389–90.

[5] *Sermones,* iv. 474/9–12. [6] B vii, 136–7; cf. note 173.

et tamen non cadit a charitate[1] which is the gist of the friar's reply. Again we find the representative of the church giving an orthodox reply which fails to convince the Dreamer.[2] The meeting with Need may be another such case. Need appears to represent a friar, the harbinger of Antichrist.[3] His speech is largely concerned with those controversial concepts 'necessity' and 'temperance' enshrined in the Bull *exiit qui seminat*;[4] he is concerned, that is to say, with Franciscan poverty. Like the Bull, he refers to the proverb 'Necessity knows no law',[5] and his praise of Temperance echoes the phrase *cum moderamine* of the Bull and controversial works concerning themselves with *usus pauper*. It is fitting that the speech should end with the praise of evangelical poverty. In fact the moderate use of what is necessary as recommended by the Bull had led to much extravagance and there is therefore an irony in the conjunction with Christ's poverty. Nevertheless, I think we may claim that this representative of the church, if such he is, is expressing orthodox views (although in this case highly contentious ones)[6] which the tenor of the poem tends to undermine.

There are, however, two ways of looking at this. Should we suppose that Langland is implicitly criticizing the church in these passages or should we assume that the apparent criticism is in fact a reflection of the Dreamer's own wilfulness, that lack of *recta*

---

[1] *Decretum*, C xxxiii, q. iii, d. iii, c. xxiii (*Corpus Iuris Canonici* (Lyons, 1624), i. 1761); cit. Raymund of Pennaforte, pp. 441-2.

[2] The same might be said of the Friar's definition of Dowel in the banquet scene, B xiii, 104-5; C xv, 112-14.

[3] Cf. Robert Adams, 'The Nature of Need in *Piers Plowman* xx', *Traditio*, xxxiv (1978), 299. It may be noted that the *meridian demon* with whom Adams identifies Need was identified by Wyclif with the friars and more generally with avarice and the corruption of the clergy as well as with Antichrist. Cf. *De Veritate*, iii. 91/4-6 and n. 5, 96/8-11; *Polemical Works*, ii, 411-25.

[4] Sexti Decret. Lib V, Tit. XII *De Verborum Significatione*, c. iii; Friedberg, ii. 1109-21.

[5] For the use of the maxim by the canonists and by political theorists such as Ockham see C. C. Bayley, 'Pivotal Concepts in the Political Philosophy of William of Ockham', *Journal of the History of Ideas*, x (1949), 199-218. But the context of the Bull is peculiarly appropriate to Need's thesis.

[6] The debate on the poverty of Christ was not ended by the Bull *Inter nonnullos* of 1323. Cf., for example, *De Civ. Dom.*, Bk. iii; Richard Maidstone, *Protectorium Pauperis*, ed. A. Williams, *Carmelus*, v (1958), 132-80; K. Walsh, 'The *De Vita Evangelica* of Geoffrey Hardeby (†c. 1385)', *Analecta Augustiniana*, xxxiii (1970), 151-261; xxxiv (1971), 5-83. It is not necessary therefore to assume that Need's posture is rigorist let alone heretical. For general discussion see Decima L. Douie, *The Nature and the Effect of the Heresy of the Fraticelli* (Manchester, 1932) and M. D. Lambert, *Franciscan Poverty* (London, 1961); 'The Franciscan Crisis under John xxii', *Franciscan Studies*, xxxii (1972), 123-43.

voluntas which constitutes his sinfulness? Is the Dreamer himself in his *robe of russet* a critic of the church?[1] Unfortunately, the robe of russet is too ambiguous to give us an answer. It was indeed a mark of Lollardy; it was also a symbol of labour. Wyclif points out in regard to the russet of the Franciscans that *russetum vero significat laborem.*[2] And Langland himself seems to support this implication.[3] This is a question which has relevance to our third and final question—the function of the polemical and satirical material in the poem as a whole. The Dreamer is a sinful man and it might be supposed that by depicting him as a wandering cleric, a *gyrovagus*, one of those hermits, *unholy of works* who appear fitfully in bishops' registers,[4] Langland is symbolizing the fluctuating will. But the Dreamer is also a symbol of a corrupt church. And in his wanderings it is at a corrupt society that he looks, an image of himself. Thus Study attacks him for the corruption of learning,[5] one of those traditional topics which the Lollards made their own; Clergy lectures him on the duties of the clergy;[6] Anima (or Liberum Arbitrium) lectures him on the corruption of the age.[7] He does indeed receive much moral instruction but much of it relates to the theme of the ploughman and the *vita apostolica* and is concerned, as Dunning pointed out, with the 'reform of Christian society'[8] and the necessity of repentance. As Gower in the *Confessio* pictures both the corruption of the individual and of society, a society in which *Boþe lettred and lewed beþ alayed now wiþ synne,*[9] so too Langland interweaves the themes of the salvation of the individual and of society. Hence the importance of the theme of repentance in the poem. It is not so much, as Knight claimed, that satire is at the centre of the poem[10] as that, as one critic put it, 'the "prophetic" character of Langland's mind is everywhere manifest in his poem'.[11] The poem is a vision in which the Dreamer, the sinful

[1] For the russet robes of the Lollards see Cannon, p. 473.

[2] *Polemical Works*, i. 27n. Cf. *Pierce the Ploughmans Crede* (ed. W. W. Skeat, *EETS* os 30 (1867)), l. 719; Pearsall, note to x, 2, and D. W. Robertson and B. F. Huppé, *Piers Plowman and Scriptural Tradition* (Princeton, 1951), p. 217.

[3] B xv, 220.

[4] See, for example, Register of Randolph Baldock on Thomas Byreford, hermit of Cripplegate (*CYS* 7 (1) (1911), pp. 141–2).

[5] A xi, 17–92; B x, 17–139; C xi, 14–83.

[6] B x, 272–335.   [7] Most of B xv and C xvi and xvii.

[8] T. P. Dunning, 'Action and Contemplation in *Piers Plowman*', *Critical Approaches*, p. 214.

[9] B xv, 354.

[10] S. T. Knight, 'Satire in *Piers Plowman*', *Critical Approaches*, p. 308.

[11] Edward Vasta, *The Spiritual Basis of 'Piers Plowman'* (The Hague, 1965), p. 13.

human will, as well as an erring cleric, learns by precept and example that *charitas* is *recta voluntas ab omnibus terrenis ac praesentibus prorsus aversa, juncta Deo inseparabiliter*.[1] The poem draws many ideas from the controversies of the period when it was written. Parallels, some of which I have indicated, can be found to the ideas of Wyclif and other heterodox thinkers of the period. Some of these ideas I have looked at in detail; others, such as the fleeting references to vernacular scripture,[2] or criticisms of worldly learning implicit in the scene with the doctor and elsewhere in the poem, I have only briefly touched upon. But in the last resort, *Piers Plowman* is less concerned with the inculcation of theories, orthodox, heterodox, or heretical, than with a prophetic vision of a corrupt society and its eschatological doom. It may, perhaps, be surmised that when Conscience sets off at the end of the poem to seek Piers Plowman, it is the *renovatio mundi* that he seeks. Perhaps Langland saw this *renovatio* as Gerhoch of Reichersberg saw it, as an age in which the church would be cleansed of all filth and simony and adorned as with crowns of gold.[3] Conscience is seeking *redde quod debes*, the spirit of justice and righteousness[4] but also the spirit of charity. The ideal is summed up by Julianus Pomerius: 'Therefore if in this life we strive to fulfil justice, whose work it is to render each man his due, let us give ourselves back to God by whom we are made . . . Let reason master the vices, let the body be subject to the soul and the soul to God and the whole perfection of man is accomplished.'[5] If we must conclude that Langland the Lollard still eludes us I think we should also conclude that Langland the reformer is due to reappear. Let Wyclif have the last word: *Spectat ad officium doctoris evangelici prophetare*[6] In this at least Langland would seem to be at one with the evangelical doctor.

[1] *De Vita Contemplativa*, III, cap. xiii (*PL* lix. 493).

[2] Cf. the definition of Dobet: *he. . . haþ rendred þe bible, and preacheþ þe peple . . . Libenter suffertis* etc. (B viii, 91–2; C x, 88–9) and Dame Study's observation that he who has Holy Writ in his mouth is little loved (B x, 32–8; C xi, 31–4). The emphasis on vernacular scripture is common among continental heretics especially the Waldensians. Cf. Lambert (1977), pp. 68, 91, 175.

[3] R. E. Lerner, 'The Refreshment of Saints: The Time after Antichrist as a Station for Earthly Progress in Medieval Thought', *Traditio*, xxxii (1976), 114.

[4] Cf. Pamela Gradon, 'John Gower and the Concept of Righteousness', *Poetica*, viii (1977), 61–71.

[5] *De Vita Contemplativa*, III, cap. xxvi (*PL* lix. 508). This sense of *redde quod debes* seems to me more likely than that proposed by R. W. Frank ('*Piers Plowman' and the Scheme of Salvation* (New Haven, 1957), p. 106 n. 2).

[6] *De Vaticinacione seu Prophetia* (Opera Minora, 165/3–4).

AUTOBIOGRAPHICAL POETRY IN THE MIDDLE AGES: THE CASE OF THOMAS HOCCLEVE

By J. A. BURROW

Read 4 November 1982

THOMAS HOCCLEVE earned his living as a clerk in the office of the Privy Seal, but he also employed his pen in the copying of poetry, his own included. Three autograph copies of his work survive, in fact; and one of these (now Huntington MS HM 744) formerly belonged to Sir Israel Gollancz, the scholar commemorated in this series of lectures. Gollancz edited poems from this manuscript as part of the edition of Hoccleve's works published by the Early English Text Society.[1] I therefore imagine that he would have sympathised with one purpose of the present lecture, which is to contribute to a revaluation of Hoccleve's poetry. The poet's own confession that he was 'dull' and learned 'little or nothing' from his master Chaucer is still commonly accepted as a fair summary of his achievement; but such self-depreciation is itself eminently Chaucerian, and I want to suggest that the disciple's poetry in fact displays, at its best, a lively intelligence and a command of English verse which give the lie to his talk of incompetence and stupidity. At the same time I shall take up some of the problems presented by those autobiographical passages which are so characteristic (and unChaucerian) in Hoccleve. Gollancz's fellow editor, F. J. Furnivall, made much of these passages, freely deriving from them conclusions about the poet's life and character; but modern critics are uneasy with such naïvely literalistic interpretation. They stress

[1] All quotations are from this three-volume edition: *The Minor Poems in the Phillipps MS. 8151 (Cheltenham)* [now Huntington MS HM 111] *and the Durham MS. III. 9*, ed. F. J. Furnivall, ES 61 (1892); *The Regement of Princes*, ed. F. J. Furnivall, ES 72 (1897); *Minor Poems from the Ashburnham MS. Addit. 133* [now Huntington MS HM 744], ed. Sir I. Gollancz, ES 73 (1925). In 1970 the two volumes of minor poems were reissued in one volume revised by J. Mitchell and A. I. Doyle, from which I cite. Selections are edited by E. P. Hammond, *English Verse between Chaucer and Surrey* (Durham, NC, 1927) and by M. C. Seymour, *Selections from Hoccleve* (Oxford, 1981). There is an admirable edition of the *Series* by M. R. Pryor (Ph.D. thesis, University of California, Los Angeles, 1968).

rather, as we shall see, the conventional and non-factual elements in Hoccleve's self-revelations. But in this as in some other areas of medieval literary studies, the reaction against autobiographical readings has begun to overreach itself, so that it now seems necessary to argue that not *all* autobiographical passages in medieval writings are simply 'conventional', and also that there are some cases, Hoccleve's included, where interest in the poetry is actually inseparable from interest in the man.

Gollancz and Furnivall would simply have taken this for granted; but modern scholars and critics have generally reacted to such declarations of biographical interest with increasing disapproval. Three distinct schools of thought, otherwise often at variance, have converged to make this anti-biographical position overpoweringly strong in recent times. Historical criticism has stressed the conventional character of authorial self-reference in medieval times (the use of traditional topics, the influence of St. Augustine, and so on); the New Criticism has discouraged biographical interest as a distraction from the words on the page; and formalist or structuralist criticism treats first-person discourse as part of the fictive world of 'le texte'. All these developments, in their different ways, have helped to make the frank man-to-man response of Furnivall to his author seem very old-fashioned indeed. Writing, as he tells us, in the British Museum on Monday, 29 February 1892, at 7.30 p.m. 'under the electric light', the Victorian editor characterised Hoccleve as a 'weak, sensitive, look-on-the-worst kind of man': 'But he has the merit of recogniz-ing his weakness, his folly, and his cowardice. He makes up for these by his sentimental love of the Virgin Mary, his genuine admiration for Chaucer, his denunciation of the extravagant fashions in dress, the neglect of old soldiers, &c. We wish he had been a better poet and a manlier fellow; but all of those who've made fools of themselves, more or less, in their youth, will feel for the poor old versifier'.[1]

The directness of Furnivall's response to his 'poor old versifier' is delightful, but it is no longer possible today after studies such as those by Curtius on the topos of affected modesty, Spitzer and Zumthor on the 'non-empirical I', Donaldson on the Chaucerian narrator, and Kane on the autobiographical fallacy.[2]

---

[1] *Minor Poems*, p. xxxviii.

[2] E. R. Curtius, *European Literature and the Latin Middle Ages*, trans. W. R. Trask (London, 1953), pp. 83-5; L. Spitzer, 'Note on the Poetic and the Empirical "I" in Medieval Authors', *Traditio* iv (1946), 414-22; P. Zumthor, *Essai de poétique médiévale* (Paris, 1972), and 'Autobiography in the Middle Ages?',

If autobiographical interpretation is to become respectable again, and if the term 'autobiographical' itself is ever to escape from that guard of inverted commas which regularly now accompanies it, the whole matter needs to be thought out afresh, so that there may be some new understanding of the proper criteria for valid and useful work in this area. Full recognition of the part played by literary tradition and free-ranging invention in first-person utterances need not deprive criticism, as it tends to do at present, of the capacity to recognize equally fully those cases where such utterances are *not* fictional or conventional.

Literary critics commonly apply the epithet 'autobiographical' quite generally to all passages where an author says things about himself which are judged to be true, at least in part. This terminology involves some awkwardness, to which I shall return later; but first let me offer a few observations on the judgement of truth. It will be clearly understood, to begin with, that in some first-person discourse the question of autobiographical truth simply does not arise, because the writer is not referring to himself at all. Thus no competent reader, knowing the relevant facts, could fail to see that the following little poem, despite its direct first-person form, is to be understood dramatically as spoken *in persona alterius*:

> I have labored sore and suffered deth,
> And now I rest and draw my breth;
> But I shall come and call right sone
> Heven and erth and hell to dome;
> And then shall know both devil and man
> What I was and what I am.[1]

The same prior question, that of reference, can be settled equally decisively in the opposite direction—in favour, that is, of formally *non*-dramatic utterance—where the first-person speaker bears the author's own proper name. This happens once in Chaucer's poetry, when the eagle calls the dreamer in the *House of Fame* 'Geoffrey', and much more frequently in Hoccleve, where the first person is many times identified as either 'Thomas' or

---

Genre 6 (1973), 29–48; E. T. Donaldson, 'Chaucer the Pilgrim', *Speaking of Chaucer* (London, 1970), pp. 1–12; G. Kane, 'The Autobiographical Fallacy in Chaucer and Langland Studies' (Chambers Memorial Lecture, London, 1965).

[1] From *English Verse 1300–1500*, ed. J. A. Burrow (London, 1977), p. 309. This anthology also contains an edition of Hoccleve's *Complaint*, ll. 1–308.

'Hoccleve'.[1] Such naming is important because it establishes clearly that the first-person pronoun does at least refer to the author, not to some other person, real or imaginary. Hence it will always be in order to raise the question of autobiographical truth in such cases. But the substantial question of truth is nearly always more difficult than the formal question of reference, because there are so many things besides the truth that one can speak about oneself (not all of which one would want to call lies).

The question can be easily and decisively settled only in those cases where an author's statement about himself can be checked in a reliable independent source. Such cases do not occur very often in medieval literature, but Hoccleve's poetry provides some instances. Like his master Chaucer, Hoccleve was a civil servant, and his career can therefore be documented, like Chaucer's, from the official archives. In Chaucer's poetry there is nothing for such documents to confirm except a passing and dismissive reference, again in the *House of Fame* (653), to his 'rekenynges' in the Customs House; but Hoccleve's writings refer quite freely to his life at the Privy Seal. He mentions, for instance, the name of the Privy Seal hostel at which he lodged (Chester's Inn, on the south side of the modern Aldwych), the amount of his annuity (£10 in 1406), and the names of fellow clerks (Baillay, Hethe, Offorde).[2] The researches in the Public Record Office of Furnivall's collaborator, R. E. G. Kirk, and of the administrative historians T. F. Tout and A. L. Brown have provided documentary confirmation of these details. Tout and Brown, both good, hard-headed historians, find nothing, it should be noted, in Hoccleve's poetry to deter them from using it as a trustworthy source of information on the workings of the Privy Seal.[3]

[1] 'Thomas': throughout the *Series*, especially in the *Dialogue* (10, 20, 25, 199, 203, etc.). 'Hoccleve': *Dialogue* 3, Roundel II (*Minor Poems*, p. 310) 1 etc., *Male Regle* 351, *Regement of Princes* 1864-5, 4360, *Balade to Maister Somer* (*Minor Poems*, p. 59) 25. Philippe Lejeune stresses the importance of identity of proper name between author and narrator in establishing the autobiographical character of a work: *Le Pacte autobiographique* (Paris, 1975). This valuable book provides an up-to-date bibliography of modern studies.

[2] Chester's Inn, *Regement of Princes* 5; annuity, *Male Regle* 421; Baillay etc., *Balade to Maister Somer* 25-6.

[3] R. E. G. Kirk, Appendix of Hoccleve Documents, *Minor Poems*, pp. li-lxx; T. F. Tout, *Chapters in the Administrative History of Mediaeval England*, vol. v (Manchester, 1930), ch. xvi; A. L. Brown, 'The Privy Seal in the Early Fifteenth Century' (D.Phil. thesis, Oxford, 1954), and 'The Privy Seal Clerks of the Early Fifteenth Century', *The Study of Medieval Records*, ed. D. A. Bullough and R. L. Storey (Oxford, 1971), pp. 260-81. Brown writes in his essay (p. 271): 'What he [Hoccleve] wrote was apparently in essence true. His service in the

The fact that in these matters, where it is possible to check, Hoccleve's poetry nowhere departs from the actual circumstances of his life must be borne in mind when approaching those other more contentious matters where documentary checks are not available. In his lecture entitled 'The Autobiographical Fallacy in Chaucer and Langland Studies', Professor George Kane has rightly insisted on the dangers and difficulties of making 'inferences from texts about . . . undocumented matters respecting the life and personality of an author'.[1] One may therefore be tempted to set the whole insoluble problem aside; but in practice this proves difficult to do. Many modern critics who profess complete agnosticism in the matter go on to talk like unblushing atheists. They slip easily, for instance, from declaring that we cannot tell whether Chaucer's poetry does or does not represent his ordinary personality into taking it for granted that it does not. This is because the reaction against the speculative excesses of older criticism has left a distinct, though unacknowledged, bias against any recognition of autobiographical reference at all in medieval literature. This bias appears in a number of ways, and most notably in the handling of the tricky and vital question of conventionality.

I want in particular to question the belief, to be traced in much recent polemic, that convention and autobiographical truth are in general to be taken as incompatible alternatives. Here again one needs to distinguish, as I did earlier, between the question of reference and the question of truth. The former tends to be a straight either/or problem: either the first-person pronoun refers to the writer or it does not. So here recognition of conventionality can indeed exclude autobiographical interpretation altogether, simply by establishing that the 'I' of the poem is not the author at all. In the *pastourelle*, for instance, one of the rules of the genre makes writers speak of themselves, in the first person, as walking out one May morning. For a competent reader the question of truth will not arise in this case. Here the conventional and the autobiographical can indeed be treated as mutually exclusive. But in those other cases where the writer does refer to himself and where the question of truth consequently arises, matters are more complex. Questions of truth rarely allow of a single either/or answer; and where they are concerned, the customary modern

Privy Seal, his annuity, his hostel, even to some extent his breakdown, can be substantiated from the records.' (I am grateful to my colleague John Guy for help with Privy Seal matters.)

[1] Kane, p. 5.

opposition between the conventional and the autobiographical,
insofar as it claims to distinguish fact from fiction, often simplifies
and distorts the issues. Let me give an example, taken from the
excellent lecture by Kane already referred to. Kane remarks that
Chaucer 'repeatedly professes inexperience, or lack of aptitude, or
lack of success as a lover'; and he goes on to ask the following
question: 'Do we accept this as autobiography, or call it a conventional pose, or take the position that we cannot possibly
know?'[1] This is indeed a difficult case, but I am concerned here
only with Kane's statement of the alternatives: 'autobiography' or
'conventional pose'. The main objection to this formulation is
simply that people strike 'poses' (conventional or otherwise) in life
as well as in literature. Furthermore, we do not always find it easy
to distinguish such attitudes, especially where they come to be
assumed as a matter of habit, from the truth or reality of a person's
life and opinions. How could such a distinction be made, for
instance, in the well-documented case of William Butler Yeats? In
such a case, the 'poses' will be of no less interest to the biographer
than to the critic.

Kane warns of an 'autobiographical fallacy', and he is right to
do so. But there is also an opposite error, which must be called the
'conventional fallacy'. Victims of the latter combine a learned and
sophisticated awareness of literary convention with an apparently
naïve and reductive notion of what real life is like—naïve and
reductive, because they talk as if non-literary experience were not
itself shaped by conventions. Of course, everyone knows that it *is*;
but the knowledge seems to desert medievalists when they argue
that the conventional character of a text *proves* that it has no
autobiographical content. In reply to this objection, it might be
argued that, insofar as life and literature do indeed share the same
conventional character, the distinction between them ceases to be
of any interest to criticism and can be ignored. From this point of
view it would be a matter of indifference whether Chaucer did or
did not in real life adopt that 'pose' of the unsuccessful lover which
he strikes in his poems. Even if he could be shown to have done so,
it might be said, the passages in question would still not count as
significantly autobiographical—not, that is, unless one could
prove that Chaucer actually *was* an unsuccessful lover. But when
modern critics deny the autobiographical character of a medieval
poem, they are not concerned only with the hard facts which
might be deduced from it. Their stress on the conventional

[1] Kane, p. 5.

character of authorial self-reference usually leads them to state, or suggest, that such reference has no bearing whatsoever on the life and experience of the author. We are offered instead, in and out of season, the purely literary, dramatic, or fictive utterances of the authorial persona, the 'I of the poem', the narrator, and so on.

Instances of the 'conventional fallacy' are not hard to find in modern discussions of Hoccleve. Let me give three examples. These concern Hoccleve's three most interesting and memorable poems: *La Male Regle de T. Hoccleve*, written in 1405 or 1406 when the poet was in his later thirties; *The Regement of Princes*, written for Prince Hal in the last years of Henry IV (1411-12); and the so-called *Series*, Hoccleve's last datable work, put together a few years before his death in 1426.[1]

La Male Regle is a highly characteristic, indeed an inimitable, literary creation. In it Hoccleve laments the present sad state both of his health and of his finances. He is suffering, he says, from a double sickness in purse and in body (337-8, 409), caused by the excesses of his riotous and unbridled youth. This is the *male regle* or misrule of the title, which Hoccleve describes with a good deal of lively detail concerning his irregular life as a young man in London and Westminster taverns and eating-houses. Furnivall treated these descriptions as direct transcripts of reality, unmediated by any literary convention; but in 1967 Eva Thornley pointed out the influence of the Middle English penitential lyrics

---

[1] The date of Hoccleve's death was established by A. L. Brown: see *The Study of Medieval Records*, p. 270. On the date of the *Male Regle*, see J. H. Kern, 'Een en ander over Thomas Hoccleve en zijne werken', *Verslagen en Mededeelingen der Koninklijke Akademie van Wetenschappen*, 5th series, i (1915), 344-47 (I am grateful to Hanneke Wirtjes for excerpting this article from the Dutch). Kern's dating, late 1405 or early 1406, is followed by Seymour, *Selections*, pp. 109-10. On the date of the *Regement*, see Kern, art. cit., 351-58. On the date of the *Series*, see Kern, art. cit., 362-71, and 'Die Datierung von Hoccleve's Dialog', *Anglia* xl (1916), 370-3. Kern dates the *Dialogue* (the second part of the *Series*, and the only part that can be dated) in 1422; but he fails to notice that the wording of the reference to a coinage statute of the Parliament of May 1421 (*Dialogue* 134-40) clearly shows that it is a later insertion in a passage written before the statute was passed. The *Dialogue* was therefore presumably first composed during Humphrey of Gloucester's first, not his second, spell as 'lieutenant' (*Dialogue* 533): between 30 December 1419 and 1 February 1421. The allusion in *Dialogue* 542-3 to Humphrey's *secundo reditu* from France must refer to his return late in 1419 from his second campaign in France, not to his return in 1422 from his third, as Seymour supposes (*Selections*, p. 136). Since Hoccleve says that he was 53 years old at the time of writing the *Dialogue* (l. 246), he was most likely born in 1366 or 1367.

on Hoccleve's poem.[1] Hoccleve's account of his wild youth, she
observed, owes something to the traditional scheme of the seven
deadly sins, commonly employed in the penitential lyrics.
Thornley herself did not draw any anti-autobiographical conclusions from her evidence, but later scholars have not hesitated
to do so. Thus Penelope Doob, in an important discussion of
Hoccleve to which I shall have occasion to return, notes approv-
ingly that Thornley 'finds the poem more conventional than
autobiographical'. Elsewhere she writes as follows: 'Hoccleve's
Male Regle is, as Thornley demonstrates, an exceptionally good
example of the conventional informal penitential lyric; and its
colourfulness and realism may relate it more closely to such works
of fiction as the *Wife of Bath's Prologue* or the lively confessions of
the seven deadly sins and of Haukyn in *Piers Plowman* . . . than to
a true confession from the heart.'[2] The weakness of this argument
lies in its tacit identification of conventionality with fictionality.
This is particularly shaky where a scheme such as that of the seven
deadly sins is concerned. That conventional scheme did indeed
figure in literary fictions such as *Piers Plowman*; but it also provided
the moral grid-system most commonly used by men of the period
whenever they attempted to map their inner lives. That was how
people thought about themselves. Hence if Hoccleve had wanted,
for whatever reason, to describe his own experiences as a wild
young man, he would most naturally have sorted them out into
sin-categories. Even if this sorting were more systematic than it in
fact is in the *Male Regle*, there would still be no reason to conclude
that the poet's confession must be a 'work of fiction'. We would
still be left free to make what we could of its 'colourfulness and
realism':

> Wher was a gretter maister eek than y,
> Or bet aqweyntid at Westmynstre yate,
> Among the tauerneres namely,
> And Cookes / whan I cam / eerly or late?
> I pynchid nat at hem in myn acate,
> But paied hem / as þat they axe wolde;
> Wherfore I was the welcomere algate,
> And for 'a verray gentil man' y-holde.   (177–84)

---

[1] E. A. Thornley, 'The Middle English Penitential Lyric and Hoccleve's
Autobiographical Poetry', *Neuphilologische Mitteilungen* 68 (1967), 295–321.
Thornley refers especially to the lyric beginning 'In my youth full wild I was',
No. 6 in F. A. Patterson, *The Middle English Penitential Lyric* (New York, 1911).

[2] P. B. R. Doob, *Nebuchadnezzar's Children: Conventions of Madness in Middle
English Literature* (New Haven, Conn., 1974), pp. 213, 226.

One must agree with Doob that such a passage does not read like a 'true confession from the heart'. The self-depreciation has a humorous, slightly weary note. We all know, it implies, what motives might prompt a cook or an innkeeper to welcome such a big spender, flattering him with titles such as 'master' and 'a real gentleman'. But the 'true confession from the heart' is only one form—and that the most vulgarly romantic—which autobiographical writing can take. When Hoccleve chooses to write about himself, as I believe he does in the *Male Regle* and elsewhere, he does so for reasons quite different from those suggested by Dr Doob's teasingly inappropriate phrase.

I shall return to this point later. For the present let us turn to a second instance of the conventional fallacy. In his most widely read work, *The Regement of Princes*, Hoccleve refers on four occasions to Geoffrey Chaucer, who had died some twelve years earlier. Hoccleve himself is sometimes referred to as an English Chaucerian, and there can be no doubt that he learned much from his predecessor's work. He imitated it quite closely on occasion, as when, at the request of a London stationer, he wrote a Miracle of the Virgin, in rhyme royal and with a Marian prologue, which derives so directly from Chaucer's *Prioress's Prologue and Tale* that it found a place in one copy of the *Canterbury Tales*.[1] Although direct echoes of Chaucer occur less frequently than one might expect in Hoccleve's verse, his metrical art and especially his mastery of the syntax of the rhyme royal stanza would have been almost impossible without Chaucer's example. Such dependence upon Chaucer is, of course, common in fifteenth-century poetry; but two of the passages in *The Regement of Princes* have been generally accepted, until quite recently, as evidence that Hoccleve actually knew Chaucer and was personally instructed by him in the art of English poetry. In the long and interesting encounter with the poor almsman which forms the prologue to the *Regement*, the old man responds to Hoccleve's disclosure of his name with these words:

> 'Sone, I haue herd, or this, men speke of þe;
> þou were aqueynted with Caucher, pardee'   (1866-7)

---

[1] *Minor Poems*, pp. 289–93. For the identity of Thomas Marleburgh, Hoccleve's patron, see *Minor Poems*, p. 272. The poem appears as the 'Ploughman's Tale' in the copy of the *Canterbury Tales* in Christ Church, Oxford. On the relation of Hoccleve's poetry to Chaucer's, see generally the remarks of M. R. Pryor in her edition of the *Series* (p. 223 n. 1 above), pp. 30–54.

Later, in dedicating his poem to the future Henry V, the poet apologizes for his lack of learning and skill:

> Mi dere maistir—god his soule quyte!—
> And fadir, Chaucer, fayn wolde han me taght;
> But I was dul, and lerned lite or naght.   (2077–9)

The meaning of this passage seems plain enough; but Jerome Mitchell, in a discussion entitled 'Hoccleve's Supposed Friendship with Chaucer', has suggested that 'this so-called autobiographical allusion is nothing more than a conventional expression of self-deprecation'.[1] Here again, the proposed alternative between autobiography and convention proves misleading. Certainly there does exist a convention of self-depreciation in polite letters, as in polite society; and no doubt Hoccleve's modest protestations, like those of Chaucer himself, owe something to the literary topic of affected modesty, studied by Curtius. Also, when Hoccleve goes on to his threnody for Chaucer, lamenting the loss of one who was a Cicero in rhetoric, an Aristotle in philosophy, and a Virgil in poetry, he is following a literary tradition already established in the vernaculars: the lament for a dead master.[2] Such considerations should certainly make one hesitate to derive from Hoccleve's words either a just estimate of his own merits or a discriminating account of his master's; but they do nothing to explain why he claimed Chaucer as an acquaintance. When John Lydgate in his *Troy Book* describes how Chaucer treated the verses of other poets, he does so from hearsay ('I have herde telle'); but Hoccleve claims direct personal knowledge.[3] Mitchell remarks that there is no indication of any friendship in the life-records of either man; but one has only to recall the character of those documents to see the absurdity of this argument. The Public Record Office is not rich in records of literary friendships.

The question of Hoccleve's friendship with Chaucer is not in itself very important; but Mitchell's discussion of the matter may be taken as representative of a general approach which can be seriously disabling. Many readers today are only too ready to accept the historical critic's pronouncement that such and such an 'autobiographical' passage is no more than conventional or

---

[1] J. Mitchell, *Thomas Hoccleve: A Study in Early Fifteenth-Century Poetic* (Urbana, Ill., 1968), p. 117.

[2] *Regement* 2080–107, cf. 1958–74. The French poet Deschamps wrote in similar terms about his master Machaut: ballades nos. 123 and 124 in Deschamps, *Œuvres*, ed. le marquis de Queux de Saint-Hilaire and G. Raynaud (Paris, 1878–1903).

[3] *Troy Book*, ed. H. Bergen, EETS, ES 97, 103, 106, 126 (1906–20), v 3519–26.

fictional. Whether they belong to the older school of the New Criticism or to the newer schools of formalism, these readers will be glad enough to be relieved of biographical considerations which both schools regard as in any case *hors de discours*. But even in medieval literature there are occasions when exclusive concentration on 'le texte' or 'the words on the page' leads to an impoverished and dehumanized reading of works whose true force and character can only be appreciated if their particular extra-textual reference is duly recognized and acknowledged. Hoccleve's *Complaint* and his *Dialogue with a Friend* are cases in point.

The *Complaint* and *Dialogue* are the first two items in Hoccleve's last and most original major work: what Hammond, for want of a better title, called the 'Series'. This consists of a sequence of linked writings, dedicated to Humphrey duke of Gloucester in the last years of Henry V. In the opening *Complaint*, Hoccleve represents himself at the age of 53 musing on the uncertainty of worldly fortunes. In particular, he recalls a 'wild infirmity' which changed his own fortunes some years before, causing him to lose his wits. He recovered from this breakdown—five years ago, he says, on All Hallows' Day—but ever since his friends and acquaintances have persisted in doubting his mental stability; and it is of this that he chiefly complains. People cannot believe that he is really better. They watch for signs of his former brain-sickness in his present ways of walking and standing and looking:

> Chaungid had I my pas / some seiden eke,
> For here and there / forthe stirte I as a Roo,
> None abode / none arrest, but all brain-seke.
> Another spake / and of me seide also,
> My feete weren aye / wavynge to and fro
> Whane that I stonde shulde / and withe men talke,
> And that myne eyne / sowghten every halke.   (127-33)

In her study of 'conventions of madness in Middle English literature' entitled *Nebuchadnezzar's Children*, Penelope Doob cites a medieval parallel to show that these are among the 'standard symptoms of the madman'.[1] She also stresses the conventional character of Hoccleve's view of the aetiology of madness: like most medieval men, he sees it as a visitation of God. These are valuable observations; but they do not, as Doob appears to believe, show that Hoccleve's account is to be understood as a conventional fiction. It is precisely those 'standard symptoms of the madman' that nervous friends would look for; and there is no reason to think

---

[1] Doob, p. 221.

that Hoccleve himself, musing on his traumatic experience, would have attempted to understand it otherwise than in the religious terms of his age, just as we today would use psychoanalytic terms.[1] Doob herself is aware of this complication, and at one point opines that 'it does not matter very much' whether one takes the account as autobiographical or not; but she reveals herself as an atheist rather than an agnostic in this matter when, for instance, she observes that the 'fairly extensive records' of Hoccleve's life contain no reference to his madness.[2] I have already objected to this kind of argument *a silentio*.

Doob offers her own interpretation of the *Complaint* and *Dialogue*, as an alternative to autobiographical readings. Hoccleve's subject, she writes, is 'the sinful madness of mankind'.[3] But is it? The poet does indeed speak of his madness as a visitation from God, and in one place he interprets it as divine punishment for his 'sinful governance' in times of prosperity (*Complaint* 393-406); but there is nothing in the text, so far as I can see, to justify Doob's conclusion that the wild infirmity is simply a 'traditional metaphor for the crippling state of sin which is the subject of the poem'.[4] On the contrary, Hoccleve clearly treats it as an actual illness, from which he recovered at a specified time, five years ago on All Hallows' Day. But if this is indeed the true subject of Hoccleve's poem, what were his reasons for writing it? Medievalists will appreciate that this is a more difficult question than it seems. It is only too easy to see why a medieval poet might write about 'the sinful madness of mankind'; but why should he choose to write about his own mental breakdown and its aftermath? Here as elsewhere the autobiographical interpretation will be in danger of seeming merely anachronistic unless it can be supported by some historically plausible account of the poet's reasons for writing about himself. Indeed, this question of the purpose or function of autobiographical writing is, as I shall try to suggest, crucial for a proper understanding of poems such as the *Complaint* or the *Male Regle*.

This is a question which the term 'autobiographical' itself most

---

[1] In his illuminating discussion of Hoccleve, S. Medcalf cites a modern psychoanalyst's judgement on the case: *The Later Middle Ages*, ed. Medcalf (London, 1981), pp. 129-30.

[2] Op. cit., p. 226. Note, however, Brown's opinion: 'In his "Complaint" . . . written about 1420-1, perhaps during Lent 1421, Hoccleve states that he regained his sanity on 1 Nov., five years previously. This may be one reason why he did not come to the Exchequer personally between May 1414 and Mar. 1417 to collect payments due to him,' *The Study of Medieval Records*, p. 271.

[3] Op. cit., p. 230.   [4] Op. cit., p. 228.

unfortunately begs. As was remarked earlier, critics commonly treat this epithet as if it were appropriate to any occasion when an author says things about himself which the reader has reason to believe are true; but in fact the word carries further implications, unwanted in most medieval contexts and generally unacknowledged there. These concern the presumed purpose of the self-referring utterance. In modern usage the term 'autobiography' denotes a genre of non-fictional narrative—a species of biography and (theoretically at least) a sub-species of history. There are, of course, many possible reasons for writing such a book; but those most commonly avowed—the official reasons, as it were—are rather grand and disinterested: to record the events of one's life for posterity, to explain how one came to be how one is, and the like.[1] Autobiographical discourse, in fact, has come to be distinguished as a literary and formal kind of talk about oneself; and as such it is not directly or primarily concerned with the ordinary practical businesses of such talk—excusing, confessing, complaining, and all those other everyday speech-acts which involve reference to one's own actions or experiences.

Did any medieval author write such an autobiography? Some scholars, notably Georg Misch, have found it possible to devote many hundreds of pages to medieval examples of the genre; but others, notably Philippe Lejeune, have argued that these so-called medieval 'autobiographies' are better called something else.[2] I think that Lejeune's judgement is correct, although the reasons which he gives are suspect. Following Zumthor, he speaks of 'absence de la notion d'auteur' and of 'absence d'emploi littéraire autoréférentiel de la première personne'; but the Middle Ages, at least from the thirteenth century onwards, had a very clear 'notion d'auteur', and their writers were perfectly capable on occasion of using the first-person pronoun 'autoreferentially'. The true difference is to be looked for rather in the realm of authorial purpose. Unlike the modern autobiography, the corresponding medieval texts will present themselves as written versions, albeit elaborated and formalized, of an everyday self-referring speech-act. They are addressed to particular recipients, and they serve

[1] Philippe Lejeune defines autobiography as follows: 'Récit rétrospectif en prose qu'une personne réelle fait de sa propre existence, lorsqu'elle met l'accent sur sa vie individuelle, en particulier sur l'histoire de sa personnalité', *Le Pacte autobiographique*, p. 14.

[2] *Pacte autobiographique*, p. 315, citing Georg Misch, *Geschichte der Autobiographie*, 8 vols (Frankfurt, 1949–69) and Zumthor, *Essai de poétique mediévale*, pp. 68–9, 172–4.

explicitly stated practical ends. The greatest of them, St. Augustine's *Confessions*, addresses itself to God with a persistence which many modern readers find disappointing; and the saint's account of his life is shaped throughout by the confessional purpose of this address. Another text frequently cited in this connection, the *Monodiae* of Gilbert of Nogent (1115), also addresses itself as a confession to God. Peter Abelard's so-called *Historia Calamitatum* takes the form of a letter to a friend offering consolation and encouragement 'based upon the experience of my misfortunes'. These works contain many facts about their authors' lives; but even they—medieval autobiographies, if ever there was such a thing—cannot be so described on any functional definition of the genre. Functionally considered, the *Confessions* and the *Monodiae* are confessions, and the *Historia Calamitatum* is a consolation.[1]

The same questions of address and function arise in the consideration of Hoccleve's autobiographical passages. To whom is he speaking? And for what purpose? Most of his works are occasional pieces, and of himself he certainly never speaks without occasion. These occasions often fall outside the province of literature as we now understand it; but they hold the key to the understanding of Hoccleve's own particular brand of autobiographical writing.

Hoccleve entirely lacked his master Chaucer's ability to speak in voices other than his own. In his *Dialogue*, the exchanges between himself and his friend display a real skill in rendering general conversational effects; but the friend never establishes himself with a distinct individual idiom, as Chaucer's Pandarus does in his talks with Troilus. The same must be said of Cupid, the speaker in *The Letter of Cupid*, of the Virgin Mary in *The Compleynte of the Virgin before the Cross*, and of the eminently forgettable characters in Hoccleve's two most ambitious verse narratives, the *Gesta Romanorum* stories in the *Series*. Even the old almsman in the prologue to the *Regement of Princes*, Hoccleve's equivalent to Wordsworth's leech-gatherer and perhaps his least insubstantial dramatic creation, is no more than a pale shadow by comparison with the old man in Chaucer's *Pardoner's Tale*. This poet's skills lay elsewhere, in the articulation of his own voice. Hoccleve speaks best when he speaks *in propria persona*, either in soliloquy, as in the *Complaint*, or when he speaks to another person, as he most often

---

[1] For a discussion of autobiography laying emphasis on functional considerations and employing the Austin/Searle concept of speech-acts, see E. W. Bruss, 'L'autobiographie considérée comme acte littéraire', *Poétique* xvii (1974), 14–26.

does. His is above all a poetry of address; and the list of persons to whom he addresses himself at one time or another is long and varied. It includes: the members of the Trinity, Health (personified), Lady Money (personified), the Virgin Mary, King Henry V and his two brothers Humphrey of Gloucester and Edward of York, John duke of Bedford, the Chancellor of the Exchequer Henry Somer, Treasurer Fourneval, the Town Clerk of London John Carpenter, and the Lollard knight John Oldcastle. Such varying occasions and purposes call for varying roles (by which I do *not* mean fictional roles); and as Hoccleve presents his self differently, to the King or to the heretic, so the character of his autobiographical writing changes accordingly. I distinguish here three main roles: the good citizen, the friend or colleague, and (most important) the dependant or petitioner.

From the present point of view (and from most others) Hoccleve the good citizen is the least interesting of the three. This is the Hoccleve who, like John Gower in the previous generation, took upon himself the role of upholding standards by giving moral counsel to the great and deploring the abuses of modern times. Examples of this kind of writing are: the poem to Oldcastle attacking the Lollard heresy, the passage on the evils of flattery in the *Male Regle* (209–88), the passage in the *Dialogue* (99–196) deploring the clipping, washing, and adulterating of coins, the story of Jonathas and Fellicula told in the *Series* as a warning to young men against the wiles of women, and above all the *Regement of Princes*. Apart from its lengthy prologue, the *Regement* devotes itself entirely to instructing Prince Hal in the proper virtues of a ruler. Such treatises 'de regimine principum' were very popular in the fifteenth century, and the *Regement* was by far and away the most successful of Hoccleve's works. It survives in more than forty manuscripts.[1] Although here as elsewhere he can command a sinewy, plain, and expressive English, it must be confessed that Hoccleve is not at his best in the role of the good citizen, loyal to country and crown, orthodox in religion, and honest in all his personal dealings. However, even Hoccleve the good citizen has his complexities, for in the *Series* especially, in the *Male Regle*, and

[1] The editors of the proposed new critical edition of the *Regement* count 43 MSS. The Robbins-Cutler *Supplement to the Index of Middle English Verse* counts 45 (including two MSS with short extracts), putting the poem ninth in their list of Middle English works preserved in the most MSS. On the popularity of such works in the fifteenth century, see R. F. Green, *Poets and Princepleasers: Literature and the English Court in the Late Middle Ages* (Toronto, 1980), ch. 5.

to a much lesser degree in the *Regement*, Hoccleve's various confessions of personal inadequacy cast fitful shadows across the adjacent passages of moral and prudential counsel. For how, after all, could a writer whose own standing was so avowedly insecure, financially, morally, and medically, take it upon himself to speak on behalf of his society, as a solid citizen, to the coiners and heretics at its margins and to the kings and lords at its centre? Readers who credit Hoccleve with no awareness of this contradiction commonly react to his orthodoxies with something of that mixture of embarrassment and derision which society reserves for those of its members who try too hard to be one of the boys; but the poet who described how he practised sane faces in front of the mirror in his room was self-aware as well as self-conscious; and that self-awareness certainly embraced some knowledge of his own weakness in seeking to be accepted as a 'verray gentil man'. I have argued elsewhere that this awareness is particularly strong in the *Series*.[1] This sequence of poems enacts, I believe, the progress of that rehabilitation in society which Hoccleve, after his wild infirmity and its unhappy aftermath, so longs for. It begins in solitude and alienation, with the *Complaint*; progresses with the ministrations of the friend; and ends with the poet comfortably ensconced in the orthodox role of *père de famille*, responding to the friend's anxious request for help with his own wild and uncontrollable son. Here at least a touch of moralizing complacency may be forgiven in a good citizen who has himself so recently suffered the miseries of alienation.

Hoccleve's 'rehabilitation' in the *Series* comes about largely through the agency of that unnamed friend who visits him, comforts and advises him, lends him books, and finally sets the seal on his recovery by asking for his help. The familiar exchanges between the two men are well rendered. Indeed, in the role of friend and companion Hoccleve generally commands a voice of notable ease and conviction, anticipating later English literary voices even more, perhaps, than Chaucer does in the *Envoy to Scogan*. He is a poet of *urban* companionship, evoking already something of that distinctive, almost cosy, sense of familiarity which unites those living in the busy 'press' of a great town who actually happen to know each other, either socially or at the office. Hoccleve's London was not big by modern standards; but, as he portrays it in such poems as the *Male Regle* or the *Series*, it is already

---

[1] 'Hoccleve's *Series*: Experience and Books', in R. F. Yeager (ed.), *Fifteenth-Century Studies: Recent Essays* (Hamden, Conn., 1984), pp. 259–73. Hoccleve describes his antics in front of the mirror in *Complaint* 155–68.

recognisably the tense, gossipy London of the satires of Donne and Pope.[1] Indeed, as Stephen Medcalf has well observed, Hoccleve can even put one in mind of a later metropolitan writer, Charles Lamb— another 'impecunious but clubbable London clerk of literary leanings'.[2] There were already clubs in Hoccleve's London. The poet belonged to one, called the 'Court de bone conpaignie', which met periodically for convivial dinners at the Temple. On behalf of this club he wrote a double ballade to one of its distinguished members, the Chancellor of the Exchequer Henry Somer.

But the most important club in Hoccleve's London life was the office of the Privy Seal, in which he served as clerk for nearly forty years. The clerks of the Privy Seal were more than simply colleagues at the office.[3] They lived communally at the *hospicium privati sigilli*, or Privy Seal hostel; and in the *Male Regle* Hoccleve uses an expressive phrase when he speaks of going 'hoom to the priuee seel' (l. 188). All the poet's 'fellawes of the prive seale', as he calls them (*Complaint* 296), shared his chronic difficulty in getting paid, and sometimes in his petitionary poems he pleads for them as well as for himself:

> We, your seruantes, Hoccleue & Baillay,
> Hethe & Offorde, yow beseeche & preye,
> 'Haastith our heruest / as soone as yee may!'[4]

He also complains feelingly of their other troubles. In a well-known passage in the *Regement of Princes*, he compares their demanding work at the writing-desk with the simpler and more companionable tasks of common craftsmen:

> This artificers se I day be day,
> In þe hotteste of al hir bysynesse
> Talken and syng, and make game and play,
> And forth hir labour passith with gladnesse;
> But we labour in trauaillous stilnesse;
> We stowpe and stare vpon þe shepes skyn,
> And keepe muste our song and wordes in.   (1009–15)

This stanza shows how especially well Hoccleve can write when he

---

[1] See for example *Complaint* 70–98 and 183 ff., describing the poet's nervous reactions to the 'press' in Westminster Hall and on the London pavements. Unlike Donne and Pope, Hoccleve does not appear to have known the satires of Horace or Juvenal.

[2] *The Later Middle Ages*, p. 127.

[3] On the life of the Privy Seal clerks, see the studies by Tout and Brown cited at p. 226 n. 3 above, especially ch. 7 of Brown's thesis.

[4] *Balade to Maister Somer* (*Minor Poems*, p. 59) 25–7; also *Balade to Henry V* (*Minor Poems*, p. 62).

is dealing with the particulars of his own experience. The contrast
between the talking, singing, and joking in a craftsman's shop and
the 'trauaillous stilnesse' of the Privy Seal office is drawn with
great precision and economy of language. Notice, for instance,
how in the line, 'We stowpe and stare vpon þe shepes skyn', the
word *stare*, neat enough already in its alliterative coupling with
stowpe, gathers extra force from the ensuing 'shepes skyn'—a
phrase which defamiliarizes the parchment and so converts the
writer's fixed gaze into a real weary, hypnotized 'stare'. A tanner
would at least have whistled.

A little later in the *Regement*, Hoccleve has another less well-
known passage where he speaks with similar force and precision
on behalf of the 'fellows of the Privy Seal', describing one of the
tricks by which they were deprived of the legitimate rewards of
their labours. A stranger comes to Westminster to get some
necessary document issued from the office of the Privy Seal. He
encounters one of those unscrupulous hangers-on so familiar from
later satirical writings—in this case, a 'lord's man' who promises
to use his influence to get the document without delay. Pocketing
the stranger's fee, he persuades the Privy Seal clerks to expedite
the business by promising them that his own influential master,
who has (he claims) the interests of the stranger at heart, will do
them a favour in return at some later date. But the lord, of course,
does not know the petitioner from Adam, and the hanger-on will
later claim to have given the clerks their fee. The clerks know what
is going on; but what can they do? 'His tale schal be leeued, but nat
ourys.' Let me quote the first part of this striking passage, which
takes the law-abiding modern reader deep into an unfamiliar
world of chicanery and influence:

> But if a wyght haue any cause to sue
> To vs, som lordes man schal vndertake
> To sue it out; & þat þat is vs due
> For oure labour, hym deyneþ vs nat take;
> He seiþ, his lord to þanke vs wole he make;
> It touchiþ hym, it is a man of his;
> Where þe reuers of þat, god wot, sooþ is.
>
> His letter he takiþ, and forþ goþ his way,
> And byddeþ vs to dowten vs no thyng,
> His lord schal þanken vs an oþer day;
> And if we han to sue to þe kyng,
> His lord may þere haue al his askyng;
> We schal be sped, as fer as þat oure bille
> Wole specifie þe effecte of oure wylle.

> What schol we do? we dar non argument
> Make ageyn him, but fayre & wel him trete,
> Leste he roporte amys, & make vs schent . . .
> (*Regement* 1499–515)

And so on. These stanzas end less well than they begin; but
the specious assurances of the lord's man are very well caught
in lines such as 'It touchiþ hym, it is a man of his' and 'His
lord schal þanken vs an oþer day'; and the complex workings
of power and influence about the king's court are displayed
with authority. This is a world where documents are 'sued out'
in return for a promise that some future 'bill' will itself be
favourably received higher up, and where petitioners depend
for their success upon the sponsorship of some great lord or else
upon the good offices of some lesser intermediary who may, for
his own reasons, agree to undertake their cause. Even established
civil servants such as Hoccleve and his colleagues could easily
come to grief on what Thomas Wyatt a century later called 'the
slipper top of court's estates'. The payment of their supposedly
regular annuities was far from being a matter of course; and the
extra fees 'due for their labour', upon which they depended
to make ends meet, could finish up in other hands, as we have
seen. They had to look after themselves as best they could, in
accordance with the harsh dictum of Arcite in Chaucer's *Knight's
Tale*:

> And therfore, at the kynges court, my brother,
> Ech man for hymself, ther is noon oother.
> (*Canterbury Tales* I 1181–82)

It is within this social context that the modern reader should try
to understand and sympathize with Hoccleve in his third and
most significant role: that of petitioner. For the image of himself
which he projects in his poetry is determined most of all by the
harsh requirements of survival in the treacherous world of the
court. Furnivall wished he had been a manlier fellow and not com-
plained so much; but the conduct of an independent nineteenth-
century gentleman would have soon led to destitution in any
medieval man dependent upon the favours of the great. When
Hoccleve speaks of himself, as he often does, 'conpleynyngly', he
does so for a purpose, and with the technique of an expert. Most
of the business with which his office dealt concerned petitions
submitted to the King or his Council and handed on, if they were
granted, to the Privy Seal clerks for the drafting of the appropriate

warrant.[1] In the formulary which he compiled in the last years of his life for the benefit of his colleagues, Hoccleve included five model 'supplications' or 'petitions ensellez du prive seel'.[2] He himself was well acquainted with the uncertainty of reward and the misery of hope deferred. One of the *sententiae* recorded in his formulary is *Expectantes excruciat dilatio promissorum* ('the putting-off of promised benefits torments those that await them').[3] It is therefore easy to understand why so much of his poetic output should take the form of a complaint about hardships or wrongs suffered, coupled with a petition for the remedy addressed either to the potential benefactor himself or else to some other person who could act as mediator on his behalf.[4] Thus Huntington MS 111 contains a group of petitionary balades addressed to the Lord Chancellor, the Subtreasurer, the King, and the Town Clerk of London; the *Male Regle* culminates in an appeal to the Treasurer for payment of his annuity; and the *Regement of Princes* makes a similar appeal for relief to Prince Hal himself.[5] Hoccleve's religious poems, too, often take the form of complaints and petitions, appealing to Christ or the Virgin Mary as mediators who can use their influence to win him favour with God the

---

[1] Brown's thesis describes the function of the Privy Seal clerks in dealing with many of the several thousand petitions presented to the King each year (ch. 2) and discusses the general importance of petitions as 'the key to all administrative action' (pp. 340–5). See also Green, *Poets and Princepleasers*, pp. 42–3, and J. A. Tuck, 'Richard II's System of Patronage', in *The Reign of Richard II*, ed. F. R. H. Du Boulay and C. M. Barron (London, 1971), pp. 1–20. Tuck writes: 'The importance of the petition in medieval government can hardly be over-emphasized: patronage as much as justice was founded upon it' (p. 4). For a collection of petitions from Hoccleve's time, see *Anglo-Norman Letters and Petitions from All Souls MS. 182*, ed. M. D. Legge, Anglo-Norman Text Society 3 (Oxford, 1941), pp. 1–41. See also J. A. Burrow, 'The Poet as Petitioner', *Studies in the Age of Chaucer* 3 (1981), 61–75.

[2] The formulary is BL MS Add. 24062. See 'The Formulary of Thomas Hoccleve', ed. E.-J. Y. Bentley (Ph.D. thesis, Emory University, 1965), item 175, p. 166. Brown discusses the formulary in his thesis, Appendix B.

[3] Ed. Bentley, item 892, p. 1030.

[4] The importance for a petitioner of having a sponsor willing to use influence on his behalf at court is stressed by Brown (thesis, pp. 30 and 345), Green (*Poets and Princepleasers*, pp. 49–52), and Tuck (*Reign of Richard II*, pp. 15–17). Hoccleve's petitionary poetry, both secular and religious, frequently refers to such intermediaries or 'menes': e.g. *Regement* 302, 3187; *Minor Poems* p. 46 l. 89, p. 53 l. 44, p. 54 l. 83, p. 63 l. 23, p. 71 l. 125, p. 135 l. 709, p. 277 l. 64.

[5] *Minor Poems*, pp. 58–64; *Male Regle* 417–48; *Regement* 4360–403. The *Regement* appeal is neatly worked into a discussion of Prodigality (to which Hoccleve confesses, as in *Male Regle*) and Largesse (for which he hopes).

Father. The pattern of complaint and supplication, as these examples show, was deeply impressed upon Hoccleve's consciousness.

He evidently gave the matter of petitioning a good deal of thought. Seneca's *De Beneficiis* taught him what he no doubt already knew, that even successful begging exacts its own high price:

> Senek seith, he haþ nat þat þing for noght
> That byeth it by speche and by prayere.
> There is no thyng þat is in eerthe wroght,
> As þat he seith, þat is y-bought so deere.[1]

But what is the alternative? As he says in the *Male Regle*, the 'shameless craver' gets what he wants by sheer importunity, while the 'poor shamefast man' stays poor. So he must learn to crave. But nagging repetition is, in fact, not the best way. Variety and inventiveness help:

> Whoso him shapith mercy for to craue,
> His lesson moot recorde in sundry wyse.
> (*Male Regle* 397–8)

There are more 'sundry wises' of petitionary approach in Hoccleve's writings than can be illustrated in this lecture; but, in view of the poet's reputation as a monotonous whiner, one should emphasize that there *is* variety, and that this variety includes a good deal of wit and comic byplay. Playing the fool, if stylishly done, can save a little face; and it also serves to keep potential benefactors entertained. Hoccleve describes one of his poems as an 'owter of my nycetee', displaying his folly to amuse, in this case, the Duke of York.[2] The phrase draws attention to an aspect of his autobiographical writing which neither Doob nor Furnivall recognizes.

An extreme example of the light petitionary touch is the group of three roundels in which the poet complains to Lady Money and receives her unfavourable reply, a *jeu d'esprit* worthy to be compared with Chaucer's *Complaint to his Purse*. But let me end by returning briefly to that more substantial piece of 'shameless craving', the *Male Regle*. In this poem the complaint, as I remarked earlier, concerns two kinds of sickness, physical and financial, both caused by the poet's excesses in his riotous youth. Thornley and

---

[1] *Regement* 4705–8. Cf. Seneca, *De Beneficiis*, ed. J. W. Basore (Loeb, 1935), II. i. 4: 'Non tulit gratis, qui, cum rogasset, accepit, quoniam quidem, ut maioribus nostris gravissimis viris visum est, nulla res carius constat, quam quae precibus empta est.'

[2] *Balade to My Gracious Lord of York* (*Minor Poems*, p. 49) 17–18.

Doob interpreted the piece as a penitential lyric; and certainly
Hoccleve does express regret for the past, as well as a resolution to
live a better-regulated life in the future. But these confessional
sentiments serve an overriding petitionary purpose, from which
the poem derives its form and its tone. Corresponding to the two
sicknesses of purse and body we find here two subtly intertwined
requests for relief, one addressed to the personified god of health,
the other to Fourneval, the King's Treasurer. The practical point
of the poem emerges clearly enough in its last four stanzas, where
Hoccleve appeals to Fourneval for payment of his annuity, which
is overdue; but this unavoidable act of importunity is approached
in the most amusingly roundabout fashion. The poem opens with
a lofty and fanciful appeal to Health, addressing that personification as if he were the great lord who could bring Hoccleve the
'socour and releef' that he needs. It then goes on to speak of the
poet's youthful misrule, referring first to the excessive and irregular
eating and drinking which have helped to ruin his constitution:

> twenti wyntir past continuelly
> Excesse at borde hath leyd his knyf with me.   (111-12)

It is in this context that Hoccleve first mentions money, when he
refers at l. 130 to the 'penylees maladie' which sometimes kept him
out of his favourite taverns. From this point on, references to his
youthful extravagance and its financial consequences occur with
more than accidental frequency. Thus immediately after the
account, quoted earlier, of his reputation with cooks and inn-
keepers as a big spender, he describes how instead of walking
'hoom to the priuee seel' he took a boat (evidently an extravagance, like a taxi in modern London). His explanations of this self-
indulgence bear all the hallmarks of his best manner: fullness of
detail specified in precise, unlaboured English. How economically,
for instance, the muted personifications of the line 'Heete & vnlust
and superfluitee' express his three reasons for taking a boat in
summer: he was hot, he had had too much to eat and drink, and he
didn't feel like walking.

> And if it happid on the Someres day
> þat I thus at the tauerne hadde be,
> Whan I departe sholde / & go my way
> Hoom to the priuee seel / so wowed me
> Heete & vnlust and superfluitee
> To walke vnto the brigge / & take a boot /
> þat nat durste I contrarie hem all three,
> But dide as þat they stired me / god woot.

> And in the wyntir / for the way was deep,
> Vnto the brigge I dressid me also,
> And ther the bootmen took vpon me keep,
> For they my riot kneewen fern ago:
> With hem I was I-tugged to and fro,
> So wel was him / þat I with wolde fare;
> For riot paieth largely / eueremo;
> He styntith neuere / til his purs be bare.   (185–200)

It may seem strange to claim of a passage such as this that it is shaped by a petitionary intention. Fourneval, one might suppose, would hardly be inclined to help replenish a purse which had been made bare by such extravagances. But the Privy Seal clerk knew what he was at:

> Whoso him shapith mercy for to craue,
> His lesson moot recorde in sundry wyse.

Hoccleve would have every reason to know that the Lord Treasurer received quite enough straight hard-luck stories in the ordinary way of business; so he could be trusted to appreciate the amusing alternative which the poet offered him—something very different from the customary 'wife and three children to support'. There is, it must be admitted, something slavish in the readiness with which Hoccleve makes a fool of himself to amuse the great man, as when he shamingly confesses that he was too shy and sheepish to do more than kiss the girls who attracted him to the Paul's Head Tavern; but he makes sure to recover his dignity in the closing pages of the poem. Here his mastery of the 'sundry wises' of petitionary address can be most clearly seen. First he addresses himself, with the warning that his modest annuity and uncertain fees make it essential for him to live a life of reason and moderation in future: 'Be waar, Hoccleue' (351). Then, in a loftier style, he addresses Health, confessing his past irregularities and renewing his pleas for relief. And finally he names Fourneval, and plainly asks him for the money that can heal all his sicknesses. It comes down to coin in the end:

> By coyn, I gete may swich medecyne
> As may myn hurtes alle, þat me greeue,
> Exyle cleene / & voide me of pyne.   (446–8)

It will be evident from this discussion that one should not look in Hoccleve's poetry for the simple truth about him, whatever that may have been. Traditional moral psychology helped to shape the account he gives in the *Male Regle* of his youthful behaviour, just as traditional morbid psychology helped to shape the account of his breakdown in the *Complaint*. Both these accounts, furthermore, owe much of their distinctive tone and emphasis to their original occasion and purpose; and the unhappy Hoccleve of these bills of complaint is not the same as the orthodox Hoccleve who reproaches Oldcastle or the gregarious Hoccleve who invites Somer to dinner at the Temple. But to put the matter in this way implies, not only that Hoccleve really does talk about himself in his poetry, but also that his departures from the imaginary norm of simple autobiographical truth are themselves best understood by reflecting upon his particular circumstances. Here, for once, we are not reduced to generalization or speculation in considering the life and the social context of a medieval poet. The details are available, in the poems themselves and in the work of historians; and it is readers least embarrassed by these details who are most likely, I think, to appreciate the character of this remarkable, though uneven, writer.

Index